Sabine von Heusinger, Annette Kehnel (Eds./Hg.)

Generations in the Cloister
Generationen im Kloster

Vita regularis

Ordnungen und Deutungen religiosen Lebens im Mittelalter

Abhandlungen

Band 36

LIT

Generations in the Cloister

Youth and Age in Medieval Religious Life

Generationen im Kloster

Jugend und Alter
in der mittelalterlichen vita religiosa

edited by/herausgegeben von

Sabine von Heusinger, Annette Kehnel

LIT

Gedruckt mit Mitteln des Stifterverbandes für die deutsche Wissenschaft

Bibliographic information published by the Deutsche Nationalbibliothek
The Deutsche Nationalbibliothek lists this publication in the Deutsche Nationalbibliografie; detailed bibliographic data are available in the Internet at http://dnb.d-nb.de.

ISBN 978-3-03735-941-9 (Schweiz)
ISBN 978-3-8258-1173-0 (Deutschland)

A catalogue record for this book is available from the British Library

Dufourstr. 31
CH-8008 Zürich
Tel. +41 (0) 44-251 75 05
Fax +41 (0) 44-251 75 06
e-Mail: zuerich@lit-verlag.ch
http://www.lit-verlag.ch

LIT VERLAG Dr. W. Hopf
Berlin 2008
Verlagskontakt:
Fresnostr. 2
D-48159 Münster
Tel. +49 (0) 2 51/620 32 - 22
Fax +49 (0) 2 51/922 60 99
e-Mail: lit@lit-verlag.de
http://www.lit-verlag.de

Auslieferung:
Deutschland/Schweiz: LIT Verlag Fresnostr. 2, D-48159 Münster
Tel. +49 (0) 2 51/620 32 - 22, Fax +49 (0) 2 51/922 60 99, e-Mail: vertrieb@lit-verlag.de
Österreich: Medienlogistik Pichler-ÖBZ GmbH & Co KG
IZ-NÖ, Süd, Straße 1, Objekt 34, A-2355 Wiener Neudorf
Tel. +43 (0) 2236/63 535-290, +43 (0) 2236/63 535 - 243, mlo@medien-logistik.at

Distributed in the UK by: Global Book Marketing, 99B Wallis Rd, London, E9 5LN
Phone: +44 (0) 20 8533 5800 – Fax: +44 (0) 1600 775 663
http://www.centralbooks.co.uk/html

Distributed in North America by:

Transaction Publishers
New Brunswick (U.S.A.) and London (U.K.)

Transaction Publishers
Rutgers University
35 Berrue Circle
Piscataway, NJ 08854

Phone: +1 (732) 445 - 2280
Fax: + 1 (732) 445 - 3138
for orders (U. S. only):
toll free (888) 999 - 6778
e-mail:
orders@transactionspub.com

CONTENTS / INHALT

Preface / Vorwort

The volume presented here combines contributions and questions that first appeared in the context of the session "Generations in the Cloister" at the International Medieval Congress in Leeds, held in July 2005. The conference theme "Youth and Age" stimulated research in the field of religious communities in the Middle Ages and in their function as "Inter-Generational-Institution". The medieval monastery, thanks to literacy, documents the history of generations, the lived 'Gleichzeitigkeit *der* Ungleichzeitigen' in the *Longue Durée*. This is the main focus of the papers assembled here, all of them inquiring about the relation between the generations in the cloister. In an interdisciplinary approach all the papers try to combine historical, theological and pedagogical traditions. The interdisciplinary communication, offered by the annual conferences in Leeds, was most supportive here for the completion of this volume.

Therefore we would like to thank Axel Müller in the very first place for the most efficient "institutionalization" of the interdisciplinary discourse in Medieval Studies in Leeds. Gert Melville was most helpful in his most patient support and the integration of the volume in *Vita Regularis*. Tanja Skambraks helped to prepare the manuscripts. Inken Diederich produced the index. A most special thanks is due to Mirko Breitenstein in Dresden for his judicious and competent help. If there was a prize for "authorfriendly editors" in academia, the series *Vita Regularis* would certainly have deserved it.

*

Der vorliegende Band bündelt Beiträge und Fragen, die zunächst im Rahmen der Sektion "Generations in the Cloister" auf dem International Medieval Congress in Leeds im Juli 2005 vorgestellt und diskutiert wurden. Das Kongressthema "Youth and Age" bot Anregung zur Untersuchung religioser Gemeinschaften des Mittelalters in ihrer Eigenschaft als genuine 'Mehr-Generationen-Institutionen'. Im Kloster wird, dank der dort kultivierten Schriftlichkeit, die Geschichte der Generationenverhältnisse, die gelebte 'Gleichzeitigkeit *der* Ungleichzeitigen' in der *Longue Durée* fassbar. Diesem Sachverhalt sind die in diesem Band versammelten Forschungsbeiträge zur Frage nach der Beziehung zwischen den Generationen im Kloster geschuldet. Im interdisziplinären Zugriff fördern die einzelnen Beiträge die hier unverzichtbare Verknüpfung historischer, theologischer und pädagogischer Forschungstraditionen. Das interdisziplinäre Gespräch, das die jährlichen Konferenzen in Leeds ermöglichen, sorgte auch hier dafür, dass die Druckfassungen weit über die ursprünglichen Vortragsfassungen hinausgehen.

In diesem Sinne sei Axel Müller mit Nachdruck für die erfolgreiche Institutionalisierung des interdisziplinären mediävistischen Gesprächs in Leeds gedankt. Gert Melville danken wir für die geduldige Unterstützung und für die Aufnahme des Bandes in die Reihe *Vita Regularis*. In Mannheim unterstützte uns dankenswerterweise Tanja Skambraks bei der Erstellung der Druckvorlage und Inken Diederich fertigte das Register an. Ein ganz besonderer Dank schließlich gilt Mirko Breitenstein in Dresden für die umsichtige und kompetente Betreuung der Drucklegung. Gäbe es das Prädikat 'autorenfreundlich' für wissenschaftliche Reihen, dann hätte *Vita Regularis* diese Auszeichnung längst verdient.

Mannheim, Mai 2008 Sabine von Heusinger / Annette Kehnel

GENERATIONS AND RELATIONS IN RELIGIOUS CONTEXTS – AN INTRODUCTION / GENERATIONENBEZIEHUNGEN IM RELIGIÖSEN KONTEXT – EINE EINFÜHRUNG

SABINE VON HEUSINGER

'Generations in the cloister' – at first sight we seem to be dealing with the companionship of young and old under one roof and with the tensions arising out of conflicts between different generations. The present proceedings show the complexity and the diversity of this topic. The articles describe much more than the polarity old – young and raise elementary questions such as: who was regarded as a child from a Christian point of view? What is the reason for man's aging – besides the elapsing of years? Is Max WEBER's dictum claiming that Christianity radically broke up kinship ties true and as a consequence there existed no family dynasties in monasteries and convents?

The concept of generations is meant to characterize the social and time-related positioning of individuals or collectives within a society and attributes to them a specific identity in the form of the generation identity.[1] The individual in his way of thinking, feeling, wanting and acting is orientated towards social perspectives that are influenced by history. We have to focus on two central questions: first, how does the belonging to a certain generation contribute to the formation of identity and secondly, how is this affiliation perceived and how does it lead to a distinction towards other generations? The members of different generations are related to each other in a personal as well as in a collective respect by intergenerational relations. They orientate themselves to each other, they influence each other and they exchange

---

1 For the following see especially K. LÜSCHER, Ambivalenz – Eine Annäherung an das Problem der Generationen. Die Aktulität der Generationenfrage, in: U. JUREIT (Ed.), Generationen. Zur Relevanz eines wissenschaftlichen Grundbegriffs, Hamburg 2005, pp. 53-78.

experiences and norms. The experience of subjective mutuality and, at the same time, of being different as well as the conditions given by an institution, e.g. in a cloister, determine the shape and the dynamics of the relations between generations. The following proceedings deal with two basic problems when discussing the questions of generations. First, the essays are about the constitution of generations and the process of attributing a specific identity to a generation, e.g. when distinguishing between those eager for reform and those who were against it within a cloister. Secondly, it is about the shaping of the relations between different generations, found for example in Irish cloisters in the early Middle Ages or manifesting themselves in the boy bishop's feast.

The following essays can be classified into two parts: The first part focuses on 'real' and 'virtual' children. Hubertus LUTTERBACH investigates the concept of "Gotteskindschaft", the state of being a child of God. Tim GORRINGE concentrates on the idea of the little child (*parvulus*) in the New Testament and Tanja SKAMBRAKS presents the boy bishop's feast as a possibility to break up structures of age and status for a short time within the protected area of a religious community. The second part consists of case studies on different themes. Annette KEHNEL discusses the relationship of generations, taking Irish monasteries as an example, whereas German convents serve as an example in the essay of Gabriela SIGNORI. Mirko BREITENSTEIN investigates the education of young people as novices of the Cistercians; Michael ROBSON's contribution explores the Franciscans' dealings with children and young people. The following is a short summary of each essay.

Hubertus LUTTERBACH deals with different types of "Gotteskindschaft". Since the 4th century monks had started to wear hoods in order to characterize themselves as religious children – a garment that in the ancient world was at first designed for children. This provoked a complex situation characterized by LUTTERBACH by the term 'hood-competition': When being baptized every believer wore a christening robe with a hood, thus showing to everybody that he was a (new) child of God. In his profess a monk was baptized for a second time. For him the hood was a sign of a special childship. According to St John's Gospel the individual turns into a child of God by baptism. Childship is a 'procreation out of God'. Therefore the children of God are of a supernatural origin. In baptism the present of the "Gotteskindschaft". manifests itself as an eschatological donation – in its centre we find the new and not the renewed individual. During the 4th century the theory of baptism had been established in monasticism, and the second baptism that had been reserved for the monks was considered to be of higher value. This estimation developed parallel to the elaboration of a theory of christening.

In antique-pagan rites little children often had a basic cultic function. This high esteem of children also became an integral part of Christendom. For example, a child's voice was regarded as especially pristine and therefore was thought appropriate to expand into celestial spheres. This particular quality of the sound of children's voices was based on sexual abstinence, an idea of increasing importance in the self-conception of the monks as well. The apostle Paul had already emphasized that the dedication to God like a child would lead to a regeneration and rejuvenation of every Christian. As a consequence, only infidels and sinners were plagued by crinkles and wrinkles. The monks transferred the idea of being spiritually young and of eternal vigour to the second baptism, regarding it as a path to a specific concept of "Gotteskindschaft". Thanks to sexual abstinence the monks preserved the purity of children (ideally, they as well preserved their clear voices). And therefore their bodies did not putrefy but still after death bore the look of a child and smelled of roses.

The specific concept of "Gotteskindschaft" required a radical subjugation to a Christian lifestyle by the servants of God. The monks renounced personal property because the godly, respectively, the monastical father cared for everything. Like any child they were to obey. Raymund KOTTJE has already pointed out the interrelation between the daily celebration of Eucharist and the demand for celibacy since the 4th century, because only now did the cultic *integritas* turn out a focal point. Only he who lived in sexual abstinence could be called a particular child of God having preserved naivety and innocence, and only these children of God could be recognized by the hood. This monastic ideal of a child is also expressed by the adoration of the 'Innocent Children', who are among the 'special martyrs': they serve as a model for young and old 'children of monasteries' when it comes to realizing a lifelong and bloodless martyrdom. Therefore, the celebration of the 'Innocent Children' is a point of reference for the liturgical celebration of child abbots and child bishops.

The idea of a special "Gotteskindschaft" was revived in the 19th century, thus transferring the contemporary ideal of the nuclear family to the monastic family. Hence, the turning into a child (Kindwerdung) in the cloister faced up to the ageing process of the world caused by sin. In his summary Hubertus LUTTERBACH succeeds in covering a wide range from the origins of the specific concept of "Gotteskindschaft" in the 4th century, referring to the doubts about it by the ideals of apostolic poverty in the 12th century, to feminine mysticism in the 13th and 14th centuries and up to the Reformation: Luther regarded the specific concept of "Gotteskindschaft" as simply blasphemous. It was only the 2nd Vatican Council that in the last century revised the distinction between ordinary and special children of God – thanks to baptism, all Christians are now equal.

In his essay Tim GORRINGE traces back the idea of the little child, the *parvulus*. Basing his argument on Matthew 18:1-5, he investigates the meaning of *parvulus* and the reception of this central text of the Bible and quotes different commentators. Thomas Aquinas stresses that the faithful should be children as far as their (missing) badness is concerned, not their comprehension. As long as a faithful believer is not innocent and pure in mind he will not be accepted into the kingdom of heaven. The *Glossa ordinaria* adds to this: He who wishes to be accepted into the kingdom of heaven has to respond to the Gospel like a child. GORRINGE stresses that *puer* characterizes a person who is worth the love of Christ. *Parvulus* may not be understood literally but indicates the wish to serve, not to be served. It also stands for that particular spirit in hearts that leads from pride to humbleness. Being innocent like a child, for example, means not persisting in one's rage.

A sermon by Radulphus Ardens handed down from the beginning of the 12th century refers to the above-mentioned text passage by Matthew. He who wishes to enter the kingdom of God has to possess the virtues and the habits of children. This means children are innocent and are not able to lie, they cannot be angry for a long time, they do not remember injuries, and they do not desire women, etc. Therefore he who humbly thinks of himself is a true child and is the greatest in the eyes of God. According to GORRINGE the goal one should strive for is the 'virtue of humility', meaning that one considers himself worthless. Based on a comment to Matthew, mistakenly attributed to Anselm of Laon, GORRINGE maintains that this passage is not about the 'true' age of a child, but about genuine humility. In his comment, Martin of Leon (†

1203) adds another aspect: He compares saints with children who died before they sinned. Ulrich LUZ points out that Matthew 18:1-5 does not explicitly explain what exactly characterizes children. That is why every epoch projects its own comprehension of children onto the text. Finally, GORRINGE contradicts this view, for starting from the age of the Church Fathers down to the late Middle Ages all preachers and commentators had read the text as a treatise on humility and had stressed the lack of a definite legal status for children. It was only in the 15th century that the idea of meekness was emphasized, a fact that, however, was related to the diatribes against humility prevailing during that time. According to GORRINGE, the silence of the commentators about Augustine's judgment that children by no means were innocent beings was noteworthy.

Tanja SKAMBRAKS deals with children playing the part of boy bishops who occasionally could take on the responsibilities and duties of a 'real' bishop. The living together of old masters and young choir boys inevitably led to conflicts and tensions. For a short time, during the boy bishop's feast, there was a possibility for a balance between the generations: existing generation conflicts were to be balanced out by means of a temporary role reversal and moderated by an implied change of status. The reduction of tensions contributed to the strengthening of the existing order. The explicit acceptance of child-like virtues in Christianity – as Hubertus LUTTERBACH, too, outlines in his essay – were celebrated, for example, in the virtue of the Christ Child and in the martyrdom of the Innocent Children.

The earliest evidence of the boy bishop's feast is to be found in the *Casus Sancti Galli* : In 911 King Conrad was witness to the celebration taking place after Christmas in St. Gallen. Research up to now has related the boy bishop's feast to the medieval theatre or to the carnival and has stressed the elements of the ridiculous or the playful. A more recent interpretation (e.g. by Arthur F. LEACH) emphasizes the recreational factor and the function as an outlet that this celebration implies. SKAMBRAKS agrees and stresses the temporary reversal of status. All these interpretations have in common that they regard the boy bishop's feast as a serious liturgical feast based on religious foundations.

The boy bishop's feast belongs to the context of clerical celebrations taking place at the end of a year. Among those celebrations are, for example, the celebration of St Stephanus on December 26th as well as the celebration of St John the Evangelist on the following day. The boy bishop's feast could be celebrated between December 6th and December 28th due to regional differences. We are dealing with a pan-European phenomenon that can be accounted for in England, Germany, France, Spain and Italy. As a rule the choirboys themselves elected the boy bishop. His true age is kept secret by the sources, but we are presumably dealing with boys aged between six and sixteen.

Taking the celebration in the Cathedral of Sarum as an example, SKAMBRAKS shows how the reversal of status was celebrated in the 11th century: The boy bishop entered the cathedral in the full array of a bishop, the choirboys took the upper seats to which the dean and the canons were usually entitled. The simple liturgical duties now had to be fulfilled by the clerics, e.g. the carrying of the censer, of the books and the candles. At the end of the ceremony the boy bishop ascended the bishop's throne and blessed those present. After the handing over of the crosier to the boy bishop everybody had to bow to him. Its official equipment as well as its ritual functions may serve as proof that we are dealing with a seriously performed act. But authority was attributed to the boy bishop not only as far as liturgy is concerned, his duties could even be more far-reaching. For example, the boy bishops in the dioceses of Mainz, Cambrai and Beauvais could decide on the re-allocation of benefices during their (short) tenure and they presumably even held the right of minting coins. In the 14th century, the boy bishop in York even set out to a visitation throughout 'his' diocese.

According to SKAMBRAKS the boy bishop's feast might be rooted in three cults. The oldest among them is the Roman Saturnalia festival, which was celebrated on December 17th in honour of Saturn and which was among the most popular celebrations in Rome. Here, a 'topsy-turvy' world was definitely established – the masters served their slaves and offered them their seats at the table. The second cult is the worshipping of the Innocent Children. It serves as a theological authorization for the authority of the boy bishop, based on his purity and innocence. The third source is to be found in the St Nicholas cult. Here meet the two elements that form part of the boy bishop's feast: The episcopate on the one hand and the patronage of children and pupils on the other. The patronage of children and pupils by St Nicholas is based on the miracle tale about three 'pickled' schoolboys and their rescue by the saint.

Finally, SKAMBRAKS presents three sermons by boy bishops from the 15th and 16th centuries, showing how the boy bishop's authority was respected. These sermons were given by the elected boy bishops. They come down to us from the time when the celebration was more and more being criticized during the Reformation and finally was officially abolished under Elizabeth I (1558 – 1603). The sermon of John Alcock (1495) emphasized the particular position of the children in the eyes of God, thus justifying the authority of the boy bishop. Richard Ramsey (1558) especially emphasized the purity of the children in his sermon and warned of the detrimental influences that children are exposed to. The boy bishop, above all, was to call for better education. Erasmus of Rotterdam (1511) used the 12-year-old Jesus in the temple as an example of a boy who, despite his youth, already possessed the wisdom of old age. By his moral action, Jesus succeeded in transcending his natural age, thus becoming an example for all Christians. The three sermons mentioned attribute authority to the boy bishop by means of the formal act of the sermon. SKAMBRAKS explicitly shows in her essay that, during the boy bishop's feast, a reversal of status with a 'reality changing effect' took place that meant far more than a playful act serving as an outlet of emotions. The cathedral as a sacred place provided the precondition for the seriousness of the ritual.

The following four essays are case studies. Annette KEHNEL and Gabriela SIGNORI deal with the generation relations and conflicts in monks' monasteries and nuns' convents. Mirko BREITENSTEIN and Michael ROBSON investigate the connection between status and different stages of age in the cloister.

Annette KEHNEL investigates why father-and-son-relations in monasteries were unwanted, although there exists no ban in the New Testament. Before its reform in the 12th century, the Irish church was ruled by family dynasties, which meant that Irish bishops often appointed their offspring to leading positions. Thus, the early Irish church may serve as an example to show how ecclesiastical life was organized on a highly spiritual level with highly ascetic standards, although celibacy was not obligatory. Looking back to the Jewish-Christian tradition, the relations between fathers and sons provide a fundamental basis. From the times of St Paul and his Letter to the

Corinthians, however, a gradual marginalization of 'fathers' holding leading positions arose. By 1200 in the Western church there developed a tendency against natural fathers in spiritual and secular leadership.

In the first part of her article KEHNEL shows important preconditions for the lack of fathers and sons in leading positions by investigating the history of asceticism and celibacy. She reminds us that married priests and bishops were the norm and not the exception in the early Middle Ages. The best-known examples are probably Gregory of Nazianz the Elder and Gregory of Nazianz the Younger. Gregory the Elder was a priest; soon after the birth of his son he was promoted to a bishopric. About 35 years later he ordained his son Gregory, the Younger to the priesthood; the latter later on took over his father's bishopric. KEHNEL emphasizes that the principle of clerical dynasties might not necessarily offend against the principle of clerical chastity: First, the successor generation of priests could be begotten and only after that did one take clerical vows. In the 4th century an opposition against fathers and sons in clerical hierarchies gradually started growing. The Synod of Elvira (around 306) is read as the beginning of disciplinary measures in the case of the sexual activities of clerics. At this time, however, clerical celibacy was still met with reservations. Up to the Merovingian and Carolingian realm priests were allowed to marry prior to taking vows. But at the same time the importance of the concept of cultic purity increased. In the 11th and 12th centuries we can talk about a 'victory of celibacy'. Measures against married clergy were now gradually tightened. It was only at the Synod of Clermont in the year 1095 that sons of priests were excluded from ecclesiastical offices. The second Lateran Council in 1139 declared every kind of clerical marriage illegal, thus ruling out all existing hereditary ecclesiastical dynasties.

The second part of the text shows how in Ireland, in the monastery of Clonmacnoise, offspring, asceticism and celibacy were connected to ecclesiastical leadership. This information is based on the Irish Annals and hagiographical legends. From the 8th to the 12th centuries 25 family members are mentioned in the sources, which means that in the case of Clonmacnoise, records of dynasties of more than 12 generations, lasting for 400 years, can be consulted! Traditionally, Irish Church history is subdivided into phases of rise and decay: From the 5th down to the 7th century, a coherent ecclesiastical structure based on high asceticism and spiritual standards was established. During the 8th century a break with old traditional values can be seen, and secularization and lay patronage increased. The time of decline is also characterized by the rise of monastic dynasties. KEHNEL expresses some doubts about this interpretation, and she emphasizes that in the first place a lot of cultural achievements coincide with the time of the 8th century and thereafter, and that secondly even the leaders of the reform movement passed on their matters of concern from father to son.

In the third part KEHNEL deals with the victory of celibacy, the consequence of which was the decision against 'fathers and sons'. Here she agrees with Arnold ANGENENDT and Hubertus LUTTERBACH, assuming less that a change took place in the ecclesiastical attitude towards sexuality than emphasizing a change in the understanding of the mass and service. These were not in the first place genuine Christian ideas but rather common religious ideas about purity. The victory of celibacy was a victory of general religious concepts over Christian ideals.

In the final part the consequences of strict celibacy – a demand, however, that even from the 12th century onwards never has been fully achieved – is discussed. KEHNEL points out that the ascetic obligation for celibacy led to a lack of offspring. There was a break with dynastic principles prevailing in medieval society, leading to the elaboration of spiritual fatherhood and kinship. At the same time, however, this meant a structural point of weakness in the ecclesiastical claims to universal power. Renouncing the pure imitation of worldly examples when claiming leadership and power, the church established spiritual models in order to successfully ensure its claim to power. Thus, the church counters the worldly claims to power by long-term effective alternatives. This concept of perpetuating one's power seems to follow the principle of 'powers of weakness'.

Taking women's convents as an example, Gabriela SIGNORI deals with generational conflicts between young and old. Although there already exists a number of investigations about children in the cloister, e.g. about oblates or pupils, there is a lack of scientific research about the elderly as well as about the living side-by-side and the living together of young and old. Virgins, widows and wives lived together in the convent. The manifold forms of life and groups in the cloister, among them especially the wives, however, up to now have been neglected by scholarly research. It is not possible to exactly determine the real age of the women involved from the most important type of sources, namely saints' lives and Sister-Books, because we get only vague data out of them. It is striking, however, that the Sister-Books mostly report on very young and very old women. On the one hand very small children who entered the convent already at the age of 3 are mentioned. On the other hand very old women who had to fight against disease and physical disability are named. It is never their real age, but their inner spiritual experience that is put in the centre of interest by the sources. As to the concept of self of the nuns, age as well was of no relevance, but it was rather important to be part of the monastic community.

Within the convent 'small families' were formed; they might consist of pairs of sisters or of a cloistral mother and their daughters. They could be daughters and nieces by birth or elective affinities (Wahlverwandtschaften). Often they shared rooms in the convent. SIGNORI shows that, in any case, we are dealing with kinship being ubiquitous even in the cloister. Here we find different kinds of kinship, such as natural, artificial, metaphorical or spiritual kinship. Max WEBER already pointed out that the intended dying out of a clan by entering a monastery or convent was one of the most radical sacrifices in the medieval system of values. SIGNORI asks that we consider how often this happened when cognatic heiresses (Erbtöchter) entered the convent, especially when siblings entered at the same time. It also frequently happened that mothers and daughters as well as aunts and nieces entered together. Up to now scholarly research has not taken the kinship in monasteries and convents between male and female relatives into consideration, such as brother and sister, uncle and niece or father and daughter.

The Sister-Books describe the living-together of the generations as harmonious, only rarely they do mention problems. But if we additionally consult visitation records, it rapidly becomes clear that also in cloisters conflicts were frequent. Especially reformatory efforts every now and then caused an overlapping of the need of reform and of generation gaps, thus provoking additional tensions. Felix Fabri, for example, reports on a reform of the Benedictine convent of Urspring where most of all young nuns had fought against the intended reform. According to Johannes Meyer those sisters were 'old' who had been living in the convent already before the reform.

The explanations of SIGNORI show that the lebensraum cloister was much more heterogeneous than is generally expected. In this regard, generational conflicts only took second place. It was much more important to have friends in the cloister with whom experiences could be shared. 'Kinship' in all its diversity divided the cloister into a microcosm resembling a family and connecting the generations. It was intended to replace the blood bonds by spiritual bonds. But a complete break with the world was never aimed at, for kinship bonds served as a guarantee of the continuation of a cloister not only as far as money was concerned, but just as well in respect of personnel resources.

In his essay Mirko BREITENSTEIN focuses on the novice master in the Cistercian Order serving as a 'hinge' between young and old. He points to a lack in research as up to now we have had only studies about the novices themselves, forgetting about the master. This gap he wants to fill in taking the novice master in the Cistercian Order as an example. Benedict of Nursia considered this office one of the most important tasks within a monastery. Nevertheless, he did not give much detail concerning this task during his rule. In the *Ecclesiastica Officia,* the Cistercians' book of customs, the tasks of the novice master are described. He introduces the novices to life in the order, he notes down the date of their entrance into the novitiate and informs the abbot about the end of probation. Practical questions of everyday life are among his tasks, such as waking up the novices in church, imposing penance on them or correcting their mistakes in general. He supports the novices with the transition from probation to monastic profession, he helps them dress and undress their habit and shows them where to sleep. In order to enable him to carry out this office, some special privileges are granted to him, e.g. the releasing from the evening lecture. The text does not mention specific qualifications or terms of suitability for the office. Later statutes mention the *magister conversorum*, who instructed the lay brothers, himself being a priest-monk. These texts, however, do not mention the novice master himself. Therefore, BREITENSTEIN looks at the implicit terms of suitability for this office. Accordingly, the novice master was able to read and write, for he noted down the day of the novices' entrance into the novitiate. He was able to keep a calendar because he informed the abbot about the progress of the novitiate. And presumably, like the *magister conversorum*, he was a priest-monk.

In order to enhance the poor sources, BREITENSTEIN consults narrative sources, providing new findings when describing three novice masters living at the end of the 12th and during the first decades of the 13th centuries: (1) Achard of Clairvaux assumed this office only in advanced age, after having been released from other tasks. His experience was especially rich and he imparted it to the young novices, and (2) The English Cistercian monk Aelred of Rievaulx entered the monastery only late in his mid-thirties and at the age of approximately forty the office of the novice master was assigned to him for one year. Probably during this time his *Speculum Caritatis* was written. He possessed high didactic abilities, and what is even more, the capacity of *discretio*. For example, a novice who returned after fleeing was not revealed to the abbot; (3) Adam, the later abbot of the Cistercian abbey of Perseigne, originally had been a regular canon, later on became a Benedictine monk and finally entered the Cistercian order. Although he had never been a novice himself – as he admitted in a letter – he nonetheless was entrusted with this office for some time. He piled up a whole list of preconditions that he considered essential for the instruction of the novices. According to them the novice master ought to be intense in belief; the fear of God as well as the love of wisdom ought to be special characteristics of him, and he ought to be an example to the novices. He ought to address the novices with true concern and understanding, and he frequently ought to hold friendly conversations with them. The novice master ought to be like a mirror for the novices, for whose salvation he was responsible. He as well bore the responsibility for preventing the novices from lapsing into melancholy. The conversations ought to help the novice – they should not only serve the purpose of instruction, but should build a confidential relationship between novice and master.

In his summary, BREITENSTEIN points out that normative texts describe the tasks of the novice master, never mentioning, however, the conditions of aptitude. They can only be deduced implicitly – e.g. age as an equivalent to experience and virtues like *discretio* were especially mentioned. It seems that one's own successful completion of a novitiate was not a precondition for assuming the post of a master. The only precondition for assuming this office possibly was a certain aptitude, meaning the competence in the successful instruction of a novice.

Michael ROBSON investigates how the Franciscan order dealt with children. First of all he talks about the pastoral care of the friars. The old monastic orders came into contact with children only through the oblates. Contrary to this, the Franciscans, following the teaching of Jesus about the innocent children, especially cared for girls and boys. Particularly in their sermons, they tried to reach people of all social categories and of every age, children included. ROBSON emphasizes the theatrical quality of the Franciscan sermon which may have had a special appeal to the young. The friars were also impressive by their experience in the ways of the world and their thorough education. For instance, Mansuetus de Castiglione Fiorentino, who was among the first generations of the friars, testifies how the Franciscans influenced him when he was a child and how they instilled in him, only ten years old, a special reverence for the body of Christ as well as strict fasting rules. A collection of sermons from Padua shows the importance of children for the Franciscan preaching. Bernhardino da Siena cast himself in an important role regarding the education of children. In the year 1424 he urged parents to bring boys and girls even at the age of five to his sermons, which he had conceived especially for the needs of the very young. In the medieval imagination deep spiritual experience was already possible even for children: It has repeatedly come down to us how they again and again became witness to Eucharistic miracles.

The second part of ROBSON's article investigates the influence of friars on children. In the year 1305 John of Montecorvino, the first bishop of Beijing, wrote a letter to his co-friars in Western Europe, informing them of how he had purchased 40 children of pagan families. They were aged between seven and eleven and they were instructed by him in religion. In addition he trained them in copying documents. Therefore, he asked his minister general to send him antiphonaries and legends of the saints for the children to copy as well. The Great Khan, too, took delight in the spiritual singing John of Montecorvino had taught the children. In the following year 1306, he announces in a letter that some of the children whom he had purchased and afterwards baptized had died. In the year 1323 Franciscan friars reported from China how they continued John's practice. They, too, purchased boys and girls and trained the boys as friars.

Frequently the Franciscans focused on the care of the children – the friars in China, for instance, gave alms to them. Peter d'Assisi, who preached in the Veneto in the year 1335, took care of abandoned children until a hospice was founded for them. Raymond Berengarii IV, count of Provence, entrusted the Franciscans with the pastoral ministry of his children. In England Franciscans lived within royal households in order to serve as chaplains and confessors and to take care of legitimate as well as illegitimate children of the royal family.

In the third part of his article ROBSON deals with the connection between Franciscan churches and children. The churches were public places where the friars came into contact with the community, for example, when they were used as places of burial for important citizens of the town. Churches offered the younger members of the community a visible guide to history of the family with their coats of arms, their chapels flanking the altar and the adjoining cemeteries. Archaeological excavations in Wales and England have revealed children's graves in the churches probably containing the bodies of novices. It is striking how often children feature in Franciscan miracles – for example, children account for 30% of the miracles coming down to us from Odorico da Pordenone († 1331). Children were as well frequently engaged to do routine tasks for the friars. For instance, in the year 1300 the Greyfriars in London repeatedly charged a boy with carrying apples and pears to Queen Margaret. The services of these boys are documented in the records as well.

The fourth part of the article deals with mendicant images of childhood. Thomas of Celano severely criticizes the circumstances of St Francis' childhood, describing him as a vain and proud boy the parents of whom are not worth being mentioned. It is only the *Vita secunda* that reports on the parents of the saint in a more conciliatory way. St John the Baptist serves as a model for the description of John of Orta. He never played with his brothers and sisters, for even when he was a child his mind already was concentrated on churches and monasteries. With deep devotion he received the Body of Christ as often as possible. The fifth part of the essay assembles indications about children who were admitted by the order, which frequently led to conflicts. Therefore, the general chapter of 1260 ordained that candidates should be at least 18 years old, whereas the general chapter of 1354 ordained a minimum age of 14. There are frequent documentations about families opposing a vocation of their sons. Salimbene, whose father Guido de Adam became known as a crusader of the 13th century, is quoted as an example. The father was inconsolable because his son had joined the order and he repeatedly tried to detach him from the order by force. He spent the rest of his life in trying to call back his son – but without success.

In his last paragraph ROBSON turns to polemics against the Franciscans. He cites Richard FitzRalph, the Archbishop of Armagh, who was one of the most vigorous critics of the friars. In a sermon for the pope and the cardinals he talks about a father whose 12-year-old son had been drawn to the friars in Oxford. The father claimed in the papal court that the order did not allow him and his wife to speak alone with their son. The parents were fully convinced that their son was being kept by the Franciscans against his will. Frequently, the sources report on similar cases. In 1358, the University of Oxford took strong measures in order to prevent the Franciscans from admitting boys below the age of 18. Nonetheless, the complaints about the friars' 'robbery' continued. The case of John Sillow once again shows how problematic the situation was: At the age of about seven he was given to the order, aged fourteen he made several attempts to leave the order, but he repeatedly was not allowed to do so. About 1476 he fled and was judged to be an apostate. It was only in 1490 that Innocent VIII cleared him of apostasy. Throughout the Middle Ages the Franciscans succeeded in attracting boys, a fact that frequently led to conflicts with the secular clergy. We do not know exactly how many children were involved. Although the sources that have come down to us are only fragmentary, we clearly understand what was the basic tendency: Children played a significant role in the Franciscans' thinking; they were to be won for the Christian message with their hearts and minds.

This collection leads us to a number of further questions. How was the affiliation with a common generation established – by age or by external factors such as spirituality, striving for reforms or the level of education? What was the relationship between age and disease like? In the Middle Ages sickness was often considered an honour (he is loved by God, who is being tested by him) – was advanced age also a gift of God? And if particular honour was to be attributed to the elderly – how did it compete with the special status of the 'innocent' children? The meaning of 'child' and 'childship' still ought to be fathomed out further: What impact can the idea of the special "Gotteskindschaft" have at its disposal, regarding for instance an intensified effectiveness of the prayers within the framework of *memoria*? How did the Christian comprehension of childhood change during the Middle Ages? How is the loss of adult authority and the upending of a divinely-sanctioned order (e.g. the replacement of bishops with children) theologically justified? How can we, finally, understand the cultural factors defining a concept of age that reaches beyond the concept of age determined by a human life-span?

The debate on the 'generations in the cloister' has brought about the first results in a historical approach to age. Inevitably, there are even more questions left open than there are questions we have been able to answer. Ideally, the volume at hand will succeed in providing an impetus to further research on this topic.

*

"Generationen im Kloster" – auf den ersten Blick geht es um das Zusammenleben von alt und jung in einer Glaubensgemeinschaft unter einem Dach und um die Spannungen, die sich aus Generationskonflikten ergeben. Der vorliegende Band belegt die Vielschichtigkeit und den Facettenreichtum dieses Themas; die Beiträge reichen weit über den Gegensatz alt/jung hinaus und werfen grundlegende Fragen auf: wer war im christlichen Verständnis ein Kind? Was lässt einen Menschen altern – jenseits vom Verstreichen der Jahre? Stimmt Max WEBERs Diktum, das Christentum habe radikal mit den Sippenbanden gebrochen und folglich gab es keine Familiendynastien im Kloster?

Der Begriff der Generation soll die sozial-zeitliche Positionierung von Individuen oder Kollektiven in einer Gesellschaft charakterisieren und schreibt ihnen eine spezifische Identität in Form der Generationenidentität zu.[2] Der Einzelne orientiert sich in seinem Denken, Fühlen, Wollen und Handeln an sozialen Perspektiven, die historisch geprägt sind. Zentral sind dabei die beiden Frage, wie erstens Generationszugehörigkeit zur Konstituierung von Identität beiträgt und diese bestimmt und wie zweitens die Zugehörigkeit wahrgenommen wird und zu einer Abgrenzung von anderen Generationen führt. In Form von intergenerationellen Beziehungen stehen die Angehörigen von unterschiedlichen Generationen in personaler und kollektiver Beziehung zueinander. Sie orientieren sich aneinander, sie beeinflussen sich gegenseitig und tauschen sich über Erfahrungen, aber beispielsweise

---

2 Zum Folgenden siehe vor allem K. LÜSCHER, Ambivalenz – Eine Annäherung an das Problem der Generationen. Die Aktulität der Generationenfrage, in: U. JUREIT (Hg.), Generationen. Zur Relevanz eines wissenschaftlichen Grundbegriffs, Hamburg 2005, S. 53-78.

auch über Normen aus. Die Erfahrung subjektiver Gemeinsamkeiten und Verschiedenheiten sowie die institutionell vorgegebenen Bedingungen, etwa im Kloster, prägen Form und Dynamik von Generationenbeziehungen. Die folgenden Beiträge beschäftigen sich immer wieder mit zwei Grundproblemen in der Auseinandersetzung mit der Generationenfrage. Zum einen geht es um die Konstituierung von Generationen und die Prozesse generationsspezifischer Identitätszuschreibungen, beispielsweise bei der Unterscheidung von Reformfreunden und -gegnern in einer Klostergemeinschaft. Zum anderen geht es um die Gestaltung von Beziehungen zwischen verschiedenen Generationen, wie wir sie im Frühmittelalter in irischen Klöstern antreffen oder wie sie sich im Kinderbischofsfest manifestieren.

Die folgenden Beiträge lassen sich in zwei Gruppen einteilen: Zuerst stehen 'reale' und 'virtuelle' Kinder im Mittelpunkt der Aufmerksamkeit. Hubertus LUTTERBACH untersucht das Konzept der Gotteskindschaft; Tim GORRINGE beschäftigt sich mit der Idee des kleinen Kindes (*parvulus*) im Neuen Testament und Tanja SKAMBRAKS stellt das Kinderbischofsfest als eine Möglichkeit vor, kurzzeitig Alter- und Statusstrukturen im geschützten Raum einer religiösen Gemeinschaft aufzubrechen. Der zweite Teil präsentiert Fallstudien zu einzelnen Themenkomplexen. Mit den Generationenbeziehungen setzt sich einerseits Annette KEHNEL am Beispiel von irischen Männerklöstern auseinander, deutsche Frauenklöster dienen als exemplarisches Beispiel im Beitrag von Gabriela SIGNORI. Die Ausbildung junger Menschen als Novizen im Zisterzienserorden untersucht Mirko BREITENSTEIN, den Umgang mit Kindern und Jugendlichen durch die Franziskaner thematisiert Michael ROBSON. Im Folgenden werden die einzelnen Beiträge kurz vorgestellt.

Hubertus LUTTERBACH thematisiert verschiedene Formen von Gotteskindschaft. Seit dem 4. Jahrhundert begannen Mönche, ein ursprünglich in der Antike für Kinder gedachtes Kleidungsstück zu tragen, die Kapuze, um sich damit als geistliche Kinder kenntlich zu machen. Dadurch entstand eine komplexe Situation, die LUTTERBACH mit dem Begriff 'Kapuzen-Konkurrenz' charakterisiert: Bei der Taufe trug jeder Gläubige ein Taufkleid mit Kapuze, und war damit als (neues) Gotteskind für alle erkennbar. Ein Mönch unterzog sich bei der Profess einer zweiten Taufe; bei ihm stand die Kapuze für eine besondere

Gotteskindschaft. In der johanneischen Theologie wird der Einzelne durch die Taufe Gottes Kind. Die Kindschaft ist eine 'Zeugung aus Gott'; damit ist den Gotteskindern eine übernatürliche Herkunft zu Eigen. In der Taufe vollzieht sich das Geschenk der Gotteskindschaft als eschatologische Gabe; zentral ist dabei der neue, nicht der erneuerte Mensch. Gleichzeitig mit einer ausdifferenzierten Theologie der Taufe setzte sich im Mönchtum seit dem 4. Jahrhundert die Ansicht durch, dass die zweite Taufe, die den Mönchen vorbehalten war, höherwertig sei.

In antik-heidnischen Riten hatten häufig kleine Kinder tragende kultische Funktionen. Diese hohe Wertschätzung der Kinder floss auch in das Christentum ein. So galt die kindliche Stimme als besonders rein und damit geeignet, bis in himmlische Sphären vorzudringen. Die besondere Klang-Qualität verdankten die Kinderstimmen der zugrunde liegenden sexuellen Abstinenz, die auch im Verständnis der Mönche immer mehr an Bedeutung gewann. Schon Paulus betonte, dass die gotteskindliche Hingabe zur Erneuerung und Verjüngung jedes Christen führe. Nur Ungläubige und Sünder würden folglich von Falten und Runzeln heimgesucht. Die Mönche übertrugen die Idee des geistlichen Jungseins und ewiger Frische auf die zweite Taufe als Weg der besonderen Gotteskindschaft. Dank sexueller Abstinenz bewahrten sich die Mönche die Reinheit der Kinder (idealiter auch deren helle Stimmen); deshalb verwesten ihre Leiber nicht, sondern zeigten nach dem Tod ein kindgleiches Aussehen und dufteten nach Rosen.

Die besondere Gotteskindschaft forderte von den Dienern Gottes eine radikale Unterwerfung unter einen christlichen Lebensstil. Die Mönche verzichteten auf eigenen Besitz, da der göttliche, respektive der klösterliche Vater für alles sorgte; wie jedes Kind sollten sie Gehorsam üben. Schon Raymund KOTTJE hatte auf den Zusammenhang zwischen dem täglichen Zelebrieren der Eucharistie seit dem 4. Jahrhundert und den Zölibatsforderungen hingewiesen, da erst jetzt die kultische *integritas* zentral wurde. Nur wer sexuell enthaltsam lebte, konnte somit ein besonderes Gotteskind sein, das sich Einfalt und Unschuld bewahrt hatte und an der Kapuze zu erkennen war. Dieses monastische Kinderideal zeigte sich auch in der Verehrung der Unschuldigen Kinder, die zu den Sonder-Märtyrern zählen: Ihnen kommt eine Vorbildfunktion für junge und alte 'Klosterkinder' bei der Verwirklichung eines lebenslänglichen und unblutigen Martyriums zu. Das Fest der Unschuldigen

Kinder ist deshalb auch ein Bezugspunkt für die liturgische Feier von Kinderäbten und -bischöfen.

Die Idee der besonderen Gotteskindschaft wurde im 19. Jahrhundert wiederbelebt; damit wurde das zeitgenössische Ideal der Kleinfamilie auf die monastische Familie übertragen. Die Kindwerdung im Kloster trat damit dem durch Sünde verursachten Alterungsprozess der Welt entgegen. In seiner Zusammenfassung gelingt es Hubertus LUTTERBACH, einen Bogen von den Ursprüngen der besonderen Gotteskindschaft im 4. Jahrhundert über ihre Infragestellung durch die Armutsbewegung im 12. Jahrhundert, durch die Frauenmystik im 13. und 14. Jahrhundert bis hin zur Reformation zu schlagen: Luther hielt die besondere Gotteskindschaft für schlicht blasphemisch. Erst das 2. Vatikanum revidierte im vergangenen Jahrhundert die Unterscheidung zwischen gewöhnlichen und besonderen Gotteskindern: Durch die Taufe sind nun alle Christen gleich.

Tim GORRINGE stellt die Idee des kleinen Kindes, des *parvulus*, in seinem Beitrag vor. Am Beispiel von Mt 18,1-5 untersucht er die Bedeutung von *parvulus* und die Rezeption dieser zentralen Bibelstelle. Dazu zieht er eine Reihe von Kommentatoren heran. Thomas von Aquin betont, dass die Gläubigen Kinder in Bezug auf ihre (fehlende) Bösartigkeit, jedoch nicht in Bezug auf ihr Verständnis sein sollen. So lange der Gläubige nicht die Unschuld und Reinheit des Geistes hat, kann er nicht ins Himmelreich eingehen. Die *Glossa ordinaria* ergänzt: Wer ins Himmelreich eingehen will, muss dem Evangelium wie ein Kind gehorsam sein. GORRINGE betont, dass *puer* eine Person bezeichnet, die der Liebe Christi würdig ist. *Parvulus* darf nicht wörtlich verstanden werden, sondern bezeichnet den Wunsch, nicht bedient zu werden, sondern zu dienen. Es bezeichnet auch denjenigen Geist in den Herzen, der vom Stolz zur Demut führt. Unschuldig wie ein Kind zu sein bedeutet beispielsweise, nicht im Zorn zu verharren.

Von Radulphus Ardens von Aquitanien ist vom Beginn des 12. Jahrhunderts eine Predigt zu besagter Matthäus-Stelle überliefert. Wer ins Himmelreich eintreten will, muss die Tugenden und Angewohnheiten von Kindern haben. Kinder sind demnach unschuldig und unfähig zu lügen, sie können Wut nicht für längere Zeit empfinden, sie erinnern sich nicht an Verletzungen, sie begehren keine Frauen etc. Wer von sich selbst demütig denkt, ist demnach das wahre Kind und in den Augen

Gottes der Größte. GORRINGE nennt als Ziel die Tugend der Demut ("virtue of humility"), nach der ein Mann in seinen eigenen Augen wertlos ist. Basierend auf einem fälschlicherweise Anselm von Laon zugeschrieben Kommentar zu Matthäus hält er fest, dass es bei dieser Stelle nicht um das 'wahre' Alter des Kindes, sondern um echte Demut geht. Martin von Leon († 1203) fügt in seinem Kommentar zu dieser Bibelstelle einen weiteren Aspekt hinzu: Er vergleicht Heilige mit Kindern, die verstorben sind, bevor sie sündigten.

Ulrich LUZ wies darauf hin, dass Mt 18,1-5 gerade nicht explizit sagt, was Kinder charakterisiert; deshalb projiziert jede Epoche ihr eigenes Verständnis von Kindern auf den Text. Dem widerspricht GORRINGE abschließend, denn von der Zeit der Kirchenväter bis zum Spätmittelalter hätten alle Prediger und Kommentatoren den Text als Traktat für Demut gelesen und das Fehlen eines eindeutigen Rechtsstatus für Kinder betont. Erst im 15. Jahrhundert sei die Idee der Sanftmut ("meekness") betont worden, was aber mit den Schmähreden auf Demut in dieser Zeit zusammenhing. Bemerkenswert sei jedoch das Schweigen der Kommentatoren über das Urteil Augustins, dass Kinder keineswegs unschuldige Wesen seien.

Tanja SKAMBRAKS beschäftigt sich mit Kindern in der Rolle von Kinderbischöfen, die temporär Aufgaben und Funktionen eines 'echten' Bischofs übernehmen konnten. Das Zusammenleben von alten Lehrmeistern und jungen Chorknaben im Kloster führte zwangsläufig zu Konflikten und Spannungen. Im mittelalterlichen Kinderbischofsfest war für kurze Zeit ein Ausgleich zwischen den Generationen möglich: Bestehende Generationenkonflikte sollten mit Hilfe eines zeitlich befristeten Rollentausches ausgeglichen und durch eine implizite Statusumkehr gemildert werden. Der Abbau von Spannungen trug auch hier zur Stärkung der bestehenden Ordnung bei. Die explizite Anerkennung kindlicher Tugenden im Christentum – wie sie auch der Beitrag von Hubertus LUTTERBACH thematisiert – wurden beispielsweise in der Tugendhaftigkeit des Jesuskindes und im Martyrium der Unschuldigen Kinder zelebriert.

Das früheste Zeugnis für das Kinderbischofsfest lässt sich in den *Casus Sancti Galli* finden: König Konrad wurde im Jahr 911 nach Weihnachten Zeuge des Festes in St. Gallen. Die bisherige Forschung ordnete das Kinderbischofsfest dem mittelalterlichen Theater oder dem

Narrenfest zu und betonte die Elemente des Lächerlichen oder Spielerischen. Eine zweite, neuere Deutung (beispielsweise bei Arthur F. LEACH) betont hingegen die Erholungs- und Ventilfunktion, die in diesem Fest enthalten sei. Dieser Argumentation folgt auch SKAMBRAKS, wobei sie einen besonderen Akzent auf die temporäre Statusumkehr legt. Allen Deutungen ist gemein, dass sie im Kinderbischofsfest ein ernst zu nehmendes liturgisches Fest mit religiöser Fundierung sehen.

Das Kinderbischofsfest gehört in den Kontext der Klerikerfeste, die am Jahresende gefeiert wurden. Zu diesen Festen zählen beispielsweise auch das Fest des heiligen Stephan am 26. Dezember oder das Fest des heiligen Johannes dem Evangelisten am darauf folgenden Tag. Das Kinderbischofsfest konnte regional unterschiedlich zwischen dem 6. und 28. Dezember begangen werden. Hierbei handelt es sich um ein gesamteuropäisches Phänomen, das in England, dem Heiligen Römischen Reich, Frankreich, Spanien und Italien nachgewiesen werden kann. Die Wahl des Kinderbischofs erfolgte in der Regel durch die Chorknaben selbst; sein genaues Alter verschweigen die Quellen, aber vermutlich handelt es sich um Jungen im Alter zwischen sechs und sechzehn Jahren.

Am Beispiel der Feier in der Kathedrale von Sarum zeigt SKAMBRAKS, wie im 11. Jh. die Statusumkehr zelebriert wurde: Der Kinderbischof zog in der Kathedrale in vollem bischöflichen Ornat ein; die Chorknaben nahmen die erhöhten Plätze ein, die gewöhnlich dem Domdekan und den Domherren zustanden. Die einfachen liturgischen Aufgaben mussten nun die Kleriker erfüllen, etwa das Tragen des Weihrauchfasses sowie der Bücher und Kerzen. Am Ende der Zeremonie bestieg der Kinderbischof den Bischofsthron und segnete die Anwesenden. Nach der Übergabe des Bischofsstabes an ihn mussten sich alle Anwesenden vor ihm verneigen. Seine materielle Ausstattung, aber auch seine rituellen Funktionen belegen, dass es sich um einen ernst zu nehmenden Akt handelte. Dem Kinderbischof wurde aber nicht nur auf der liturgischen Ebene Autorität zugeschrieben, sondern seine Pflichten konnten noch weiterreichen. So konnten die Kinderbischöfe in den Diözesen Mainz, Cambrai und Beauvais während ihrer (kurzen) Amtszeit über die Neuvergabe von Pfründen entscheiden und hatten vermutlich sogar kurzzeitig das Münzprägerecht inne; in York machte sich der Kinderbischof im 14. Jahrhundert überdies zu einer Visitationsreise durch 'seine' Diözese auf.

Die möglichen Ursprünge für das Kinderbischofsfest sieht SKAMBRAKS in drei Kulten. Am ältesten ist das römische Saturnalienfest, das am 17. Dezember zu Ehren Saturns begangen wurde und zu den populärsten Festen Roms zählte. Hier wurde eindeutig eine 'verkehrte' Welt konstituiert: Die Herren bedienten ihre Sklaven und mussten ihnen am Tisch ihre Plätze räumen. Die Verehrung der Unschuldigen Kinder ist der zweite Kult; er bietet die theologische Legitimation für die Autorität des Kinderbischofs, die sich auf seiner Reinheit und Unschuld gründet. Die dritte Quelle liegt im Nikolauskult. Hier treffen die beiden Elemente des Bischofsamtes und des Patronats über Kinder und Schüler zusammen, die in das Kinderbischofsfest einflossen. Das Schutzpatronat von Nikolaus über Kinder und Schüler gründet auf der Wundererzählung von drei eingepökelten Schulknaben und ihre Errettung durch den Heiligen.

Abschließend stellt SKAMBRAKS drei Kinderbischofspredigten aus dem 15. und 16. Jahrhundert vor, die zeigen, wie dem Kinderbischof Autorität beigemessen wurde. Diese Predigten wurden von den gewählten Kinderbischöfen vorgetragen; sie stammen aus einer Zeit, als das Fest im Zuge der Reformation zunehmend kritisiert und schließlich unter Elizabeth I. (1558-1603) offiziell abgeschafft wurde. Die Predigt von John Alcock (1495) hob die besondere Stellung der Kinder in den Augen Gottes hervor und rechtfertigte damit die Autorität des Kinderbischofs. Richard Ramsey (1558) betonte in seiner Predigt vor allem die Reinheit der Kinder und warnte vor den schädlichen Einflüssen, denen Kinder ausgesetzt sind. Der Kinderbischof sollte vor allem eine bessere Erziehung anmahnen. Erasmus von Rotterdam (1511) zog den zwölfjährigen Jesus im Tempel als Beispiel für den altersweisen Knaben heran. Durch sein moralisches Handel gelang es Jesus, sein natürliches Lebensalter zu transzendieren und damit zum Vorbild für alle Christen zu werden. Alle drei vorgestellten Predigten sprechen dem Kinderbischof durch den formalen Akt des Predigens Autorität zu. SKAMBRAKS zeigt mit ihren Ausführungen eindrücklich, dass beim Kinderbischofsfest eine Statusumkehr mit "wirklichkeitsverändernder Wirkung" stattfand, die weit über einen spielerischen Akt mit Ventilfunktion hinausreichte. Die Kathedrale als dafür gewählter sakraler Raum schuf die Voraussetzung für die Ernsthaftigkeit des Rituals.

Die folgenden vier Beiträge sind Fallstudien; Annette KEHNEL und Gabriela SIGNORI beschäftigten sich mit Generationenbeziehungen und -konflikten in Männer- und Frauenklöstern. Mirko BREITENSTEIN und Michael ROBSON gehen der Verbindung von Status und verschiedenen Altersstufen im Kloster nach.

Annette KEHNEL untersucht, warum Vater-Sohn-Beziehungen innerhalb der Klöster unerwünscht waren, obwohl es im Neuen Testament kein Verbot dafür gibt. Die irische Kirche wurde vor ihrer Reform im 12. Jahrhundert von Familien-Dynastien regiert; dabei setzten irische Äbte und Bischöfe häufig ihren Nachwuchs in Führungspositionen ein. Am Beispiel der frühen irischen Kirche kann also nachverfolgt werden, wie das kirchliche Leben auf einem hohen spirituellen Niveau mit hohen asketischen Standards organisiert wurde, obwohl das Pflicht-Zölibat fehlte. Blickt man auf die jüdisch-christliche Tradition zurück, so bilden Vater-Sohn-Beziehungen eine fundamentale Basis. Seit den Briefen von Paulus an die Korinther beginnt jedoch eine schrittweise Marginalisierung von 'Vätern' als Führungspersönlichkeiten. Bis 1200 bildete sich dann in der westlichen Kirche eine Tendenz heraus, die sich gegen die natürlichen Väter in spirituellen und zeitlichen Führungspositionen richtete.

In ersten Teil zeigt KEHNEL wichtige Voraussetzungen für das Fehlen von Vätern und Söhnen in Führungspositionen. Dazu untersucht sie die Geschichte des Asketentums und Zölibats und betont, dass verheiratete Priester und Bischöfe im Frühmittelalter nicht die Ausnahme, sondern die Norm waren. Das bekannteste Beispiel dürften Gregor von Nazianz der Ältere und der Jüngere sein. Gregor der Ältere war Priester, kurz nach der Geburt des Sohnes übernahm er das Bischofsamt. Seinen Sohn Gregor von Nazianz den Jüngeren weihte er rund 35 Jahre später ebenfalls zum Priester; dieser übernahm von ihm danach das Bischofsamt. KEHNEL betont, dass das Prinzip der klerikalen Dynastie nicht notwendigerweise gegen das Prinzip der klerikalen Enthaltsamkeit verstoßen musste: Zuerst konnte die nächste Priestergeneration gezeugt werden, erst danach wurden die höheren Weihen empfangen. Seit dem 4. Jahrhundert formierte sich allmählich eine Opposition gegen Väter und Söhne in kirchlichen Hierarchien. Die Synode von Elvira (um 306) gilt als Beginn von disziplinarischen Maßnahmen bei sexueller Aktivitäten von Klerikern; in dieser Zeit stieß aber ein Zölibat für Priester noch auf breite Ablehnung. Bis in die Zeit der Merowinger und Karolinger war eine Eheschließung für Priester vor Ablegung der Gelübde erlaubt; gleichzeitig gewann aber das Konzept der kultischen Reinheit immer mehr an Bedeutung. Von einem "Sieg des Zölibats" kann im 11. und 12. Jahrhundert gesprochen werden. Die Maßnahmen gegen verheiratete Priester nahmen nun zu. Erst die Synode von Clermont im Jahr 1095 schloss Söhne, deren Väter Priester waren, von kirchlichen Ämtern aus. Das II. Laterankonzil erklärte 1139 alle Priester-Ehen für illegal und beendete damit alle bestehenden kirchlichen Erbdynastien.

Am exemplarische Beispiel des Klosters Clonmacnoise in Irland wird im zweiten Teil dieses Beitrags gezeigt, wie Nachwuchs, Askese und Zölibat zu kirchlicher Führung ("leadership") verbunden werden. Als Quelle werden irische Annalen und hagiographische Legenden herangezogen. Vom 8. bis zum 12. Jahrhundert werden 25 Familienmitglieder in den Quellen erwähnt, d.h. für Clonmacnoise können Dynastien über 12 Generationen, die sich auf 400 Jahre erstrecken, herangezogen werden! Traditionellerweise wird die irische Kirchengeschichte in klare Phasen von Aufstieg und Verfall eingeteilt: Vom 5. bis zum 7. Jahrhundert gab es demnach eine kohärente kirchliche Struktur mit hohen asketischen und spirituellen Maßstäben; im 8. Jahrhundert erfolgte ein Bruch mit den alten, traditionellen Werten und Verweltlichung und Laienpatronage griffen um sich. Diese Zeit des Verfalls wird auch durch die monastischen Dynastien charakterisiert. Dieser Sicht misstraut KEHNEL, und sie gibt zu Bedenken, dass erstens eine Reihe von kulturellen Höhepunkten in die Zeit des 8. Jahrhunderts und danach fallen und zweitens sogar die Führer der Reformbewegung ihr Anliegen vom Vater auf den Sohn weitergaben.

Im dritten Teil stellt KEHNEL Erklärungsmöglichkeiten für den Siegeszugs des Zölibats vor, der eine Entscheidung gegen 'Väter und Söhne' mit sich brachte. Dabei folgt sie den Argumentationen von Arnold ANGENENDT und Hubertus LUTTERBACH, die weniger einen Wandel in der Haltung der Kirche gegenüber Sexualität annehmen, sondern vielmehr einen Wechsel im Verständnis von Messe und Gottesdienst betonen. Dabei geht es weniger um genuin christliche Ideen als vielmehr um allgemeine Ideale der Reinheit. Der Sieg des Zölibats war ein Sieg allgemeiner religiöser Ideen über christliche Ideale.

Im Schlussteil werden die Konsequenzen eines konsequenten Zölibats diskutiert, das aber auch nach dem 12. Jahrhundert nicht umfassend durchgesetzt werden konnte. KEHNEL betont, dass die asketische Verpflichtung zum Zölibat zu einem Mangel an Nachwuchs führte. Es kam zu einem Bruch mit dynastischen Prinzipien, die in der mittelalterlichen Gesellschaft vorherrschend waren. Dadurch entstanden spirituelle Vaterschaften und Verwandtschaften. Gleichzeitig brachte dies aber einen strukturellen Schwachpunkt im Anspruch der Kirche auf universale Macht mit sich. Durch den bewussten Verzicht auf weltliche Vorbilder von Führung und Macht konnten spirituelle Modelle entstehen, die die weltliche Herrschaft ersetzten und Teil eines übergeordneten Konzeptes von 'Macht durch Schwäche' ("power of weakness") wurden.

Generationenkonflikte zwischen jung und alt nimmt Gabriela SIGNORI am Beispiel von Frauenkonventen in den Blick. Obwohl es bereits zahlreiche Untersuchungen zu Kindern im Kloster gibt, beispielsweise zu Oblaten oder Klosterschüler und -schülerinnen, so fehlen doch Beiträge zu Alten ebenso wie zu dem Neben- und Miteinander von jung und alt. Jungfrauen, Witwen und Ehefrauen lebten gemeinsam im Kloster. Die vielfältigen Lebensformen und Gruppen im Kloster, vor allem die Ehefrauen, wurden jedoch bisher von der Forschung vernachlässigt. Wie alt oder jung die Frauen tatsächlich waren, lässt sich anhand der wichtigsten Quellengruppe, den Viten und Schwesternbüchern, nicht genau bestimmen, da immer nur vage Angaben gemacht werden. Auffällig ist jedoch, dass die Schwesternbücher meist von sehr jungen und sehr alten Frauen berichten. So werden einerseits sehr kleine Kinder erwähnt, die zum Teil schon mit drei Jahren ins Kloster kamen; andererseits ist von sehr alten Frauen die Rede, die mit Krankheit und körperlicher Behinderung zu kämpfen hatten. Ihr absolutes Alter spielt in den Quellen aber nie eine Rolle, sondern ihr inneres, spirituelles Erleben steht im Vordergrund. Im Selbstverständnis der Schwestern spielte Alter ebenfalls keine Rolle, sondern es war wichtig, dass sie Teil der klösterlichen Gemeinschaft waren.

Innerhalb des Konvents formierten sich häufig 'kleine Familien', die aus Geschwisterpaaren oder aus einer Klostermutter und ihren -töchtern zusammengesetzt sein konnten. Hier konnte es sich um leibliche Töchter, Nichten oder Wahlverwandtschaften handeln. Häufig bewohnten sie gemeinsam dieselben Räume im Konvent. SIGNORI macht deutlich, dass es sich auf jeden Fall um Verwandtschaft handelte, die auch im Kloster allgegenwärtig war; dabei konnte es sich um so unterschiedliche Formen wie leibliche, künstliche, metaphorische oder spirituelle Verwandtschaft handeln. Max WEBER wies bereits darauf hin, dass das intendierte Erlöschen der Sippe durch den Eintritt ins Kloster eines der radikalsten Opfer im mittelalterlichen Wertesystem war. Diesen Gedanken führt SIGNORI weiter und gibt zu Bedenken, dass dies auch häufig durch den Eintritt von Erbtöchtern passierte, vor allem beim gemeinsamen Eintritt von Geschwistern. Ebenfalls traten häufig Mütter und Töchter sowie Tanten und Nichten gemeinsam ein. Bisher von der Forschung übersehen wurden die Verwandtschaftsbande im Kloster zwischen männlichen und weiblichen Verwandten, etwa Bruder und Schwester, Onkel und Nichte oder Vater und Tochter.

Die Schwesternbücher stellen das Miteinander der Generationen harmonisch dar, nur selten ist von Problemen die Rede. Werden aber Visitationsprotokolle zur Ergänzung herangezogen, so wird rasch deutlich, dass es auch im Kloster regelmäßig Konflikte gab. Vor allem Reformvorhaben führten immer wieder dazu, dass sich Reformanliegen und Generationsunterschiede überlagerten und zu zusätzlichen Spannungen führten. Felix Fabri berichtet beispielsweise von der Reform des Benediktinerinnen-Klosters Urspring, vor allem junge Nonnen hätten sich gegen die geplante Reform zur Wehr gesetzt. 'Alt' sind für Johannes Meyer diejenigen Schwestern, die schon vor der Reform im Kloster lebten.

Deutlich wird bei den Ausführungen von SIGNORI, dass der Lebensraum Kloster viel inhomogener war, als gemeinhin angenommen wird. Generationenkonflikte spielten dabei nur eine nachgeordnete Rolle, viel wichtiger war es, im Kloster Freunde zu haben, mit denen Erfahrungen geteilt werden konnten. 'Verwandtschaft' in ihren vielfältigen Ausprägungen unterteilte das Kloster in kleine familienähnliche Welten, die generationsübergreifend strukturiert waren. Ziel war es, die Blutsbande durch spirituelle Bande zu ersetzten. Ein völliger Bruch mit der Welt war aber nie intendiert, denn Verwandtschaftsbande garantierten den Fortbestand des Klosters, nicht nur in materieller, sondern eben auch in personeller Hinsicht.

Mirko BREITENSTEIN stellt den Novizenmeister im Zisterzienserorden als 'Scharnierstelle' zwischen jung und alt in den Mittelpunkt seiner Ausführungen. Er lenkt damit den Blick auf eine Forschungslücke, da bisher nur die Novizen Beachtung fanden, ihr Meister aber übersehen wurde. Diese Lücke will er am Beispiel des Novizenmeisters im Zisterzienserorden schließen. Für Benedikt von Nursia zählte dieses Amt zu den wichtigsten Aufgaben innerhalb des Klosters; dennoch führte er diesen Punkt in seiner Regel nicht weiter aus. Die *Ecclesiastica Officia,* einem Werk zu den zisterziensischen Gewohnheiten, beschreiben die Aufgaben des Novizenmeisters. Er führt die Novizen ins Ordensleben ein, er notiert ihren Eintritt ins Noviziat und informiert den Abt über das Ende dieser Zeit. Er ist für praktische Fragen zuständig, wie das Wecken der Novizen in der Kirche, die Festsetzung von Strafen oder das prinzipielle Korrigieren von Fehlern. Beim Übertritt in den Mönchsstand steht er den Novizen bei und hilft ihnen beim An- und Ablegen der Ordenstracht und weist ihnen ihren Schlafplatz zu. Damit er dieses Amt ausüben kann, genießt er spezielle Privilegien, zum Beispiel die Befreiung von der Abendlektüre. Der Text nennt keine speziellen Qualifikationen oder Voraussetzungen für das Amt. Spätere Statuten erwähnen den *magister conversorum*, der die Laien-Brüder unterwies und ein Priester-Mönch war; diese Texte schweigen sich aber über den Novizenmeister aus. So fragt BREITENSTEIN nach den impliziten Voraussetzungen für dieses Amt. Der Novizenmeister konnte demnach lesen und schreiben, denn er notierte den Eintritt in den Novizenstand; er konnte einen Kalender führen, da er den Abt über den Ablauf informierte; und vermutlich war er, wie der *magister conversorum*, ein Priester-Mönch.

Um die karge Quellenlage zu verbessern, zieht BREITENSTEIN auch erzählende Quellen heran, die zu neuen Erkenntnissen am Beispiel von drei Novizenmeisters aus der Zeit des ausgehenden 12. und den ersten Jahrzehnten des 13. Jahrhunderts führen. (1) Achard von Clairvaux übernahm erst im fortgeschrittenen Alter dieses Amt, nachdem er von anderen Aufgaben befreit worden war. Er verfügte über einen besonders reichen Erfahrungsschatz, von dem er den jungen Novizen berichtete. (2) Der englische Zisterziensermönch Aelred von Rievaulx trat erst spät ins Kloster ein, in seinen Mittdreißiger-Jahren, und wurde mit ca. vierzig Jahren für ein Jahr lang Novizenmeister. Vermutlich in dieser Zeit verfasste er sein *Speculum Caritatis.* Er verfügte über hohe didaktische Fähigkeiten und vor allem über *discretio.* Als beispielsweise ein Novize entlaufen und wieder zurückgekehrt war, teilte er dies dem Abt nicht mit. (3) Adam, der spätere Abt von Perseigne, war zuerst Regularkanoniker gewesen, wurde dann Benediktinermönch und trat schlussendlich bei den Zisterziensern ein. Obwohl er selbst nie Novize gewesen war – wie er in einem Brief selbst bekannte – hatte er dennoch zeitweise das Amt des Novizenmeisters inne. Er formulierte eine ganze Liste von Voraussetzungen, die für die Unterweisung der Novizen in seinen Augen zentral waren. So musste der Novizenmeister gefestigt im Glauben sein; ihn sollten ebenso Angst vor Gott wie eine Liebe zur Weisheit auszeichnen und sein religiöses Verhalten sollte ein Vorbild für die Novizen sein. Den Novizen sollte er mit echter Anteilnahme und Sorge gegenübertreten und mit ihnen häufige und freundliche Unterhaltungen suchen. Der Novizenmeister sollte ein Spiegel für die Novizen sein, für deren Seelenheil er Sorge trug. In seiner Verantwortung lag es auch, dass die Novizen nicht melancholisch wurden. Dies sollten die Gespräche bewirken, die nicht nur zur Unterweisung dienen, sondern ein vertrauensvolles Verhältnis zwischen Novize und Meister begründen sollten.

In seiner Zusammenfassung betont BREITENSTEIN, dass normative Text die Aufgaben der Novizenmeister nennen, aber nirgends die Zugangsvoraussetzungen erwähnt werden. Sie können nur implizit abgeleitet werden; so wurde Alter mit Erfahrung gleichgesetzt und Tugenden wie *discretio* wurden eigens erwähnt. Anscheinend war der eigene erfolgreiche Abschluss des Noviziats keine Voraussetzung, um Novizenmeister zu werden. Vermutlich war die einzige Voraussetzung für das Amt ein gewisses Talent (“aptitude”), eine *virtus*, die es ermöglichte, den Novizen erfolgreich zu unterweisen.

Michael ROBSON untersucht den Umgang mit Kindern im Hinblick auf den Franziskanerorden. Als erstes wendet er sich der Seelsorge der Brüder zu. Die alten Mönchsorden hatten nur durch die Oblaten Kontakt zu Kindern. Der Lehre von den unschuldigen Kindern folgend, die Jesus vertrat, kümmerten sich hingegen die Franziskaner gezielt um Mädchen und Jungen. Vor allem in ihren Predigten versuchten sie, alle Bevölkerungsgruppen und alle Altersklassen zu erreichen, auch die Kinder. ROBSON betont die theatralische Qualität der franziskanischen Predigt, die vermutlich besonders Jüngere ansprach. Ebenso beeindruckten die Brüder durch ihre Weltgewandtheit und gute Ausbildung. So berichtet Mansuetus de Castiglione Fiorentino, der zur ersten Generation der Brüder zählte, wie ihn die Franziskaner als Kind prägten und er bereits als Zehnjähriger eine besondere Verehrung des Leibes Christi sowie strikte Fastenpraktiken einübte. Eine Predigtsammlung aus Padua zeigt die Bedeutung von Kindern für die franziskanische Predigt. Bernhardino da Siena wies sich selbst eine wichtige Rolle bei der Ausbildung von Kindern zu. Im Jahr 1424 forderte er die Eltern auf, bereits ihre fünfjährigen Kinder zu seinen Predigten zu bringen, die er speziell für die Jüngsten konzipiert hatte. Tiefes spirituelles Erleben war im mittelalterlichen Verständnis auch schon Kindern möglich: So wird mehrfach überliefert, wie sie immer wieder Zeugen von eucharistischen Wundern wurden.

Im zweiten Teil wird der Einfluss von Brüdern auf Kinder untersucht. Johannes von Montecorvino, der erste Bischof von Peking, schilderte im Jahr 1305 in einem Brief an seine westlichen Glaubensbrüder, wie er heidnischen Familien 40 Kinder abgekauft hatte. Sie waren zwischen sieben und elf Jahren alt und erhielten von ihm religiöse Unterweisungen. Zudem brachte er ihnen das Kopieren von Schriften bei. Deshalb bat er seinen Generalminister, ihm Antiphonare und Heiligenlegenden sowie Graduale und Psalter zu schicken, damit die Kinder auch diese kopieren konnten. Die geistlichen Gesänge, die er den Kindern beibrachte, begeisterten auch den Großen Khan. Im folgenden Jahr, 1306, berichtet er in einem Brief, dass einige der Kinder verstorben waren, die er zuerst gekauft und dann getauft hatte. Im Jahr 1323 berichteten Franziskanerbrüder aus China, wie sie die Praxis von Johannes fortführten. Auch sie kauften Jungen und Mädchen und bildeten die Jungen zu Brüdern aus.

Immer wieder kümmerten sich Franziskaner eigens um das Wohlergehen von Kindern: so spendeten die Brüder in China gezielt für sie Almosen. Petrus von Assisi predigte im Jahr 1335 im Veneto und kümmerte sich so lange um verlassene Kinder, bis ein Spital für sie gegründet worden war. Raimund Berengar IV., Graf der Provence, ließ die Franziskaner die Seelsorge für seine eigenen Kinder übernehmen. In England hielten sich Franziskaner in königlichen Haushalten auf, um als Kapläne und Beichtväter zu dienen und sich um legitime wie illegitime Kinder der königlichen Familie zu kümmern.

Die Verbindung zwischen den franziskanischen Kirchengebäuden und Kindern untersucht ROBSON im dritten Teil. Die Kirchen waren öffentliche Räume, in denen die Brüder mit der Gemeinde in Kontakt traten, beispielsweise wenn sie zu Begräbnissorten für bedeutende Bürger der Stadt wurden. Den jungen Gemeindemitgliedern boten sie sichtbare Wegweiser zur Familiengeschichte mit ihren Familienwappen,

Seitenkapellen und angrenzenden Friedhöfen. Archäologische Grabungen aus Wales und England entdeckten in Kirchen Kindergräber, die vermutlich von Novizen stammten. Auffällig häufig kommen Kinder in franziskanischen Wundererzählungen vor; so besteht bei 30 % aller Wunder, die zu Odorico da Pordenone († 1331) überliefert sind, ein Zusammenhang zu Kindern. Kinder stehen auch immer wieder im Dienst der Brüder. So beauftragten beispielsweise die Londoner Greyfriars im Jahr 1300 wiederholt einen Knaben, um Äpfel und Birnen zu Queen Margaret zu tragen. Diese 'dienstbaren' Knaben tauchen auch in Rechnungsbüchern für ihre Hilfsdienste auf.

Der vierte Teil behandelt mendikantische Vorstellungen von Kindheit. Scharfe Kritik an den Umständen der Kindheit von Franziskus von Assisi übte sein Biograph Thomas von Celano, der ihn als eitlen und stolzen Jungen beschreibt, dessen Eltern der Erwähnung nicht wert sind. Erst die *Vita secunda* berichtete versöhnlicher von den Eltern des Heiligen. Johannes der Täufer ist die Vorlage für die Darstellung des Johannes von Orta. Er spielte nie mit seinen Geschwistern, denn schon sein kindliches Denken war ganz auf Kirchen und Klöster ausgerichtet. Mit großer Hingabe empfing er so oft wie möglich die Eucharistie. Der fünfte Teil des Aufsatzes sammelt Hinweise auf eine Aufnahme in den Orden von Kindern. Dies führte immer wieder zu Konflikten, weshalb das Generalkapitel von 1260 ein Mindestalter von 18 Jahren, das Generalkapitel von 1354 von 14 Jahren festsetzte. Immer wieder wird von Familien berichtet, die sich gegen eine Berufung ihrer Söhne wehrten. Als Beispiel wird Salimbene vorgestellt, dessen Vater Guido von Adam als Kreuzfahrer des 13. Jahrhunderts bekannt wurde. Der Vater war untröstlich, dass sein Sohn in den Orden eingetreten war und versucht mehrfach, ihn gewaltsam dem Orden zu entziehen. Er verbrachte sein restliches Leben damit, seinen Sohn zurückzuholen – jedoch ohne Erfolg.

Im letzten Abschnitt wendet sich ROBSON der Polemik gegen Franziskaner zu. Er lässt Richard FitzRalph, den Erzbischof von Armagh, zu Wort kommen, der einer der größten Kritiker der Brüder war. In einer Predigt für den Papst und die Kardinäle erzählt er von einem Vater, dessen zwölfjähriger Sohn in Oxford von den Franziskanern angezogen wurde. Der Vater klagte vor dem päpstlichen Gericht, der Orden lasse nicht zu, dass er und seine Frau alleine mit ihrem Sohn sprechen dürften. Die Eltern waren der festen Überzeugung, dass ihr Sohn gegen seinen Willen von den Franziskanern festgehalten würde. Vielfach berichten die Quellen von ähnlichen Fällen. Im Jahr 1358 ergriff die Universität Oxford Gegenmaßnahmen und erließ Statuten, die den Franziskanern die Aufnahme von unter Achtzehnjährigen verbat. Dennoch hielten die Klagen über den 'Diebstahl' der Brüder an. Der Fall des John Sillow zeigt noch einmal die ganze Problematik: Mit ca. sieben Jahren wurde er in den Orden gegeben; mit 14 versuchte er mehrfach, auszutreten, aber dies wurde ihm immer wieder verboten. Um 1476 floh er und wurde als Apostat verurteilt. Erst Innozenz VIII. sprach in 1490 vom Vorwurf der Apostasie frei. Das ganze Mittelalter gelang es den Franziskanern, Jungen anzuziehen; dies führte immer wieder zu Spannungen mit dem Säkularklerus. Wie viele Kinder davon betroffen waren, kann nur geschätzt werden. Obwohl nur fragmentarische Quellen überliefert sind, wird doch die zugrunde liegende Tendenz deutlich: Kinder hatten einen hohen Stellenwert in den Augen der Franziskaner, sie sollten mit ihrem Herz und Verstand ("mind and heart") für die christliche Botschaft gewonnen werden.

Die vorliegenden Beiträge führen zu einer Reihe von weiterführenden Fragen. Wie wurde die Zugehörigkeit zu einer gemeinsamen Generation hergestellt: Über Alter oder über externe Faktoren wie Spiritualität, Reformanliegen oder Ausbildungsgrad? Wie sieht die Beziehung zwischen Alter und Krankheit aus? Häufig galt im Mittelalter Krankheit als Auszeichnung (wen Gott liebt, den prüft er) – war damit automatisch ein hohes Alter auch ein Geschenk Gottes? Falls den Alten besondere Ehre zukam – wie stand diese in Konkurrenz zum besonderen Status der 'unschuldigen' Kinder? Die Bedeutung von 'Kind' und 'Kindschaft' müsste noch weiter ausgelotet werden: Welche Strahlkraft hatte etwa die Idee der besonderen Gotteskindschaft, beispielsweise in Bezug auf eine gesteigerte Wirksamkeit der Gebete im Rahmen der *memoria*? Wie wandelte sich das christliche Verständnis von Kindheit im Laufe des Mittelalters? Wie wird der Autoritätsverlust von Erwachsenen zugunsten von Kindern, hier am Beispiel von Bischöfen aufgezeigt, theologisch gerechtfertigt, da doch hier die gottgewollte Ordnung auf den Kopf gestellt wurde? Wie können wir die kulturellen Faktoren fassen, die Alter jenseits von Lebensalter überhaupt erst definieren?

Die Auseinandersetzung mit den "Generationen im Kloster" brachte erste Befunde für das in vielen Bereichen noch unbestellte Feld der historischen Altersforschung. Zwangsläufig sind noch mehr Fragen offen, als hier beantwortet werden konnten. Idealerweise gelingt es dem vorliegenden Band, Anstöße für künftige Studien zu diesem Themenkomplex zu bieten.

DIE MÖNCHE – BESONDERE GOTTESKINDER?

Die Bedeutung der geistlichen Kindschaft für das christliche Klosterleben

HUBERTUS LUTTERBACH

Ob religiös unmusikalisch oder christlich gebunden, ob weltanschaulich neutral oder esoterisch verwurzelt – auf die Frage nach dem Aussehen eines christlichen Mönches wird wohl kaum einer den Verweis auf die Kapuze als das typische Kennmerkmal eines Klostermenschen schuldig bleiben. So eröffnet der ehemalige Trappistenmönch und Schriftsteller Bernardin SCHELLENBERGER seine Beschreibung des klösterlichen Lebens mit der Erinnerung an einen kapuzenbekleideten Mönch, der seinen Blick von einem Berg aus in die Ferne schweifen lässt. In diesem Bild erblickt der Autor den Spiegel für all jene Ideale, die viele 'Weltmenschen' auf einen Mönch projizierten: Weltflucht und Traumwelt, Zierde und Schönheit. Freilich sieht SCHELLENBERGER den durch und durch idealisierten Kapuzenmönch näher an die Gestalt eines gleichfalls kapuzenbedeckten Gartenzwerges herangerückt als inmitten eines Klosterlebens angesiedelt, stehe dieses doch einem Leben mit Familie und 'Weltberuf' an Alltäglichkeit in nichts nach.[1] – Szenenwechsel 1: Im Jahre 2006 feierten die Benediktinermönche des 'Dormitio-Klosters' in Jerusalem ihr 100-jähriges Klosterjubiläum. Die Wachsapplikationen auf den Jubiläumskerzen zeigen vor der Silhouette des Zions-Klosters einen in einem Buch lesenden und kapuzenbedeckten Mönch in der Seitenansicht. Offenbar soll sich der Betrachter der Kerze – mit oder ohne Kapuze – durch diese idealisierte Version des Mönchtums eingeladen fühlen, sich dem Blick des Mönches anzuschließen: Abgeschottet von allen Einflüssen und Einflüsterungen der Welt gilt das Augenmerk dem heiligen Text und die innere Ausrichtung dem Zion als jenem Ort, von dem die Christen glauben, dass Christus dort am Ende der Tage zur Erde zurückkehren wird. –

---

1 B. SCHELLENBERGER, Ein anderes Leben. Was ein Mönch erfährt, Freiburg/Basel/Wien ^{3}1981, S. 11f.

Szenenwechsel 2: Im Jahre 2006 machte das Folkwang-Museum in der Ruhrgebietsstadt Essen mit einer Ausstellung auf sich aufmerksam, die bedeutende Werke des romantischen Malers Caspar David Friedrich († 1840) präsentierte. Unter anderen umfasste diese Jahrhundertschau einige Bilder, auf denen der Künstler das Klosterleben detailreich in Szene setzt. Hier fällt auf, dass fast alle seine Darstellungen, die sich dem christlichen Mönchtum widmen, von kapuzenbedeckten Mönchen bevölkert sind: Mönche auf Friedhöfen, Mönche beim Gebet, Mönche vor gotischen Ruinen – immer angetan mit Kapuze.

Die drei Schlaglichter können die Frage provozieren, wo die Verbindung zwischen dem Mönch und seiner Kapuze eigentlich ihre ursprüngliche Wurzel hat. Es mag überraschen, dass die Anfänge der Mönchskapuze bis in die Anfänge des christlichen Mönchtums zurückreichen – also bis etwa in das 4. Jahrhundert nach Christus. Ebenso sehr mag es verwundern, dass der ursprüngliche Sinn der Mönchskapuze allein darin bestand, die Mönche als geistliche Kinder auszuweisen. Damit knüpfte das Mönchtum an eine sozialgeschichtliche 'Vorgabe' an; denn die Kapuze galt in der antiken Alltagswelt gemeinhin als Kinderkleidung: Kinder trugen eine Kapuze.

Über die Ausstattung der Mönche mit den Kapuzenkleidern hinaus besannen sich die Christen auf das Kapuzenkleid, um die einem Täufling mit der Taufe geschenkte geistliche Verjüngung – näher hin die Gabe der Gotteskindschaft – zu inszenieren. Damit allerdings standen die Christen im 4. Jahrhundert vor einer komplexen Situation: Einerseits bekam jeder Getaufte ein Kapuzen-Taufkleid, andererseits erhielt jeder Mönch ein klösterliches Kapuzenkleid, insofern er sein Mönchsversprechen im Sinne einer Zweiten Taufe verstand. So verweist die 'Kapuzen-Konkurrenz' auf die hintergründige Konkurrenz zwischen der Ersten Taufe mit Wasser und Geist sowie der Zweiten Taufe der Mönchsprofess. Schließlich spiegelt sich in der Konkurrenz zwischen der Ersten Taufe und der Zweiten Taufe die Konkurrenz zwischen der einfachen und der besonderen Gotteskindschaft wider, wie im Anschluss an einen kurzen Einblick in den Stand der Metaphern-Forschung zu analysieren sein wird.

Bislang war in der Christentums- und Kulturgeschichte von einer 'Kinder- und Kapuzen-Theologie' noch kaum die Rede. Der vergewissernde Blick auf aktuelle Tendenzen innerhalb der mönchsgeschichtlichen Forschung bestätigt diese weitgehende

Vernachlässigung der Bildersprache. Während der soeben verstorbene Mönchshistoriker Karl Suso FRANK dem Verständnis des klösterlichen Lebens als *vita angelica* in den 1960er Jahren seine Dissertation widmete,[2] ist dieser ebenso horizonteröffnende wie vielversprechende Forschungsansatz seitdem kaum wieder aufgegriffen worden. Dieses Desiderat muss umso mehr verwundern, da FRANK die Erklärungskraft der *vita angelica*-Metapher sowohl für das diesseitige als auch für das jenseitige Leben in vielerlei Hinsicht veranschaulicht, ja die Lebenden und die Verstorbenen als eine Gemeinschaft von Engeln in den Blick nimmt;[3] nicht zuletzt weist die klösterlich rückgebundene Engel-Metaphorik auf die Wurzeln monastischen Lebens in der Martyriumstheologie hin.[4]

Das Ziel der vorliegenden Studie besteht darin, den von FRANK ins Bewusstsein gehobenen metaphorischen Zugang zum Klosterleben – also zum Leben in der Zweiten Taufe – um die stufenweise Erschließung eines weiteren Bildes für den klösterlich Lebenden zu ergänzen: der Mönch als das besondere Gotteskind. Während – wie noch zu erläutern sein wird – gemäß dem Neuen Testament jeder Getaufte als Gotteskind gilt, differenzierte sich diese ursprünglich 'ungeteilte' Gotteskindschaft mit dem Aufkommen des Gemeinschaftsmönchtums seit dem 4. Jahrhundert aus: zum einen in die (gewöhnliche) Gotteskindschaft der einmal Getauften und empfangsbereit in der Welt mit Familie und Kindern lebenden Christen; zum anderen in die besondere Gotteskindschaft der 'zweitgetauften' Mönche, welche sich aufgrund außerordentlicher Verzichtleistungen im Diesseits entsprechend außerordentliche Gegenleistungen im Jenseits zu verdienen suchten.

Das in der vorliegenden Studie zu rekonstruierende Selbstverständnis der Mönche als besondere Gotteskinder liegt umso näher, da sich die Untersuchung dieser bislang von Theologen und Historikern nicht erschlossenen Metapher in geisteswissenschaftlich aktuelle Forschungsperspektiven einfügt: So hat der Münsteraner Altgermanist Friedrich OHLY seit 1977 in seinen "Schriften zur mittelalterlichen

---

2 K. S. FRANK, Angelikos bios. Begriffsanalytische und begriffsgeschichtliche Untersuchungen zum "engelgleichen Leben" im frühen Mönchtum (Beiträge zur Geschichte des alten Mönchtums und des Benediktinerordens 26), Münster i. W. 1964.

3 Ebd., S. 97-122, 198.

4 Ebd., S. 177-182.

Bedeutungsforschung" sowohl methodisch-theoretisch[5] als auch anhand konkreter Einzelbeispiele[6] verdeutlicht, dass Metaphern nicht als ausschmückende Rede angesehen werden dürften, sondern vielmehr als inhaltliche Substanz gelten müssten; besonders die Theologie der Alten Kirche und des Mittelalters bleibe ohne diesen Zugang unverständlich.[7] Neben anderen zeitgenössischen Theologen[8] hebt auch Hans BLUMENBERG hervor, dass Metaphern nicht 'Restbestände', sondern 'Grundbestände' menschlichen Lebens, allzumal religiöser Weltdeutung seien. Gewiss hätte die Metaphorik seit dem Umschlag der Theologie in reine Begrifflichkeit, wie er für die Scholastik kennzeichnend ist, an Bedeutung eingebüßt; gleichwohl konnte die begriffliche Theologie die 'Bildertheologie' niemals vollständig absorbieren.[9] – Im Sinne eines Beleges für die vorgetragene Hypothese sei das Augenmerk, geschärft durch eine knappe Revision der neutestamentlichen Schlüsselaussagen

---

5 F. OHLY, Schriften zur mittelalterlichen Bedeutungsforschung, Darmstadt ²1983.

6 DERS., Die Perle des Wortes. Zur Geschichte eines Bildes für Dichtung, Frankfurt a. M./Leipzig 2002.

7 DERS., Metaphern für die Sündenstufen und die Gegenwirkungen der Gnade (Rheinisch-Westfälische Akademie der Wissenschaften: Geisteswissenschaften, Vorträge 302), Opladen 1990, S. 165-169.

8 Aus theologischer Perspektive sekundiert Eberhard JÜNGEL: Besonders die Sprache des Glaubens sei angewiesen auf metaphorische Rede, weil sich allein auf diese Weise Überweltliches in menschlicher Sprache und in irdischen Bildern ausdrücken lasse; gewissermaßen sei die Metapher die Lösung eines hermeneutischen Notstandes: "Von Gott ist also eigentlich nur dann die Rede, wenn metaphorisch von ihm geredet wird." (E. JÜNGEL, Metaphorische Wahrheit. Erwägungen zur theologischen Relevanz der Metapher als Beitrag zur Hermeneutik einer narrativen Theologie, in: E. JÜNGEL / P. RICOEUR [Hgg.], Metapher. Zur Hermeneutik religiöser Sprache, München 1974, S. 71-122, hier S. 112; auch ebd.: "Die Differenz von Gott und Welt, Gott selbst also, kann nur metaphorisch zur Sprache kommen.") In der Konsequenz ist "die Sprache des christlichen Glaubens [...] durchweg metaphorisch" (ebd., S. 121; siehe auch ebd., S. 80, 100, 109f.). Bemerkenswerterweise stellt auch der Heidelberger Neutestamentler K. BERGER, Was ist biblische Spiritualität, Gütersloh 2000, S. 17, das Ungenügen einer allein begrifflichen Theologie ("scholastische Theologie") heraus, wenn er sich ergänzend für die Erschließung der bildreichen "monastische[n] Theologie" einsetzt, um auf diese Weise einen "Beitrag zur Erneuerung der Exegese" zu leisten.

9 H. BLUMENBERG, Paradigmen zu einer Metaphorologie, in: A. HAVERKAMP (Hg.), Theorie der Metapher (Wege der Forschung 389), Darmstadt 1983, S. 285-315, hier S. 289.

zur Taufe, auf die schrittweise Rekonstruktion der langlebigen Vorstellung vom Mönch als besonderes Gotteskind gerichtet.

Die neutestamentliche Rede von der Gotteskindschaft

Für das Verständnis der christlichen Tauftheologie war die johanneische Theologie seit alters her von besonderer Impulskraft. Ihr zufolge ist die Vollmacht bzw. Gabe der Kindschaft als eine 'Zeugung aus Gott' zu beschreiben; grundsätzlich wird dieser Prozess aus dem 'Geist' bzw. aus dem Empfang der Taufe abgeleitet.[10] Ebenso wie die Rede von der Ersten Taufe in der johanneischen Tradition situiert ist, sollte sich später auch die Vorstellung von der besonderen monastischen Gotteskindschaft auf diesem Wurzelgrund ansiedeln.

"Allen aber, die ihn aufnahmen, gab er die Macht, Kinder Gottes zu werden; denen, die an seinen Namen glauben, die nicht aus dem Blute, [...] sondern aus Gott gezeugt sind." Joh 1,12-13 zufolge wird man zu einem Gotteskind nicht als Schlusspunkt einer natürlichen Entwicklung oder als Folge eines menschlichen Angenommenseins; vielmehr ist das Geschehen von überweltlich-göttlicher Qualität und entzieht sich menschlichem Verfügen und Begreifen. So werden 'Fleisch und Blut', die entsprechend semitischer Ausdrucksweise eine Umschreibung für 'Mensch' sind, als Wege der Zeugung grundsätzlich ausgeschlossen. Umso schärfer akzentuiert das Johannes-Evangelium mit Hilfe der zitierten Antithese die übernatürliche Herkunft der Gotteskinder; das für Israel typische Erwählungsbewusstsein gewinnt auf diese Weise eine neue Qualität, insofern die dem einzelnen Christen eingeräumte Eröffnung des "Heimatrechtes bei Gott" ein "schlechthinniges Wunder" ist:[11] "Das Bewusstsein der Gottgehörigkeit und des Gottgezeugtseins prägt das 'johanneische' Christentum und gibt ihm die Gewissheit, der 'Welt' überlegen zu sein."[12]

---

10 O. MICHEL, Art. nios tou theou, in: Theologisches Begriffslexikon zum Neuen Testament, Budapest [9]1993, S. 1166-1175, hier S. 1174.

11 U. WILCKENS, Das Evangelium nach Johannes (Das Neue Testament Deutsch 4), Göttingen 1998, S. 31.

12 R. SCHNACKENBURG, Das Johannesevangelium (Herders theologischer Kommentar zum Neuen Testament 4,1-4) 4 Bde., Freiburg i. Br. 1965-1975, hier Bd. 1, S. 239.

Der zeitgenössische christliche Leser des Johannes-Evangeliums wusste die Rede von der Zeugung aus Gott als Umschreibung des Taufgeschehens zu deuten. Diese Aussageabsicht tritt in den zitierten Versen umso augenfälliger hervor, da Gott allen, die an ihn glauben, die Möglichkeit einräumt, mit Hilfe der Taufe Kinder Gottes zu werden. In der Taufe vollzieht sich das Geschenk der Gotteskindschaft als eschatologische Gabe,[13] wie auch Joh 3,5 unterstreicht[14]; bei der geistlichen Geburt des Kindes Gottes in der Taufe geht es um den "neuen, nicht um eine Erneuerung des alten Menschen".[15] Die Rede davon, dass ein Mensch neu geboren werden muss, um das Reich Gottes zu sehen, darf als charakteristisch für die johanneische Theologie herausgestellt werden (Joh 3,3)[16] und durchzieht besonders den 1. Johannesbrief (1 Joh 2,29; 3,9f.; 4,7; 5,1.4.18);[17] in diesem Kontext geht es nicht um die Kategorien von 'Vergeistigung' oder 'Verinnerlichung', sondern um das "Durchhalten einer eschatologischen [eben auf Dauer angelegten, über die Welt hinausweisenden] Perspektive."[18]

Die Ausrichtung des Katechumenen bzw. Getauften, schließlich des Klosterkandidaten am christlichen Ideal der Nachfolge lässt eine weitere, für die Tauftheologie bedeutsam gewordene, neutestamentliche Perikope in den Mittelpunkt der Reflexion rücken: Entsprechend der synoptisch überlieferten Kinderbegegnung Jesu stellt der göttliche Sohn den Erwachsenen die Kinder als Modell für die Jüngerschaft vor Augen: "Amen, das sage ich euch! Wer das Reich Gottes nicht annimmt, als wäre er ein Kind, wird nicht hineinkommen." (Mt 18,3) Dieser Vers findet sich im Markus- und Lukas-Evangelium um die Segnung der Kinder erweitert: " Und er nahm die Kinder in seine Arme, legte ihnen die Hände auf und segnete sie." (Mk 10,16; Lk 18,17) Im Zentrum sprechen die angeführten Verse von der Gotteskindschaft, die durch Jesus angenommen worden ist und als Ausdruck des eigentlichen nachösterlichen Geschehens mittels der Taufe auf alle Gläubigen

---

13 J. GNILKA, Johannesevangelium (Die Neue Echter Bibel. Kommentar zum Neuen Testament mit der Einheitsübersetzung 4), Würzburg 1983, S. 15.

14 Joh 3,5: "Wenn jemand nicht aus Wasser und Geist geboren wird, kann er nicht in das Reich Gottes kommen."

15 GNILKA, Johannesevangelium (wie Anm. 13), S. 27.

16 WILCKENS, Das Evangelium nach Johannes (wie Anm. 11), S. 65.

17 MICHEL, Art. nios tou theou (wie Anm. 10), S. 1174.

18 Ebd., S. 1174.

ausgeweitet wird: "Sie [die Gotteskindschaft] ruht ganz auf der zuvorkommenden Gnade Gottes, die es in bescheidenem Kindessinn einfach anzunehmen gilt."[19] Nicht zuletzt wird in der vorliegenden Studie zu zeigen sein, in welcher Weise die Mönche die angeführten und im ursprünglichen Sinne auf die Empfangsbereitschaft der Christen ausgerichteten Tauf-Perikopen exklusiv auf das Klosterleben beziehen konnten.

Die besondere Gotteskindschaft – Ein mönchisches Ideal

Die geistliche Ausdeutung der Taufe auf der Basis der aufgezeigten neutestamentlichen Schlüsselstellen begann kaum vor dem 4. Jahrhundert: "Eine Theologie der Taufe gibt es im Grunde erst seit dem vierten Jahrhundert, denn erst jetzt werden ihre überkommenen Riten oder wird sie selbst als Ganze auf die Schrift bezogen und von der Schrift her ausgelegt."[20] Beinahe zeitgleich griff auch das aufkommende christliche Mönchtum auf die entsprechenden Perikopen zurück, um die Notwendigkeit der Zweiten Taufe als einer höherwertigen Taufe zu rechtfertigen.

Die oben beschriebene 'Kapuzen-Konkurrenz' aufgrund der Ausdifferenzierung zwischen der Ersten und der Zweiten Taufe war von einer Dramatik, bei der es geradezu um Leben und Tod des Menschen

---

19 A. OEPKE, Art. *pais*, in: Theologisches Wörterbuch zum Neuen Testament 5 (1954), S. 636-653, hier S. 651; K. BERGER, Theologiegeschichte des Urchristentums. Theologie des Neuen Testaments, Tübingen/Basel 1994, S. 32 unterstreicht: "Paulus [Röm 8,14; Gal 4,6] und Johannes [Joh 20,17] bezeugen gleichermaßen, dass die Ausweitung der einzigartigen Vater-Kind-Relation, in der Jesus stand, auf alle Christen als das eigentliche nachösterliche Geschehen angesehen wird. Nur diese beiden Theologen kennen die Bezeichnung 'Kinder (griech.: *tekna*) Gottes' zur Bezeichnung der Glaubenden." Zur Thematik sei auch hervorgehoben W. BEILNER, "Wenn ihr nicht werdet wie die Kinder [...]". Die Unwichtigkeit und Verdrängung der Kinder in Gesellschaft und Kirche und das Kindsein im Neuen Testament, in: W. ACHLEITNER / U. WINKLER (Hgg.), Gottesgeschichten. Beiträge zu einer systematischen Theologie (FS G. BACHL), Freiburg/Basel/Wien 1992, S. 287-304.

20 G. KRETSCHMAR, Die Geschichte des Taufgottesdienstes in der Alten Kirche, in: K. F. MÜLLER / W. BLANKENBURG (Hgg.), Leiturgia. Handbuch des evangelischen Gottesdienstes 5, Kassel 1970, S. 1-348, hier S. 264.

ging; denn im Hintergrund erhebt sich die Frage, welche Heilsbedeutung der Ersten Taufe gegenüber der Zweiten Taufe zukommt. Anders gesagt: Konnte sich ein Christ mit der Zweiten Taufe – also mit der besonderen Gotteskindschaft – im Diesseits und im Jenseits *coram Deo* einen Vorteil ausrechnen gegenüber jenen Mitchristen, die allein die Erste Taufe und damit die gewöhnliche Gotteskindschaft empfangen hatten? Zugespitzt gefragt: Kam der Ersten Taufe – und damit der gewöhnlichen Gotteskindschaft – im Vergleich zur Zweiten Taufe und der besonderen Gotteskindschaft überhaupt noch eine Bedeutung zu im Blick auf das ewige Leben?

Stellvertretend für viele andere monastische Voten sei hier allein die Stimme des Magisters mit seiner zwischen 500 und 525 in der Gegend von Rom abgefassten so genannten Magisterregel zu Gehör gebracht.[21] Kompromisslos proklamiert er die exklusive Heilsrelevanz der Zweiten Taufe bereits in der Einleitung seiner Regel:

> Hören wir nochmals die Stimme vom Brunnen her, der uns neu belebt hat. Sie spricht: Nehmt mein Joch auf euch und lernt von mir, denn ich bin milde und demütig von Herzen, und ihr werdet Ruhe finden für eure Seelen. Denn mein Joch ist sanft und meine Last ist leicht (Mt 11,29-30). Hören wir das, so lasst uns zu einander sagen: Neu belebt durch einen solchen Quell und angesprochen vom Herrn, der uns einlädt, wollen wir die Last der Sünden, [...] denen wir auf dem Gang zum Brunnen der Taufe entsagt haben, uns nicht wieder aufladen. [...] Entsagen wir also der früheren Sündenlast. Mag ein weltlicher Wandel den Lässigen die schwere Bürde ihrer Vergehen aufladen.[22]

Und an anderer Stelle heißt es: "Und als er [der Klosterkandidat] noch ein Laie in der Welt war, hat ihn der Teufel nicht versucht, denn er vollzog ja stets dessen Willen, als er noch sein Arbeiter war."[23] Trefflich

---

[21] Zu den differierenden Positionen zu Lokalisierung und Datierung der Magisterregel siehe H. LUTTERBACH, Monachus factus est. Die Mönchwerdung im frühen Mittelalter. Zugleich ein Beitrag zur Frömmigkeits- und Liturgiegeschichte (Beiträge zur Geschichte des alten Mönchtums und des Benediktinertums 44), Münster 1995, S. 124f.

[22] Regula Magistri, Beginn des Themas 13-19.21-22, in: La Règle du Maitre 1, ed. A. DE VOGÜE (Sources Chrétiennes 105), Paris 1965, S. 298-300.

[23] Ebd., Bd. 2, S. 390.

charakterisiert der Mönchshistoriker Terrence KARDONG die rezitierte Position des Magisters im Blick auf die Zweite Taufe: "Wenn der Magister die Aufnahme des monastischen Lebens als eine wiederholte Taufabsage an die Sünde versteht, tut er das in einer Weise, die nahe daran ist, die Welt ebenso wie das gewöhnliche christliche Leben als böse und sündig abzuqualifizieren."[24] Das überaus Erstaunliche dieser Vorstellung liegt darin, dass der Magister sogar die Kirche in seine umfassende Abwertung einbezieht: "Der Bruch trennt den Mönch und die Welt voneinander, eingeschlossen die Kirche"[25] – übrigens eine Position, die die Magisterregel weiter dadurch radikalisiert, dass sie von der Wirkung der Auferstehung für die ganze Welt absieht, um sie stattdessen allein auf das Kloster zu beschränken.[26] Dieses in der Vorstellung von der besonderen Gotteskindschaft aufgipfelnde und nunmehr detailliert zu rekonstruierende Selbstverständnis des christlichen Mönchtums sollte sich im Abendland bis in das 20. Jahrhundert hinein erhalten. Von allem Anfang an gründete das Ideal der besonderen Gotteskindschaft auf der Wertschätzung der reinen Stimmen.

"Kindergebet dringt durch die Wolken"

Innerhalb der antik-heidnischen Kulte nahmen kleine Kinder tragende liturgische Funktionen wahr, wie sozial- und religionsgeschichtliche Studien zu antiken Kulten ergaben. So hat Hilde RÜHFEL die Mitwirkung von Kindern an kultischen Handlungen anhand von ikonographischen Darstellungen auf griechischen Vasen genauestens rekonstruiert.[27] Insofern die Kinder über zarte, vom Stimmbruch noch unverdorbene Stimmen verfügten, konnten sie auch als Sängerknaben zum Einsatz

24 T. KARDONG, The World in the Rule of Benedict and the Rule of the Master, in: Studia Monastica 26 (1984), S. 185-204, hier S. 203.

25 DERS., The Devil in the Rule of the Master, in: Studia Monastica 30 (1988), S. 41-62, hier S. 47.

26 LUTTERBACH, Monachus factus est (wie Anm. 21), S. 152.

27 H. RÜHFEL, Kinderleben im klassischen Athen. Bilder auf klassischen Vasen (Kulturgeschichte der antiken Welt 19), Mainz 1984, S. 82f.; dazu auch P. MÜLLER, In der Mitte der Gemeinde. Kinder im Neuen Testament, Neukirchen-Vluyn 1992, S. 121f.

gelangen. Die 'landläufige Begründung' besagt, dass "die Kinder den Göttern besonders lieb seien [...] [und] die Gottheit am meisten auf sie höre und zwar auf sie allein, weil sie als völlig keusch das volle Recht hätten."[28] Mitunter betätigten sich während ihrer Kindheit sogar Persönlichkeiten in heidnischen Kulten, die nach ihrer Konversion zum Christentum daselbst einflussreiche Amtsträger werden sollten. Erinnert sei hier allein an den späteren Bischof Cyprian von Karthago († 258), der als Kind von noch nicht einmal sieben Jahren im Mithraskult ministrierte, als Zehnjähriger im Kult der Demeter und Kore assistierte sowie anschließend auf der Athener Akropolis im Kult der Schlange von Pallas Athene kultische Funktionen übernahm.[29]

In das Christentum drang der Gedanke von den Gott besonders wohlgefälligen Kinderstimmen durch die Interpretation des biblischen Wortes Sir 35,21 ein. Genauerhin erfuhr der Vers "Das Gebet dessen, der sich vor Gott klein macht, dringt durch die Wolken" seine Wertschätzung seit altkirchlicher Zeit als ein allerdings ursprünglich gesinnungsethisch gemeintes Wort. Innerhalb der Anweisungen zum rechten Gebet ermutigt der Vers den Beter, sich seiner Wenigkeit angesichts der Größe Gottes bewusst zu sein. Zum einen bezieht sich die durchdringende Kraft des Gebetes von Geringen und Demütigen darauf, dass diese beharrlich sind und aufgrund des Ausmaßes ihrer Not nicht vorzeitig aufgeben. Zum anderen bestärkt der Kontext des Verses (35,21-22) das Vertrauen darauf, dass Gott auf das Gebet des Geringen und Demütigen tatsächlich reagiert: "Das Gebet eines Menschen, der sich klein macht/sich demütigt, durchdringt Wolken. Es ruht nicht, bis es am Ziel ist. Es weicht nicht, bis Gott eingreift und Recht schafft als gerechter Richter."

Aus zwei Gründen konnten die Christen diese eigentlich auf die innere Haltung des Beters ausgerichtete Schriftstelle auf die Kinder beziehen: Erstens wertschätzten die Christen die Kinder von Anfang an so kompromisslos wie keine andere frühere oder zeitgenössische Weltanschauung – übrigens mit zivilisationsgeschichtlichen

---

28 OEPKE, Art. *pais* (wie Anm. 19), S. 636-653, hier S. 643; auch H. HERTER, Das unschuldige Kind, in: Jahrbuch für Antike und Christentum 4 (1961), S. 146-162, hier S. 154, der auf die "unbeeinträchtigte Reinheit" der hellenistischen Kinderliturgen hinweist.

29 RÜHFEL, Kinderleben (wie Anm. 27), S. 94; zur Assistenz von Kindern in Geheim- und Mysterienkulten siehe auch OEPKE, Art. *s* (wie Anm. 19), S. 643f.

Auswirkungen bis in unsere Tage;[30] zum zweiten zeigten sich die Christen beeinflusst von jener in den antik-heidnischen Kulten verbreiteten Vorstellung, dass Kinder aufgrund ihrer reinen Stimmen in der Liturgie bei Gott auf die Erhörung ihrer karitativen Anliegen in besonderer Weise hoffen durften.[31] So können die sozialgeschichtlichen Folgen des Zusammenhangs von kindlichen Stimmen, christlicher Liturgie und karitativer Wirkung mit Blick auf die abendländische Geschichte ohne Übertreibung als weitreichend bezeichnet werden.

Genauerhin begann man christlicherseits bereits in der Alten Kirche, die unterschiedlichen Eigenarten menschlicher und himmlischer Stimmen auf ihre Gottnähe hin zu differenzieren und ihnen eine je unterschiedliche Aussicht auf göttliche Erhörung zuzusprechen. So schrieb man die "engelgleiche Stimme" (*uox angelica*) oder die "helle Stimme" (*uox clara*) den Engeln und Heiligen zu, also Wesen, die sexuell unberührt – gewissermaßen in der Situation vor dem 'Stimmbruch' – geblieben sind; eine dunkle(re) Stimme hingegen verstand man – so schwer verständlich das in einer heutzutage 'nach-aufgeklärten' Gesellschaft sein mag – als untrüglichen Ausdruck für den vorangegangenen Kontakt mit der per se als beschmutzend erachteten Sexualität.[32] Daraus ergab sich seit altkirchlicher Zeit eine über das in Sir 35,21 geforderte demütige Gebet hinausweisende Erkenntnis von schlüsselhafter Bedeutung: Je heller und reiner die Stimme eines

---

30 Dazu grundlegend H. LUTTERBACH, Gotteskindschaft. Kultur- und Sozialgeschichte eines christlichen Ideals, Freiburg/Basel/Wien 2003, S. 165-256; auch DERS., Der zivilisationsgeschichtliche Beitrag der christlichen Bußbücher zum christlichen Kinderschutz, in: Historisches Jahrbuch 123 (2003), S. 3-25; DERS., "Was ihr einem dieser Kleinen getan habt, das habt ihr mir getan [...]" Der historische Beitrag des Christentums zum "Jahrhundert des Kindes", in: Jahrbuch für biblische Theologie 17 (2002), S. 199-223, hier besonders S. 210-223; DERS., Die christliche Sorge um Kinder, in: Stimmen der Zeit 220 (2002), S. 3-11.

31 M. KLEIJWEGT u.a., Art. Kind, in: Reallexikon für Antike und Christentum 20 (2004) Sp. 865-947, hier Sp. 879f.; OEPKE, Art. *pais* (wie Anm. 19), S. 643f.

32 Zu Genese und Ursachen der Abwertung von Sexualität sowie zu den negativen Folgen für die Frauen im Christentum siehe umfassend H. LUTTERBACH, Sexualität im Mittelalter. Eine Kulturstudie anhand von Bußbüchern des 6. bis 12. Jahrhunderts (Beihefte zum Archiv für Kulturgeschichte 43), Köln/Weimar 1999; A. ANGENENDT, "Mit reinen Händen". Das Motiv der kultischen Reinheit in der abendländischen Geschichte, in: G. JENAL (Hg.), Herrschaft, Kirche, Kultur. Beiträge zur Geschichte des Mittelalters (FS F. PRINZ) (Monographien zur Geschichte des Mittelalters 37), Stuttgart 1993, S. 297-316.

himmlischen oder irdischen (vor allem eines männlichen) Wesens als Ausweis seiner (gottgegebenen oder menschlich-freiwilligen) sexuellen Abstinenz ist, umso näher ist es Gott und dem Himmel, ja umso mehr vermag es in der Sphäre des Himmlischen zugunsten der Irdischen an göttlichem Beistand zu bewirken.

Kurzum: Während Sir 35,21 die Rede vom 'Sich-klein-Machen' des Menschen vor Gott auf die innere Haltung des Beters hinorientiert, bezog man dieses Wort in späterer Zeit auf die von Natur aus kleine Gestalt der Kinder; aus einem metaphorischen Verständnis der Schriftstelle entwickelte sich ein 'dinglich-reales', wie es in (frühmittelalterlichen) Zeiten reduzierter Bildung auch in anderen Bereichen des christlichen Lebens zu beobachten ist.[33] Damit war die 'wolkendurchdringende' Kraft des Gebetes mehr von der körperlichen Kleinheit des Beters und der Reinheit seiner Stimme abhängig als von der inneren Haltung der Demut. Indem man seit altkirchlicher Zeit überdies die Idee von der Wirkmächtigkeit des stellvertretenden Gebetes wertschätzte[34], ergaben sich für das von reinen (Kinder-)Stimmen vorgetragene Bitten vielfältige Einsatzmöglichkeiten: als Sänger, als Lektor oder als Fürbitter am Heiligtum. – Bemerkenswerterweise blieb das Ideal kindlicher *puritas* nicht auf die Kinder beschränkt; die alten Mönche waren ihm als Träger der Liturgie gleichfalls derart verpflichtet, dass auch sie schließlich im geistlichen Sinne als Kinder gelten konnten.

Das geistliche Jungsein aller Mönche

Von Anfang an haben die Christen herausgestellt, dass die Taufe sowie eine an diesem Initiationssakrament ausgerichtete Lebensführung

---

33 H. LUTTERBACH, Bonifatius – Mit Axt und Evangelium. Eine Biographie in Briefen, Freiburg/Basel/Wien ²2005, S. 65-67, 267f.; A. ANGENENDT, Das Frühmittelalter. Die abendländische Christenheit von 400 bis 900, Stuttgart/Berlin/Köln ²1995, S. 223-226, hier besonders S. 226; V. SAXER, Art. Petrus III. (Kultverbreitung), in: Lexikon des Mittelalters 6 (1993), Sp. 1957-1958; P. RÉFICE, Le chiavi del Regno, in: Arte medievale, 2. Ser. 4/2 (1990), S. 59-64.

34 Zu den biblischen Grundlagen des Stellvertretungsgedankens in der christlichen Frömmigkeit siehe K.-H. MENKE, Art. Stellvertretung II. (Biblisch-theologisch) und IV. (Spirituell), in: Lexikon für Theologie und Kirche 9 (2000), Sp. 952-953, 955-956.

geistliches Jungsein bewirken und zu ewiger Frische führen könne;[35] allein wer das Evangelium missachte, erfahre die 'Entwertung' der natürlichen Zeit nicht und altere mit den äußerlichen Merkmalen von Makeln und Runzeln (Eph 4,23): "Die [durch die Jesus-Anhänger seit Anbeginn hochgehaltene] Erneuerungsidee führte wie von selbst zur Vorstellung der 'Jugend' des gläubigen Christen und damit auch zu deren dunklem Gegenbild, zum Gedanken an die 'Greisenhaftigkeit' des Ungläubigen und Sünders, d. h. eben des 'alten' Menschen."[36]

Diese geistliche Wertschätzung des Kindseins griff das Mönchtum zu einem Zeitpunkt auf, als die urreligiöse, allerdings vom Neuen Testament außer Kraft gesetzte, vornehmlich durch den Verzicht auf Sexualität erreichbare kultische Reinheit eine im Christentum zuvor unbekannte Wertschätzung erfuhr;[37] gleichzeitig betonten die Mönche den Wert asketischer Lebenspraxis: "Die Überwindung der natürlichen Altersgrenzen gehörte [...] zu den festen Zielen asketischen Lebens, ja, kann geradezu als umfassende Formel für das ganze asketische Programm gelten."[38] Konsequent sollten im Rahmen des Gemeinschaftsmönchtums auf der einen Seite die Klosterkinder über ihre altersbedingte sexuelle Reinheit hinaus zugleich die asketische Erfahrung der bereits betagten Mönche antizipieren. So heißt es über den späteren Nordlandmissionar Ansgar († 865) mit Blick auf seine Zeit als Klosterkind in der Mönchsgemeinschaft von Corbie: "Er sonderte sich von den anderen Kindern ab. Desgleichen kümmerte er sich jetzt eifriger um Lesen, Lernen und andere nützliche Beschäftigungen."[39] Auf der anderen Seite war den klösterlichen *seniores* abgefordert, über ihre monastische Erfahrung hinaus die sexuelle Reinheit der Kinder zu

---

35 Dazu umfassend LUTTERBACH, Gotteskindschaft (wie Anm. 30), S. 39-105.

36 C. GNILKA, Aetas spiritalis. Die Überwindung der natürlichen Altersstufen als Ideal frühchristlichen Lebens (Theophaneia 24), Bonn 1972, S. 245.

37 Zur Vorstellung der kultischen Reinheit in religionsgeschichtlicher Perspektive siehe LUTTERBACH, Sexualität im Mittelalter (wie Anm. 32), besonders S. 20-63; mit Fokus auf die Bedeutung der kultischen Reinheit in altkirchlicher Zeit siehe D. WENDEBOURG, Die alttestamentlichen Reinheitsgesetze in der frühen Kirche, in: Zeitschrift für Kirchengeschichte 95 (1984), S. 149-170.

38 GNILKA, Aetas spiritalis (wie Anm. 36), S. 149, 210.

39 Vita Anskarii auctore Rimberto 2, ed. G. WAITZ (MGH SS rer. Germ. 55), Berlin 1884, S. 21. Dazu im Kontext siehe H. LUTTERBACH, Ansgar und das fränkische Mönchtum. Zeituntypische Spuren eines monastischen Werdegangs, in: Studia Monastica 37 (1995), S. 79-99.

verkörpern. Demnach sollten idealiter sowohl die an Jahren noch jungen Mönche als auch die *seniores* unter den Klosterbewohnern über eine kindergleiche, helle und klare Stimme verfügen, so dass ihre Leiber nach ihrem irdischen Tod nicht verwesten, sondern vielmehr ein rosafarbenes, also kindergleiches Aussehen zeigten und rosengleich dufteten.[40] Immerhin, so die damals auf Ps 15,10 gründende Überzeugung: Die Heiligen – im Mittelalter allzumeist identifiziert mit den sexuell Enthaltsamen – lasse Gott die Verwesung nicht schauen.[41]

Halten wir fest: Während der Apostel Paulus die Erneuerung und Verjüngung noch in der jedem Christen möglichen Hinkehr zur christlichen Empfangsbereitschaft und gotteskindlichen Hingabe wurzeln sieht, bezieht das aufstrebende Asketen- und Mönchtum dieses Paulus-Wort auf die Ergreifung des sexuell enthaltsamen Lebens im Einsatz am klösterlichen Heiligtum: auf die Mönchwerdung als Zweite Taufe und als Weg in die besondere Gotteskindschaft. Somit gilt für das zu Exklusivität hin tendierende Selbstverständnis des christlichen Mönchtums: "'Kind' soll man sein, weil dem Kinde Unschuld, Einfalt und Leidenschaftslosigkeit eignen."[42] – Die Prägekraft des geistlichen Kinderideals hat sich für das Mönchtum unter anderem in der Begründung des 'Rätelebens' ausgewirkt, überdies die äußere Erscheinung der Mönche geprägt, zu eigenartigen klösterlichen Festbräuchen geführt und bis in die Moderne überdauert.

Ehelosigkeit, Armut und Gehorsam im Dienste der besonderen Gotteskindschaft

Bei der Entscheidung des Christen zugunsten von Ehelosigkeit, Armut und Gehorsam geht es zutiefst um "die innere und äußere Freiheit für die Nachfolge Jesu."[43] Idealiter soll sich der Mensch von allen weltverhafteten inneren und äußeren Banden freihalten, um im Dienste

---

40 A. ANGENENDT, Corpus incorruptum. Eine Leitidee der mittelalterlichen Reliquienverehrung, in: Saeculum 42 (1991), S. 320-346.

41 Das entsprechende Psalmwort lautet: [...] *non dabis sanctum tuum videre corruptionem.*

42 GNILKA, Aetas spiritalis (wie Anm. 36), S. 247.

43 J. GRÜNDEL, Art. *Consilia Evangelica*, in: Theologische Realenzyklopädie 8 (1981), S. 192-196, hier S. 193.

der Gottes- und Nächstenliebe allein als Gotteskind gegenüber dem göttlichen Vater zu leben. Tatsächlich diente die lebenspraktische Umsetzung von Ehelosigkeit, Armut und Gehorsam von allem Anfang an dem "radikalen Vollzug des christlichen Glaubens."[44] Erst nachdem die Hoffnung auf die baldige Wiederkunft Christi nicht in Erfüllung gegangen war, ließen viele Christen von den biblischen Maximalforderungen ab, während die Mönche sie mit zunehmender Exklusivität zu ihrer Sache und zu einem Kennzeichen der besonderen Gotteskindschaft machten. Entsprechend mühte sich fortan das besondere Gotteskind – in Anlehnung an ein Kind aus Fleisch und Blut – darum, von aller Sexualität unberührt zu bleiben, um allein dem göttlichen Vater und der klösterlichen Familie zu leben. Weiter noch sah man das besondere Gotteskind in der Notwendigkeit, auf eigenen Besitz zu verzichten, weil der göttliche Vater bzw. der Klostervorsteher analog zu jedem leiblichen Vater die Garantie dafür bietet, das für das Kind Lebensnotwendige stets bereitzuhalten. Schließlich sollte sich das besondere Gotteskind wie jedes andere Kind im Gehorsam üben, hier: gegenüber Abt und Regel. Im folgenden Abschnitt wird beispielhaft rekonstruiert, wie die Anforderung der Ehelosigkeit von den gewöhnlichen auf die besonderen Gotteskinder überging.

Die von der Naherwartung durchdrungene neutestamentliche Jesus-Botschaft gibt sich im Blick auf die Ehe ambivalent: Einerseits redet sie dieser Verbindung als Ausdruck gottgewirkter Einheit zwischen zwei Menschen das Wort (Mk 10,6-9; Mt 19,4ff.); andererseits sind Traditionen überliefert, denen zufolge die Heirat den Menschen vor Gott sogar schuldig macht, weil er darüber sein Verhältnis als geistliches Kind zum göttlichen Vater in den Hintergrund rückt (Lk 14,20; Mt 24,38f.; Lk 17,27) – ein Tatbestand, der auch deshalb von Relevanz ist, weil die Ehe lediglich als eine Lebensform der Weltzeit gilt (Mk 12,25). In diesem Sinne mahnt der Apostel Paulus in seinem Brief an die Gemeinde von Korinth (1 Kor 7,7), dass die Eheleute "ihren ehelichen Beziehungen nicht so unterworfen sein [dürfen], dass sie ohne sie gar nicht existieren könnten."[45] Es ist das 'ungeteilte Dem-Herrn-Gehören',

---

44 Ebd.

45 E. WALTER, Der erste Brief an die Korinther (Geistliche Schriftlesung 7), Düsseldorf 1969, S. 134.

mit anderen Worten: die ohne eheliche Bindungen gelebte Gotteskindschaft, die Paulus auch in 1 Kor 7,28-35 als Ideal einschärft.[46]

Entscheidend für die Durchsetzung der zölibatären Lebensform sollte sich das Wort von den Eunuchen auswirken, die sich im Dienste der ungeteilten Gotteskindschaft freiwillig zur ehelosen Lebensweise entscheiden (Mt 19,12): "Der Verzicht auf Ehe, Zeugung, Kinder geschieht [hier] um des Himmelreiches willen, nicht so sehr um es persönlich zu gewinnen, sondern um ungeteilt und mit allen Kräften für die Basileia und ihre Gerechtigkeit wirken zu können."[47] Gleichfalls im Sinne eines von allen irdisch-ehelichen Bindungen freien Verständnisses der Gotteskindschaft erwägt Ulrich LUZ als Grund für diese Weise freiwilliger Ehelosigkeit: "damit sie [die Ehelosen] nicht durch die Sorgen um ihre Familie von ihrer Aufgabe am Gottesreich abgelenkt werden."[48]

Im 4. Jahrhundert, als die Großkirche aufgrund ihrer Expansion zwischen einer gewöhnlichen und einer besonderen Gotteskindschaft zu unterscheiden begann, um in der Konsequenz die ehelose Lebensform als Ausdruck der besonderen Kindschaft aufzuwerten, trat im Christentum auch die Idee der kultischen Reinheit ihren Siegeszug an. Deren Einfluss sollte sich auf die Entwicklung des priesterlichen Zölibats prägend auswirken.[49] Raymund KOTTJE verdanken wir die Erkenntnis, dass erst das Aufkommen der täglichen Eucharistiefeier im 4. Jahrhundert zur Zölibatsforderung führte.[50] Aufgrund der *integritas* des Leibes Christi, mit dem der Priester während der Eucharistie in Kontakt gerät, bedarf auch sein eigener Leib der *integritas* im Sinne des Freiseins von sexueller Betätigung. Weiter: Nicht zuletzt in dem Maße, wie seit

---

46 Ebd., S. 138; auch A. STROBEL, Der erste Brief an die Korinther (Zürcher Bibelkommentare NT 6,1), Zürich 1989, S. 125-129.

47 J. GNILKA, Das Matthäusevangelium. II. Teil (Herders theologischer Kommentar zum Neuen Testament 1), Freiburg/Basel/Wien 1988, S. 155.

48 U. LUZ, Das Evangelium nach Matthäus (Mt 18-25) (Evangelisch-Katholischer Kommentar zum Neuen Testament 1,3), Zürich/Düsseldorf/Neukirchen-Vluyn 1997, S. 11.

49 D. WENDEBOURG, Die alttestamentlichen Reinheitsgesetze (wie Anm. 37), S. 149-170; mit zahlreichen Belegen auch G. DENZLER, Die Geschichte des Zölibats, Freiburg/Basel/Wien 1993, S. 60-79.

50 R. KOTTJE, Das Aufkommen der täglichen Eucharistiefeier in der Westkirche und die Zölibatsforderung, in: Zeitschrift für Kirchengeschichte 82 (1971), S. 218-228, hier besonders S. 225.

frühmittelalterlicher Zeit die Klerikalisierung des Mönchtums und die Monastisierung des Klerus zu einer Angleichung von Klerikertum und Mönchtum mit der Folge führten, dass fortan gleichermaßen Priester und Mönche dem Ideal der besonderen Gotteskindschaft verpflichtet waren, durfte sich die Lebensweise sowohl des Klerikers als auch des Mönches im Blick auf den Umgang mit der Sexualität nicht von derjenigen eines gewöhnlichen Kindes unterscheiden.[51]

Im 11. und 12. Jahrhundert glaubte man der hervorragenden Beziehung des kultisch rein lebenden Priesters zum Jesuskind besonders während der Eucharistiefeier ansichtig zu werden, wenn sich die konsekrierte Hostie in das Jesuskind verwandelte. Der "Hauptzweck [dieser Verwandlungswunder] wird die gnadenvolle Beseligung und Belohnung [des Priesters] für Frömmigkeit und [asexuelle] Heiligkeit [gewesen sein]. Das ist das Neue", wie maßgeblich Peter BROWE unterstreicht.[52] So berichtet eines der ältesten Zeugnisse aus dem Benediktinerkloster Déols von 1116 über die sakralen Folgen der priesterlichen Zölibatserfüllung: "Als der Priester im Kloster Déols die Messe feierte, erschien an der Stelle der Hostie ein Junge (*puer*) über dem Altar."[53] Gleichfalls zeigte sich der kleine Jesus dem offensichtlich zölibatär lebenden Zisterzienserabt Walthenus († 1159) in Schottland, als dieser bei der Elevation statt der Hostie unversehens den Jesusknaben (*puer Jesus*) in der Hand hielt, der ihn zudem herzlich liebkoste.[54] Der Kartäuserabt Hugo und spätere Bischof von Lincoln († 1200) galt in

---

51 Zur Bedeutungsvielfalt der Termini *clericus* und *monachus* im Frühmittelalter siehe H. LUTTERBACH, Monachus factus est (wie Anm. 21), S. 118ff.

52 P. BROWE, Die eucharistischen Wunder des Mittelalters (Breslauer Studien zur historischen Theologie 4), Breslau 1938, S. 100, der zugleich darauf hinweist, dass "vor dem 11. Jahrhundert nur ein Beispiel bekannt" ist für derart eucharistische Kind-Verwandlungswunder. Dazu grundlegend auch DERS., Die eucharistischen Verwandlungswunder des Mittelalters, in: DERS., Die Eucharistie im Mittelalter: liturgiehistorische Forschungen in kulturwissenschaftlicher Absicht, mit einer Einleitung hgg. von H. LUTTERBACH / T. FLAMMER (Vergessene Theologen 1), Münster/Hamburg/London 2003, S. 265-289; auch DERS., Die scholastische Theorie der eucharistischen Verwandlungswunder des Mittelalters, in: Ebd., S. 251-263.

53 Wilhelm von Nangiaco, Chronica, ed. H. GERAUD, (Chronique latine de Guillaume de Nangis de 1113-1300), 8 Bde., hier Bd. 1, Paris 1843, S. 7.

54 Vita Waltheni I 8, ed. Acta Sanctorum, Aug. I, Venedig 1750, S. 242.

dieser Hinsicht sogar als derart begabt[55], dass ihn die Ikonographie von Anfang an mit dem Attribut des göttlichen Knaben dargestellt hat.[56] Auch im *Exordium Magnum* der Zisterzienser ist eine Erzählung überliefert, die belegt, dass die sittlich-zölibatäre Lebensführung des Priesters direkt mit dem Erscheinen Jesu als *puer* verbunden ist: Während ein Mönch im Kloster Clairvaux an der Messfeier teilnahm, sah er, wie das Jesuskind vor dem Kelch stand, wenn der unsittliche Priester ihm den Rücken zukehrte, um zu predigen oder die Oblationen entgegenzunehmen; sobald sich der Priester dem Kelch zuwandte, verbarg sich das Jesuskind hinter dem Kelch.[57] Wie man sich diese Verwandlungs-Erscheinungen dachte, ist in vielen ikonographischen Darstellungen überliefert, die in hoch- und spätmittelalterliche Messbücher Eingang gefunden haben.[58]

Hier kann nicht auf das "in seiner Bedeutung für den Zölibat kaum hoch genug einzuschätzende [und vor allem aus der Hohelied-Exegese abgeleitete] Motiv der Brautschaft zwischen Christus und Kirche bzw. Kleriker"[59] eingegangen werden; gleichwohl zeigt sich auch aus diesem Blickwinkel seit dem 4. Jahrhundert die Bedeutung der Leistungsfrömmigkeit für die Gotteskindschaft: Nur wer als Mönch oder Priester "die Zukunft vorwegnimmt, in der es keine Trennung nach Geschlechtern mehr geben wird",[60] vermag als besonderes Gotteskind zu gelten. Analog dem Bräutigam bringt das besondere Gotteskind, also Mönch oder Priester, der durch die Ehe seiner geistlichen Braut verbunden ist, mit Hilfe des Heiligen Geistes geistliche Kinder hervor:[61]

---

55 Zu den Jesuskind-Erscheinungen des Abtes siehe Vita Hugonis episcopi Lincolniensis 5,4, ed. J.-P. MIGNE (Patrologia Latina 153), Paris 1888, Sp. 1036.

56 J. BRAUN, Tracht und Attribute der Heiligen in der deutschen Kunst, Stuttgart 1943, Sp. 344.

57 Exordium Magnum Cisterciense sive Narratio de initio Cisterciensis Ordinis auctore Conrado monacho Claravallensi postea Eberbacensi ibidemque abbate, ed. B. GRIESSER (Corpus Christianorum. Continuatio Mediaevalis 138), Turnholt 1994, S. 245, Z. 104 - S. 246, Z. 127.

58 M. BRILLANT, Eucharistia. Encyclopédia populaire sur l'eucharistie, Paris 1934, S. 166.

59 T. LENTES, Art. Zölibat, in: Lexikon des Mittelalters 9 (1998) Sp. 663-664, hier Sp. 664.

60 KRETSCHMAR, Die Geschichte des Taufgottesdienstes in der Alten Kirche (wie Anm. 20), S. 128.

61 LUTTERBACH, Sexualität im Mittelalter (wie Anm. 32), S. 106-114.

vor allem wer im Kloster oder als Priester der mystischen Gottesgeburt teilhaftig und unter Abt oder Bischof selbst Gottes hervorragendes Kind geworden ist, kann als Bräutigam der Kirche bei der Zeugung von Gotteskindern hilfreich sein.

Das Äußere der besonderen Gotteskinder: Die Kapuze

Wie eingangs bereits angedeutet, gibt es seit dem 4. Jahrhundert eine Fülle von rituellen Parallelen zwischen der Ersten und der Zweiten Taufe. Sie reichen von einer sowohl für die einfachen als auch für die besonderen Gotteskinder notwendige Probezeit bis hin zu einem auf Dauer angelegten Tauf- bzw. Mönchsversprechen. Aus der Vielzahl der 'Doppelungen' sei exemplarisch die einleitend schon zur Sprache gebrachte Kapuze herausgegriffen, um sie entwicklungsgeschichtlich herzuleiten.

Aus den Anfängen der griechischen Kirche wissen wir, dass den Neugetauften im Anschluss an die Chrisam-Salbung die Kapuze aufgesetzt wurde, mit der sie ihr Haupt sieben Tage lang verhüllt halten sollten, um ihre Taufsalbung zu schützen. Die Kirche verband mit der Taufe so sehr die Idee der Neugeburt des Menschen, dass man die Täuflinge unabhängig von ihrem biologischen Alter als *infantes* bezeichnete.[62] Wenn die Mönche seit altkirchlicher Zeit eine Kapuze tragen, weist diese nicht zuletzt auf die Zweite Taufe der Klosterbewohner hin: "Der Kukullus war Kinderkleid" und galt als "Zeichen der Gotteskindschaft." In dieser Auffassung stimmten den maßgeblichen Untersuchungen von Philipp OPPENHEIM zufolge "fast alle […] [altkirchlichen und mittelalterlichen] Erklärer der Mönchstracht überein".[63] Schon in der Vita des Mönchsvaters Pachomius († 347) findet sich der Hinweis, dass seine Brüder ihre Fellkleider, Ledersandalen und

---

62 Diese Sicht konnte sich auf 1 Petr 2,1-2 gründen: […] *deponentes igitur omnem malitiam et omnem dolum et simulationes et invidias et omnes detractiones sicut modo geniti infantes.* Eben diese biblische Aussage hallt auch wider im Introitus des 1. Sonntags nach Ostern: *Quasi modo geniti infantes.*

63 P. OPPENHEIM, Symbolik und religiöse Wertung des Mönchskleides im christlichen Altertum. Vornehmlich nach Zeugnissen christlicher Schriftsteller der Ostkirche (Theologie des christlichen Ostens. Texte und Untersuchungen 2), Münster i. W. 1932, S. 65 (Zitat), 68.

Gürtel ablegten, wenn sie zum Zeichen ihrer Gotteskindschaft allein mit einem Leinengewand und der Mönchskapuze auf dem Kopf die Kommunion empfingen.[64] In dieser Kleidervorschrift ist eine Erinnerung an den Tauftag zu sehen, da auch das Taufkleid aus Leinen gewebt sein sollte; angetan mit diesem durch die Mönchwerdung in seiner Unschuld erneuerten Leinenkleid empfingen sie auch die Kommunion. Ein Brief des Evagrius Ponticus († 399) bestätigt diese Vermutung: "Der Kukullus beschützt und hütet das Kindsein der Mönche in Christus."[65] Entsprechend heißt es in der zwischen 433 und 435 abgefassten Kirchengeschichte des Sozomenos: "Die Kopfbedeckung jedoch, welche [die Mönche aus Ägypten] als Kukullus bezeichnen, setzen sie auf, um in Einfalt und Reinheit zu leben, genau als ob sie Kinder sein würden, die noch mit der Muttermilch versorgt werden. Eben solchen nämlich setzt man üblicherweise derartige Kapuzen auf, um ihre Köpfchen zu bedecken und zu schützen."[66] Und der für das mittelalterlich-okzidentale Mönchtum einflussreiche Johannes Cassian († um 430) hebt im Rückblick auf seine Reiseerfahrungen hervor: "Die ägyptischen Mönche tragen die Kapuzen, um beständig daran gemahnt zu werden, dass sie auch die Unschuld und die Einfalt der Kinder bewahren sollen, deren Verhüllung sie nachahmen. So wieder Kind geworden, singen sie Christo [Lob]."[67] Mit entsprechendem Rückbezug auf den altchristlichen Taufgedanken heißt es auch bei dem Griechen und späteren Erzbischof Theodor von Canterbury († 690) im 7. Jahrhundert: Der Mönch dürfe die bei der Mönchwerdung empfangene Kapuze sieben Tage nach der Klosteraufnahme nicht abnehmen – analog also der Forderung, wie sie auch soeben Getauften galt.[68] Zwar entwickelten sich im Mönchtum unterschiedliche Kapuzen-

---

64 Vita Pachomii 22, ed. J.-P. MIGNE (Patrologia Latina 73), Paris 1888, Sp. 242C; auch Palladius Heleopolitanus, Historia Lausiaca 38, ed. J.P. MIGNE (Patrologia Latina 73), Paris 1875, Sp. 1137D.

65 Evagrius Ponticus, Capita practica ad Anatolium, ed. J.-P. MIGNE (Patrologia Graeca 40), Paris 1863, Sp. 1220C.

66 Sozomenos, Kirchengeschichte 3,14, ed. J.P. MIGNE (Patrologia Graeca 67), Paris 1881, Sp. 1069ff.

67 Johannes Cassian, De Institutis coenobiorum I 3, ed. J.-C. GUY (Sources Chrétiennes 109), Paris 1965, S. 42-45.

68 Discipulus Umbrensium II 3,3, ed. P. W. FINSTERWALDER, in: Die Canones Theodori Cantuariensis und ihre Überlieferungsformen (Untersuchungen zu den Bußbüchern des 7., 8. und 9. Jahrhunderts 1), Weimar 1929, S. 315. Weitere

Moden; von diesen Variationen blieb die Taufsymbolik der Mönchskapuze allerdings unberührt. Philipp OPPENHEIM unterstreicht die Reichweite, zu der es die Deutung der Kukulle als Kinderkleid brachte: "Eine ununterbrochene Deutung reicht von den Altvätern der Wüste bis ins späteste Mittelalter hinein. Immer wieder werden Stimmen laut, die in dem Mönchskukullus ein Zeichen der Unschuld und Reinheit und des Kindseins in Christo sehen."[69]

Kinderäbte und Kinderbischöfe als Brennpunkte des monastischen Kinderideals

Zu den heutigem Verstehen wohl unzugänglichsten Phänomenen des kirchlichen Lebens in Mittelalter und Neuzeit zählt die – in ihrer Gültigkeit allerdings zeitlich befristete – Wahl von Kindern zum Abt oder Bischof.[70] Diese Tradition wurde verstanden als Ausdruck des geistlichen Kindseins, das alle Christen im Anschluss an die Taufe zu hüten hatten, vor allem aber die besonderen Gotteskinder aufgrund ihrer Profess bzw. Weihe.

Die im Hintergrund der Kinderäbte und -bischöfe stehende liturgische Verehrung der so genannten 'Unschuldigen Kinder' ruht auf einer nur schmalen neutestamentlichen Basis: "Als der König Herodes sah, dass er von den Magiern an der Nase herumgeführt worden war, wurde er sehr zornig. Er sandte Leute aus und ließ alle Knaben (*pueri*) in Bethlehem und im gesamten Gebiet töten, die jünger als zwei Jahre alt waren." (Mt 2,16). Wenn zum rituellen Gedenken an dieses Ereignis auch die Wahl eines Kinderabtes gehörte, dann liegt dies gewiss mit darin begründet, dass der liturgische Inhalt dieses Festes insgesamt als "Besinnung auf die vier Begriffe 'heilig', 'unschuldig', 'Märtyrer' und

---

Beispiele bei O. CASEL, Die Mönchsweihe, in: Jahrbuch für Liturgiewissenschaft 5 (1925), S. 1-47, hier S. 30 und OPPENHEIM, Symbolik (wie Anm. 63), S. 69-72.

69 OPPENHEIM, Symbolik (wie Anm. 63), S. 66, 101; auch DERS., Das Mönchskleid im christlichen Altertum (Römische Quartalschrift. Supplementheft 28), Freiburg i. Br. 1931, S. 149.

70 Dazu K. ARNOLD, Kinderbischof, in: Lexikon des Mittelalters 5 (1991), Sp. 1149; P. RICHE, L'enfant dans la société chrétienne aux XIe-XIIe siècles, in: La cristianità dei secoli XI e XII in occidente, Mailand 1983, S. 281-302.

'Kinder' angesehen" werden kann.[71] Genauerhin stimmen die patristischen ebenso wie die mittelalterlichen Ausdeutungen des Festgeheimnisses darin überein, dass die unschuldigen Kinder als 'Sonder-Märtyrer' zu sehen sind: Im Unterschied zu allen übrigen christlichen Märtyrern gaben sie ihr Leben nicht hin zum Zeugnis für den gestorbenen Jesus; vielmehr kamen sie zu Tode, um dem neugeborenen Jesuskind sein Leben zu erhalten.[72]

Das Brauchtum der Kinderäbte und -bischöfe wird als Erinnerung daran aufzufassen sein, dass der dem Martyrium entgegenstrebende Mönch dem Leitbild des Kindes verpflichtet war; in diesem Zusammenhang kam den Kindern, die das blutige Martyrium zum Schutze Jesu auf sich genommen hatten, für die alten und jungen 'Klosterkinder' eine besondere Vorbildfunktion zu bei deren Verwirklichung eines lebenslänglichen und unblutigen Martyriums.

Während das früheste Zeugnis für den Kinderabt auf Ekkehards († um 1060) *Casus Sancti Galli* zurückgeht,[73] stammt eine besonders ausführliche Überlieferung aus dem 11. Jahrhundert und beschreibt die Liturgie am Festtag der Unschuldigen Kinder in Rouen: Am Vorabend, unmittelbar nach der Feier des St.-Johannes-Festes, begaben sich zwei Chorknaben, in Chorhemd und Talar gekleidet, ihr Haupt mit dem Amikte bedeckt und jeder eine brennende Kerze in der Hand haltend, aus der Sakristei in den Chor. Hierauf kamen auch die übrigen in gleicher Ausrüstung in die Kirche und zuletzt derjenige, der im Voraus dazu bestimmt worden war, an diesem Tage den bischöflichen Titel zu tragen und die Huldigung zu empfangen. Er zog einher, feierlich, mit den Pontifikalien geschmückt, die Mitra auf seinem Haupte und den Hirtenstab in der Hand. So begab sich das Gefolge der Knaben quer durch den Chor gegen den Altar der Unschuldigen Kinder. Während des Zuges sang der Chor für die Feier geeignete Hymnen und Responsorien. Vor dem Altare der Heiligen Kinder wurde dann unter dem Vorsitze des Knabenbischofs eine feierliche Statio gehalten. Gegen deren Ende erging an das Volk die Mahnung, sich zu beugen, um den Segen des jungen

---

71 J. HENNIG, Zur liturgischen Lehre von den Unschuldigen Kindern, in: Archiv für Liturgiewissenschaft 9/1 (1965), S. 72-85, hier S. 73.

72 Ebd., S. 74, 84.

73 Ekkehard, Casus Sancti Galli, ed. H. F. HAEFELE (Freiherr vom Stein-Gedächtnisausgabe 10), Darmstadt 1980, Kap. 14, S. 40.

Prälaten zu empfangen. Am Festtage selber wurden die Knaben mit der gleichen Auszeichnung beehrt. Mit Ausnahme der Heiligen Messe, die in ihrer Gegenwart ein *canonicus* las, hielten sie in festlichem Pompe alle Funktionen des Chores.[74]

Als ursprünglicher Zeitpunkt für die Einsetzung des Kinderabtes bzw. des Kinderbischofs (*episcopus puerorum*, *episcopus scholarium*, *episcopus innocentium*) darf das Fest der Unschuldigen Kinder gelten, wie die nach wie vor maßgebliche Untersuchung von Karl MEISEN unterstreicht, der für dieses Faktum Beispiele aus vielen Teilen Europas zusammenträgt.[75] Erst seit dem Ende des 13. Jahrhunderts lassen sich, ausgehend von Nordfrankreich, erste Zeugnisse dafür beibringen, dass der Brauch des Kinderabtes bzw. Kinderbischofs mit dem Gedenktag des Heiligen Nikolaus in Beziehung tritt.[76]

Eine Notiz im Inventar der Abtei Westminster von 1388 lässt die geradezu preziose Ausstattung des Kinderbischofs beispielhaft erkennen. So umfasst das Verzeichnis eine "Mitra für das Fest des Heiligen Nikolaus, geschneidert für den Kinderbischof, mit silbernen Streifen sowie mit verschiedenen goldenen Steinen verziert; auf der Vorderseite beschrift mit der Anrede '*Sancte Nicholae*', auf der Rückseite mit den Worten '*Ora pro nobis*'; alle Buchstaben sollen aus Perlen gefertigt sein."[77] Aus Bamberg ist eine ähnliche Ausstattung überliefert, die überdies noch ikonographisch festgehalten ist. Unter der Überschrift *An Sanct Nicolai Abent zu der Vesper wie vnd welcher gestalt der Erwelt Bischoff vnder den schulern mit seinen Asseclis in Chor geht* lesen wir in einer Handschrift, die zwischen 1581 und 1583 verfasst wurde:

---

74 Abbé PICARD, Quelques cérémonies allégoriques anciennements en usage dans l'église de Rouen, in: Précis analytique des trauvaux de l'Académie royale des sciences, belles-lettres et art de Rouen, Rouen 1847, S. 373ff., zit. nach dem Abdruck bei J. D'ORTIGUE, Dictionnaire liturgique, historique et théorétique du plain-chant et de musique d' Eglise, in: J.-P. MIGNE (Hg.), Nouvelle Encyclopédie théologique, IIe série 29 (1860), Sp. 538f.

75 K. MEISEN, Nikolauskult und Nikolausbrauch im Abendlande. Eine kultgeographisch-volkskundliche Untersuchung, Düsseldorf 1931 (ND 1981), S. 312-317.

76 Zu den Hintergründen siehe umfassend ebd., S. 289-306.

77 J. WICKHAMM LEGG, On an Inventory of the Vestry in Westminster Abbey. Taken in 1388, in: Archaeologia. Or Miscellaneous Tracts Relating to Antiquity 52 (1890), S. 195-286, hier S. 220f.

> *Wen man am Abent Nicolai Zu der Vesper sammen leut, so geht der knab, welcher Bischoff, von der schul herab, in einem korrock, vnnd darueber ein schones rotes korkeplein Ein Jnful* [= Mitra] *auf seinem haupt vnnd den Baculum pastorale oder Bischofstab in seiner handt, Zu beden seiden nebe Jme die zwen Asseclae, oder ministranten, auch mit korrocken, vnnd gespreckletetn khorkeplein, daruber angethan.*[78]

Fassen wir zusammen: Die 'Kinder-Liturgie' vom Fest der Unschuldigen Kinder korrespondiert direkt mit dem Verständnis des Mönches als geistliches Kind, ja als besonderes Gotteskind. Dem 'Kinderliturgen', der das Kind als Leitbild des mönchischen Lebens veranschaulicht, sollte tatsächlich ein langes Leben beschieden sein: Noch aus dem 1863 gegründeten Benediktinerkloster Beuron an der Donau ist bekannt, dass die jungen Novizen an den Festtagen der Heiligen Maurus (15. Januar) und Placidus (5. Oktober) wichtige liturgische Funktionen übernahmen; den Dialogen von Papst Gregor dem Großen († 604) zufolge sollen die genannten Heiligen dem Heiligen Benedikt bereits im Kindesalter anvertraut worden sein.[79]

Das Revival der besonderen Gotteskindschaft im19. Jahrhundert

Nachdem das Mönchtum im Gefolge der aufklärerischen Bewegung im 18. Jahrhundert seine materielle und personelle Basis beinahe vollständig verloren hatte, indem die Klostergebäude staatlicherseits konfisziert und deren ehemalige Bewohner vertrieben worden waren,[80] lag ein Wiedererwachen des Mönchtums im 19. Jahrhundert außerhalb jeden Erwartungshorizontes. Wenn derlei trotzdem gelang, dann beruhte diese überraschende Entwicklung grundlegend auf dem jahrhundertealten Ideal der besonderen Gotteskindschaft.

---

[78] Zit. nach J. DÜNNINGER / H. SCHOPF (Hgg.), Bräuche und Feste im fränkischen Jahreslauf. Texte vom 16. bis zum 18. Jahrhundert (Die Plassenburg. Schriften für Heimatforschung und Kulturpflege in Ostfranken 30), Kulmbach 1971, S. 10. Weitere Ritusbeschreibungen aus den Jahren 1520 und 1534, siehe ebd., S. 11.

[79] Gregor I., Dialogi II 3,14, ed. A. DE VOGÜÉ (Sources Chrétiennes 260), Paris 1979, S. 150f.

[80] B. STOLLBERG-RILINGER, Europa im Jahrhundert der Aufklärung (Reclam Universal-Bibliothek 17025), Stuttgart 2000, S. 97-104.

Vor allem das bereits angesprochene Benediktinerkloster Beuron fußt auf der Vorstellung vom Mönch als besonderes Gotteskind; unter dieser traditionsreichen Prämisse sahen die Klostergründer Maurus und Placidus Wolter das Kloster als den eigentlichen Hort von Kinder- und Familienleben an. Das Charisma der Kindlichkeit ist Maurus WOLTER zufolge an kein natürliches Alter gebunden. Vielmehr versteht er es in Übereinstimmung mit romantischem Gedankengut als eine Grundhaltung, wie sie alle Mönche einzuüben hätten: "Aus jedem Alter und Stande kommen diese 'Kinder' der Gnade, die das Wort verstehen: 'Wahrlich, ich sage euch, wenn ihr euch nicht bekehret und wie die Kinder werdet, so werdet ihr nicht in das Himmelreich eingehen (Mt 18,3).'"[81] Entsprechend der monastischen Familientradition sieht Maurus WOLTER die Kindschaft des Mönches zweifach verankert: Auf der einen Seite steht der Professe in einem besonderen, auch emotional innigen Kindschaftsverhältnis zu Gott, dem Vater, auf der anderen Seite darf er als Kind des Abtes, des Christus-Stellvertreters im Kloster, gelten: "Für den Religiosen ist der Obere mit der Autorität Christi bekleidet, dessen Stellvertreter und lebendiges Bild, ein Vater, dem er als Kind vertrauend sich hingibt, um ins Himmelreich einzugehen. Gerade diese Rücksicht heiliger Ehrfurcht und kindlicher Liebe, die Folge des übernatürlichen Familienverhältnisses, erklärt jene altehrwürdige klösterliche Observanz [der Gewissenseröffnung]."[82] Der Gehorsam bildet das Band zwischen dem Vater Abt und dem Mönchskind: "Er [der Religiose] ist gekommen, nicht um sich selber zu leiten, sondern um in Kindeseinfalt sich leiten zu lassen."[83] Genauerhin werden alle Lebensvollzüge der im 19. Jahrhundert populären Kleinfamilie im geistigen Sinne auch auf die monastische Familie übertragen:

> Das Wort: 'Siehe, Kinder sind des Herrn Erbe', gilt dem Vater der Klosterfamilie, der in allem Gottes Willen sucht. Je größer die Treue in der Observanz, desto zahlreicher werden die 'Kinder', die Novizen sein, die seiner Leitung sich unterstellen. Wunderbare 'Kindschaft', die, ganz übernatürlich und geistig, nur Christo, der 'Leibesfrucht' der

---

81 M. WOLTER, Psallite sapienter. Psallieret weise! Erklärung der Psalmen im Geiste des betrachtenden Gebetes und der Liturgie, 5 Bde., Freiburg i. Br. 1871-1890, (deutsche Übersetzung) hier Bd. 5, S. 107.

82 Ebd., Bd. 1, S. 501.

83 Ebd., Bd. 5, S. 36.

> himmlischen Jungfrau, ihren Ursprung verdankt. [...] Sie werden im Noviziate 'neu geboren' und schauen 'Gottes Reich'.[84]

Wie Mönche die besondere geistliche Verjüngung persönlich erlebten, ist uns aus einer 1888 erschienen und vielfach neu aufgelegten Lebenserzählung des Beuroner Mönches Odilo WOLFF überliefert. Als Motivation für seinen eigenen Eintritt in das Kloster hebt Wolff hervor, dass ihn das Leben in der Welt vorschnell hatte altern lassen:

> Ich verstand auf einmal, dass ich in der Welt schon zu alt geworden, wiewohl ich noch erst im Anfang der zwanziger Jahre stand. Die Welt altert sehr schnell und macht alles schnell alt, was in ihr ist. Ein Kind zu sein, ist ja heutzutage dem Kind selbst schwer gemacht; nur wenige retten den kindlich geraden Sinn nur in die Jünglingsjahre hinüber.[85]

Den Kontrast zwischen der in Sünde beständig alternden Welt und der gewissermaßen entgegengesetzten Kindwerdung im Kloster stellt er auch an anderer Stelle deutlich heraus: "Die erste Lehre, die ich in den Mauern des Klosters erhielt, war die: 'Wenn ihr nicht werdet wie die Kindlein, werdet ihr nicht in das Himmelreich eingehen (Mt 18,3)', 'und auch nicht ins Kloster', fügte später der Novizenmeister oft ergänzend hinzu."[86] WOLFF erklärt sich das Wunder der monastischen Kindwerdung anhand eines naturwissenschaftlichen, aus dem Kontext der Industrialisierung des 19. Jahrhunderts entnommenen Vorgangs:

> Das [die Kindwerdung] scheint ein großes Stück Arbeit. Dem alten Nikodemus im Evangelium (Joh 3,4) dünkt es schon allzu schwer, wenn er, fast den Mut verlierend, an den Herrn die Frage richtet: 'Wie kann ich denn noch einmal geboren und ein Kind werden, da ich schon alt bin?' Indes, wirf ein Stücklein Erz in den glühenden Strom geschmolzenen Metalles – es widersteht nicht lange: bald ist es mit dem übrigen Metalle eins geworden.[87]

---

84 Ebd., S. 107.

85 O. WOLFF, Beuron. Bilder und Erinnerungen aus dem Mönchsleben der Jetztzeit, Freiburg i. Br. [4]1923, S. 17.

86 Ebd.

87 Ebd.

Als Beispiel für eine gelungene mönchische Kindwerdung führt Wolff seinen Mitbruder Pius VON DRAIS († 1883) an, der nach seiner Profess am 15. Juni 1866 über die beiden Wolter-Brüder als die eigentlichen Klostergründer hinaus der dritte Mönch der neuen Gemeinschaft war; trotz dessen im Vergleich zu seinen beiden Klosterbrüdern höheren Alters sei der Greis aufgrund des Klostereintritts geistlich wieder jung geworden: "Pater Pius war als weltlicher Herr schon hochbetagt ins Kloster eingetreten, um unter den kleinen jungen Novizen wieder ein Kind (*sic*) zu werden. Kurz vorher war er in die hl. Katholische Kirche zurückgekehrt, nachdem er einer hohen Stellung am badischen Hofe und langjährigem Staatsdienste entsagt hatte."[88] Zu seinem 80. Geburtstag dichteten die Novizen dem Jubilar und den übrigen Brüdern zu Ehren: "Kinder, die Welt betrügt, Gott nur genügt."[89]

Kurzum: Das Wiederaufleben des Mönchtums mit dem Kloster Beuron erklärt sich wesentlich aus dem Rückbezug auf das traditionsreiche Ideal der besonderen Gotteskindschaft. Ja, von dem bedeutenden Donau-Kloster aus sollte diese Maxime im 19. Jahrhundert ihren unaufhaltsamen Siegeszug aufgrund der von Beuron zahlreich ausgegangenen und europaweit vernetzten Klostergründungen[90] (unter anderen Maredsous, Belgien; Abtei Emaus in Prag; Fort Augustus, Schottland; Erdington, England) antreten.

Ausblick

Ohne Zweifel wurde das bis ins 4. Jahrhundert zurückreichende Ideal der besonderen – eben askese-betonten – Gotteskindschaft während der abendländischen Christentumsgeschichte mehrfach in Frage gestellt: ein erstes Mal durch die Armutsbewegung im 12. Jahrhundert sowie zweitens durch die Bewegung der mittelalterlichen Frauenmystik im 13. und 14. Jahrhundert, die jeweils an die Stelle des monastisch-leistungs-

88 Ebd., S. 34.

89 Ebd.

90 Dazu siehe knapp S. PETZOLT, Art. Beuron, in: Lexikon für Theologie und Kirche 2 (1994), Sp. 344-345; umfassender DERS., Die Gründungs- und Entwicklungsgeschichte der Abtei Beuron im Spiegel ihrer Liturgie (1863-1908), Würzburg 1990.

betonten Kindesideals erneut das neutestamentliche Ideal des Empfangens als Grundhaltung aller Gotteskinder rückten;[91] zum dritten durch die Reformation, hielten doch Martin Luther[92] und die übrigen Reformatoren[93] aufgrund ihrer Vergewisserungen im Neuen Testament nur eine einzige Gotteskindschaft aller Getauften für denkbar bzw. eine Unterteilung in eine gewöhnliche und eine besondere Gotteskindschaft für blasphemisch; zum vierten schließlich durch die Bewegung der Aufklärung, die einen neuerlichen Versuch unternahm, um die Frömmigkeit der Gotteskindschaft auf ein neutestamentliches Level zurückzuführen.[94] Angesichts dieses Hintergrundes ist es bemerkenswert, dass sich das Ideal der besonderen Gotteskindschaft bis in das 20. Jahrhundert hinein immer wieder durchzusetzen oder zumindest: durchzuhalten vermochte.

Erst das 2. Vatikanische Konzil während der 1960er Jahre bezeichnet einen auf 'Säkularisierung' hindeutenden Paradigmenwechsel, insofern es – römisch-lehramtlich übrigens erstmalig – die seit dem 4. Jahrhundert grundlegende Unterscheidung zwischen der gewöhnlichen und der besonderen Gotteskindschaft revidierte und stattdessen die biblisch eine, alle Christen aufgrund der Taufe verbindende Gotteskindschaft in das Bewusstsein der Gläubigen zurückholte:[95]

> "Eines ist also das auserwählte Volk Gottes: 'Ein Herr, ein Glaube, eine Taufe (Eph 4,5)'; gemeinsam die Würde der Glieder aus ihrer Wiedergeburt in Christus, gemeinsam die Gnade der Kindschaft, gemeinsam die Berufung zur Vollkommenheit. [...] Wenn auch einige nach Gottes Willen als Lehrer, Ausspender der Geheimnisse und Hirten für die anderen bestellt sind, so waltet doch unter allen eine

---

91 Dazu ausführlich LUTTERBACH, Gotteskindschaft (wie Anm. 30), S. 417f.

92 B. LOHSE, Mönchtum und Reformation. Luthers Auseinandersetzung mit dem Mönchsideal des Mittelalters, Göttingen 1963, S. 277f.; auch O. H. PESCH, Luthers Kritik am Mönchtum in katholischer Sicht, in: H. SCHLIER / E. VON SEVERUS / J. SUDBRACK (Hgg.), Strukturen christlicher Existenz. Beiträge zur Erneuerung des geistlichen Lebens, Würzburg 1968, S. 81-96, hier S. 89.

93 H. LUTTERBACH, Der Weg in das Täuferreich von Münster, Ein Ringen um die heilige Stadt (Geschichte des Bistums Münster 3), Münster 2006, S. 222-238, 249-255.

94 Dazu ausführlich LUTTERBACH, Gotteskindschaft (wie Anm. 30), S. 420f.

95 J. SCHMIEDL, Das Konzil und die Orden. Krise und Erneuerung des gottgeweihten Lebens, Vallendar/Schönstatt 1999, S. 522.

> wahre Gleichheit in der allen Gläubigen gemeinsamen Würde und Tätigkeit zum Aufbau des Leibes Christi."[96]

Tatsächlich erteilten die Konzilsväter dem traditionellen Schema der doppelten Gotteskindschaft und damit der Höherbewertung des klösterlich-klerikalen Lebens nach mehr als anderthalb Jahrtausenden eine Absage. An dessen Stelle trat das neutestamentlich-kraftvolle Plädoyer zugunsten der durch die Taufe gegebenen Egalität und Heiligkeit aller Christen.[97]

---

[96] Lumen Gentium 32, ed. K. RAHNER / H. VORGRIMLER, Kleines Konzilskompendium (Herderbücherei 270), Freiburg/Basel/Wien 1966, S. 162.

[97] SCHMIEDL, Das Konzil und die Orden (wie Anm. 95), S. 522.

PARVULUS: THE IDEA OF THE LITTLE CHILD IN MEDIEVAL PREACHING AND COMMENTARY

TIM GORRINGE

There are five words sometimes translated 'child' in the Greek New Testament: τέκνον, τεκνίον, παίς, παιδίον, and νήπιος. Like υιός ('son') Jerome translates τέκνον by 'filius'. τεκνίον, which is only used by John amongst the evangelists is translated by *filiolus*. παίς is translated twice by 'puer' and once by 'filius'. νήπιος is translated once by *infantium* (Mt 21.16) and twice by *parvulus*. παιδίον is the commonest word for 'child' in the New Testament. In his translations of the gospels Jerome occasionally translates it by *filius* (Mk 5.35-43, Lk 7.32), eighteen times by *puer* or *puella* (Mt 2.8, 2.9, 2.11, 11.16; Mk 7.27,28,30, 9.24, 9.36; Lk 1.59, 1.66, 1.76, 1.80, 2.17, 2.27, 2.40, 9.43, 9.48, 11.7, 18.16, 18.17) and eight times by *parvulus* (Mk 10.13f.; Mt 14.21, 15.38, 18.1-5, 19.13,14). In the Synoptic passages Jerome sometimes uses *puer* and sometimes *parvulus* for παιδίον, indicating that he was guided more by stylistic than by theological considerations. I am going to look at the reception history of two important passages which speak of the *parvulus* (Mt 18.1-5), where Jesus says that unless we become as little children we shall not enter the kingdom of heaven, and Mt 19.13-15, 'Suffer the little children'. Matthew 18. 1-5 reads, in the Vulgate:

> *In illa hora accesserunt discipuli ad Iesum dicentes quis putas maior est in regno caelorum. Et advocans Iesum parvulum statuit eum in medio eorum. Et dixit amen dico vobis nisi conversi fueritis et efficiamini sicut parvuli non intrabitis in regnum caelorum. Quicumque ergo humiliaverit se sicut parvulus iste hic est maior in regno caelorum. Et qui susceperit unum parvulum talem in nomine meo me suscipit.*

Because of the mention of angels in v. 10 this was also the gospel set for the feast of St Michael and all angels. What I want to attempt is a brief reception history for this passage as a way of seeing how *parvulus* was understood in the medieval church. I begin with the Catena Aurea where Aquinas summarises comments primarily by Origen, Chrysostom and

Jerome. Noting the context of the dispute about greatness, Aquinas' citations run as follows:[1] Chrysostom: "He chose, I suppose, quite an infant, devoid of any passions." Jerome: "One whose tender age should express to them the innocence which they should have. But truly he set himself in the midst of them, a little one who had come 'not to be ministered unto, but to minister' that he might be a pattern of holiness." Others interpret the little one of the Holy Spirit whom he set in the hearts of his disciples, to change their pride into humility. He does not enjoin on the Apostles the age, but the innocence of infants which they have by virtue of their years, but to which these might attain by striving, that they should be children in malice, not in understanding. As though he had said, as this child, whom I set before you as a pattern, is not obstinate in anger, when injured does not bear it in mind, has no emotion at the sight of a fair woman, does not think one thing while he speaks another; so you, unless you have the like innocence and purity of mind, shall not be able to enter into the kingdom of heaven. Hilary: "He calls infants all who believe through the hearing of faith; for such follow their father, love their mother, know not to will that which is evil, do not bear hate, or speak lies, trust what is told them, and believe what they hear to be true." Glossa interlinear:

> 'Except ye be converted' from this ambition and jealousy in which you are at present, and become all of you as innocent and humble in disposition as you are weak in your years, 'you shall not enter the kingdom of heaven', and since there is none other road to enter in, 'whoso shall humble himself as this little child, the same is the greatest in the kingdom of heaven;' for by how much a man is humble now, so shall he be exalted in the kingdom of heaven.

Remigius: "In the understanding of grace, or in ecclesiastical dignity, or at least in everlasting blessedness." Jerome: "Or otherwise, 'Whoso shall humble himself as this little child', that is, whoso shall humble himself after my example, 'he shall enter into the kingdom of heaven'." It follows:

---

1 Catena aurea, Commentary on the Four Gospels, collected out of the works of the Fathers by S. Thomas Aquinas, translated from the Latin by Mark Pattison, J. D. Dalgairns and T. D. Ryder, Oxford 1841, p. 625.

> And whoso receiveth one such little one in my name, receiveth me [...] For whoever is such that he imitates Christ's humility and innocence, Christ is received by him, and by way of caution, that the Apostles should not think, when such are come to them, that it is to themselves that the honour is paid. He adds, that they are to be received not for their own desert, but in honour of their Master.

The *glossa ordinaria* notes that the one who wants to enter the kingdom of heaven must obey the gospel 'like a child (*puer*) which does not contradict its teachers.'[2] By *puer* we understand a humble person worthy of Christ's love and embrace. We must not take *parvulus* literally but it signifies the desire not to be served but to serve; or it is the Spirit in our hearts leading us from pride to humility. Christ calls us to be like children which is to say to have innocence and humility. To be innocent as a child is not to persevere in anger. In this author's view Jesus did not have in mind not desiring a woman.

Radulphus Ardens of Aquitaine has a sermon on this text from the beginning of the twelfth century.[3] What the text means, he says, is that those of you who have the ambition to be greatest in the kingdom of heaven will in no way enter it. You cannot enter by ambition, but only by humility. If you wish to enter the kingdom of heaven you must manifest the virtues and habits of children. The child is characterised by innocence, an inability to lie, not perservering in anger, not remembering injuries, not desiring women, and so forth. When it says therefore that the one who humbles himself as a child is the greatest in the kingdom of heaven, what it means, is that the one who genuinely thinks of himself with humility is the true child and the one who is greatest in God's sight. What we are interested in is not simply talk about humility, nor its semblance, but truly believing in your heart that you are less than others, confessing it and showing it. For this is the virtue of humility, that a man becomes worthless in his own sight.

Also in the twelfth century there is a commentary on Matthew wrongly ascribed to Anselm of Laon and included under his work in

2 The glossa is assigned to Walafrid Strabo, Glossa ordinaria, Evangelium secundum Mattheum, ed. J.-P. MIGNE (Patrologia Latina 114), Turnholt 1969, col. 0146B, but is thought to come from the school of Anselm of Laon in the 12th century.

3 Radulphus Ardens of Aquitaine, Homiliae de tempore, ed. J.-P. MIGNE (Patrologia Latina 155), Turnholt 1975, col. 1460.

MIGNE.[4] According to this commentator the point of taking the child was to overturn (*contundere*) the disciples' pride. Jesus stood the child in the midst "so that its innocence, which it has by nature, might be imitated both diligently and in moral perfection (*virtute*)." The point of comparison is not the age of the child but true humility, like Christ not coming to be served but to serve. Humbling oneself includes, as Origen thought, not fancying beautiful women, neither making any remark about their beauty nor even thinking about it.

Abbot Godfrey of Admonte has a sermon on the Feast of St Michael on this text, which he makes a sermon on humility:[5]

> The one who is a true child, is the one whom Jesus sweetly and rightly calls, seeking after him with a clear mind and following him in purity and innocence. For this is true humility, which restrains a carnal and proud mind, that Jesus calls us to love and service towards God whilst previously the stubborn heart was obsessed with wicked things. The bottomless pit of the human condition is constantly roaming around, tossed about in a thousand things, and always tends to overlook or neglect the grace of humility. For this reason Jesus placed a child in their midst, clearly making the spirit of humility stable and immovable in their hearts, so that they should not be stirred by pride. Unless you become as one of these little children you shall not enter the kingdom of heaven. No one will receive such excellent and singular humility who has not deserved in this life to taste of the divine grace (*suavitatis*). Whence it is clear that the blessed, or rather the truly happy soul, when joined with its spouse, which is to say Christ, valuing the humble position in the whole of this mortal life, casting down the injurious and troublesome state of mind and desiring the fullness of mutual love. In this way, therefore, the faithful become *parvuli*, placing no obstacles before the gates of the kingdom of heaven.

From the late fourteenth or early fifteenth century we have a Wycliffite sermon for the feast of St Michael.[6] Jesus took a little child, "in quantity

---

4 Anselmus Laudunensis, Enarrationes in Evangelium Matthaei, ed. J.-P. MIGNE (Patrologia Latina 162), Paris 1889, cols. 1227-1499.

5 Godefridus Abbas Admontensis, Homiliae Festivales, ed. J.-P. MIGNE (Patrologia Latina 174), Turnholt 1966, col. 1040B.

6 English Wycliffite Sermons, ed. P. GRADON, 5 vols., Oxford 1988, here vol. 2, pp. 310-314.

and in soul, for he was little in body, and therewith he was meek." We do not know who this child was and it does not matter. The key thing is that:

> For ever as man is more meek, ever the better man he is. And as Christ is best man, so he is the meekest man; and as nought may be lower than centre, so none may be more meek than Christ [...] no man may have any virtue but if he have meekness, ground of all, and since no man may come to heaven but if he be clothed in virtues, it is open to true men that no man may come to heaven but if he have meekness to ground his tour up to heaven.

The preacher later generalises this to a warning to the rich, who have many servants and are accounted great, but later may be damned to hell. Equally the poor should not be despised for we honour the heir apparent of England or France, but in that case how much the more should we honour the heir apparent of the bliss of heaven. Matthew 19; 13-15 runs in the Vulgate:

> *Tunc oblate sunt ei parvuli, ut manus eis imponeret, et oraret. Discipuli autem increpabant eos. Jesus vero ait eis: Sinite parvulos, et nolite eos prohibere ad me venire: talium est enim regnum coelorum. Et cum imposuisset eis manus, abiit inde.*

Once again I begin with the *catena aurea.* Aquinas begins by citing pseudo Chrysostom:[7] "The Lord had been holding discourse of chastity; and some of his hearers now brought to him infants, who in respect of chastity are the purest; for they supposed that it was the pure in body only whom he had approved [...]" Origen:

> For they now understood from his previous mighty works, that by laying on of his hands and by prayer evils were obviated. They bring therefore children to him, judging that it were impossible that after the Lord had by his touch conveyed divine virtue into them, harm or any demon could come near them.

Chrysostom: "[...] the Lord teaching them holy thoughts, and to subdue the pride of this world, took the children into his arms [...]" Pseudo

---

[7] Catena aurea, (see note 1 above), p. 660.

Chrysostom: "For who were worthy to come to Christ if simple infancy is thrust away?" Jerome:

> [...] and he said distinctly, 'Of such (*talium*) is the kingdom of heaven', not 'Of these' (*istorum*), to shew that it was not years, but disposition that determined his judgement, and that the reward was promised to such as had like innocence and simplicity.

Pseudo Chrysostom:

> The present passage instructs all parents to bring their children to the priests, for it is not the priest who lays his hand on them, but Christ, in whose name hands are laid. For if he that offers his food in prayer to God eats it sanctified, for it is sanctified by the word of God [...] how much rather ought children to be offered to God, as sanctified?

Origen:

> Mystically, we call them children who are yet carnal in Christ, having need of milk. They who bring babes to the Saviour, are they who profess to have knowledge of the word, but are still simple, and have for their food children's lessons, being yet novices. They who seem more perfect, and are therefore the disciples of Jesus, before they have learnt the way of righteousness which is for children, rebuke those who by simple doctrine bring to Christ children and babes, that is, such as are less learned. But the Lord exhorting his disciples now become men to condescend to the needs of babes, to be babes to babes, that they may gain babes, says, 'For of such is the kingdom of heaven'. For he himself also, when he was in the form of God, was made a babe. These things we should attend to, lest in esteeming that more excellent wisdom and spiritual advancement, as though we were become great we should despise the little ones of the church, forbidding children to be brought to Jesus. But since children cannot follow all things that are commanded them, Jesus laid his hands on them, and leaving virtue in them by his touch, went away from them, seeing they were not able to follow him, like the other more perfect disciples.

Remigius: "Also laying his hands upon them, he blessed them, to signify that the lowly in spirit are worthy of his grace and blessing." Hilary:

> The infants are a type of the Gentiles, to whom salvation is rendered by faith and hearing. But the disciples, in their first zeal for the

> salvation of Israel, forbid them to approach, but the Lord declares that they are not to be forbidden. For the gift of the Holy Spirit was to be conferred upon the Gentiles by laying on of hands, as soon as the Law had ceased.

Bede, in his commentary on Matthew,[8] like almost all the rest of the tradition, echoes Jerome in distinguishing between *talium* and *istorum* to make the point that it is habits (*mores*) not age which is at stake. The Lord lays hands on those who seek the help of his grace so that they can follow his precepts. Rabanus Maurus, likewise citing Jerome, glosses it further by noting "that it is those who have innocence and simplicity who are children", citing 1 Corinthians 14.20 to make his point ("Do not be children in your thinking; but be infants in evil"). The commentary ascribed to Anselm of Laon mentioned previously[9] notes that *parvulos* means that the truly humble and temperate come to God. With the rise in heresy in the twelfth century, and people challenging infant baptism, the text is very naturally used to defend baptism and confirmation.[10] Preaching on All Saints Day, Martin of Leon runs through the various ranks of the saints and cites this verse for his ninth and highest step. The saints are those who may be compared to children who have died before plunging into sin.[11]

There is also a Wycliffite sermon on this text, though using the Markan version.[12] The preacher begins by noting that:

> *Iesu louyde litil children in kynde and figure: for sith Christ ordeyned litil children to growe to men and eft to seyntis, it is no drede Crist louyde this age, as alle othere agis of men. But for children of this age lyuen oft as innocentis, and ben not brokun with worldly falsed, therefore Christ louyde this figure.*

---

8 Beda Venerabilis, Expositio in Evangelium S. Matthaei, in: Opera exegetica genuina, ed. J.-P. MIGNE (Patrologia Latina 92), Paris 1862, col. 86C.

9 Anselmus Laudunensis, Enarrationes, ed. MIGNE (note 3 above), col. 1413B.

10 For example, Cardinal Robert Pulli in 1153, cf. Robertus Pullus, Sententiae, ed. J.-P. MIGNE (Patrologia Latina 186), col. 847A.

11 S. Martinus Legionensis, Sermones de sanctis, ed. J.-P. MIGNE (Patrologia Latina 209), col. 50B.

12 English Wycliffite Sermons, ed. A. HUDSON, 5 vols., Oxford, 1990, here vol. 3, pp. 39f.

Referring to 1 Peter 2.2 the preacher notes that people are nourished on belief as children on milk. Christians must love belief, because this is how they indwell Christ. The corollary is that those who persecute those who try to spread belief, are 'worse than Herod'.

In a recent commentary on Matthew Ulrich LUZ notes that since the text does not explicitly say what is characteristic of children it is not surprising that every age to a great degree has read into the text its own understanding of what a child is.

> In the process a fundamental change in the meaning of the text seems to have prevailed throughout the history of the text's interpretation. Interpreters ask not what children *are* but what they *should* be. More often that not they read the text as if it said: 'Become like good, well behaved children […]' 'Like children' has been regarded as empty space that the exegete has been only too willing to fill in in terms of their own relationship to children.[13]

In terms of these texts this seems to be not quite true. From the patristic age to the late Middle Ages preachers and commentators read them consistently as treatises on humility, recognising the child's lack of legal status, and their status vis a vis adults of all kinds. Only in the fifteenth century, so far as I can ascertain, is the idea of meekness glossed to warn hearers about not despising the humble. This is partly because the audience is often monastic, and diatribes on humility can be read as grumbles about the strains and tensions which always arise in community life. The idea of the *parvulus* is treated remarkably abstractly. Even more surprising is the absence of Augustine in the *Glossa ordinaria* and in the other scholastic commentary. In the *Confessions* Augustine demonstrates vividly the marks of original sin in very small children, and believed that unbaptised infants would, on that account, receive *mitissima damnatio*. On

---

[13] Matthew 8-20, ed. U. LUZ, Fortress/Minneapolis 2001, p. 428. I have only been able to find one example where the idea of the child, in this case *filius*, was used to argue for human equality, and that only in relation to baptism. Agobard of Lyons Ep iv. While God has ordered that men should serve each other with their bodies he does not allow the inner man to be subject to any one but himself. The inner man is free. For this reason he protests against the prohibition of the baptism of slaves without the consent of their masters: *Propter quod omnes sancti praedicatores, socii apostolorum…omnes baptizaverunt, omnes in uno corpore redigerunt, omnesque fratres et filios Dei esse docuerunt, ita tamen ut unusquisque in quo vocatus est, in hoc permaneret, non studio sed necessitate.*

his own observation he discounted any romantic views of the innocence of children. Perhaps other commentators did not have his first hand experience, for Jerome certainly had as dismal a view of the proclivities of human nature. This silence seems to indicate a wish to be deceived. Children, in the texts we have looked at, are a vestige of the golden age, before Eve took the apple. A deep inconsistency was thereby introduced into Christian anthropology, preparing the way for the sentimentality of the romantic fiction of the child. Alternatively, although it is hard to say this of Jerome, perhaps we might say that human experience prevailed over the doctrinaire gloominess of Christian orthodoxy, something we see in comparing fourteenth century sermons with Chaucer and Boccacio. As Blake put it, what he saw in the garden of love was:

> Priests in black gowns,
> walking their rounds,
> and binding with briers
> our joys and desires.

Perhaps in their refusal to vilify the child and tar it with the Augustinian brush the commentators obstinately clung on to some gleams of innocence which they observed in real life. But then again, perhaps not…

Im Spannungsfeld zwischen Spiel und Ernsthaftigkeit

Einige Bemerkungen zum Kinderbischofsfest in England

Tanja Skambraks

Begreift man die mittelalterliche vita religiosa als eine Form des Zusammenlebens verschiedener Generationen, so liegt es nahe das hiermit verbundene Rollenverständnis verschiedener Altersstufen sowie die Momente des Konfliktes und der Spannung ins Auge zu fassen. Diese sind gleichsam unvermeidlich und ergeben sich zum Beispiel aus der Konstellation zwischen Novizenmeister und Novize, Lehrer und Schüler, Chormeister und Chorknabe etc. Das Kinderbischofsfest soll im Folgenden als eine Form der Kommunikation zwischen den Generationen in religiösen Gemeinschaften und darüber hinausgehend in der mittelalterlichen Kirche und Gesellschaft interpretiert werden. Hier erfolgte eine vorübergehende Statusumkehr, die es erlaubte in Ritualen des temporären Rollentausches latente Spannungen und Konflikte zwischen Jung und Alt auszutragen oder zumindest spielerisch auszugleichen und somit die bestehende Ordnung zu stärken.

Zugleich kann in einer Feier, welche durch die Bezugnahme auf das Martyrium der Unschuldigen Kinder und die Tugendhaftigkeit des Jesuskindes ausschließlich auf der Anerkennung kindlicher Tugenden basiert, eine Bestätigung des vorbildhaften Status des Kindes gesehen werden. Es kommt also diesem Fest, welches im vorliegenden Aufsatz untersucht werden soll, eine wesentliche Bedeutung im Hinblick auf das Verhältnis der Generationen in der mittelalterlichen vita religiosa – und darüber hinaus – zu, welche das Thema zugleich anschlussfähig für den vorliegenden Sammelband macht.

Das früheste Zeugnis dieses Festes findet sich an prominenter Stelle in den *Casus Sancti Galli* Ekkehards IV. Dort wird berichtet, wie König Konrad nach Weihnachten 911 auf Empfehlung des Bischofs Salomo III. ins Kloster St. Gallen reiste, um dort Zeuge dieses Klerikerfestes zu werden. Ekkehard beschreibt den Eindruck des Königs folgendermaßen: *Longum est dicere, quibus jocunditatibus dies exegerit, maxime in processione infantum.* Daraufhin ließ der König auf dem Boden der Kirche Äpfel zu den Füßen der Knaben hinschütten und *cum nec unum parvissimorum moveri nec ad ea adtendere vidisset, miratus est disciplinam.*[1]

Das Kinderbischofsfest erfuhr seine Einschätzung in der bisherigen Forschung bis auf wenige Ausnahmen durch die Einordnung in den Kontext des mittelalterlichen Theaters sowie der Narrenfeste, welche die Elemente des Lächerlichen, Burlesken und Spielerischen betont. Diese erste These wurde vor allem von für die Rezeption des Festes maßgeblichen Autoren wie CHAMBERS, WARTON oder YOUNG vertreten.[2] Obgleich er dem Kinderbischof eine "mature responsibility" zuerkennt, schlussfolgert YOUNG in seiner Darstellung:

> The episcopellus, to be sure, does in a sense, pretend to be the real bishop, and in some of his doings he may be said to imitate that dignified personage. It should be remembered, however, that the chief action in which he is engaged is not an imitation of the liturgy, or a dramatic representation of it, but the usual, authorized worship of the day. He is therefore, not an impersonation of the true presiding bishop, but merely a ludicrous substitute.[3]

Diese Forschungsmeinungen lassen sich wiederum auf frühere Darstellungen wie beispielsweise die DU TILLIOTS[4], aber auch auf

---

1 Vgl. Ekkehardus IV., Casus Sancti Galli, übersetzt von H. F. HAEFELE (Ausgewählte Quellen zur deutschen Geschichte des Mittelalters 10), Darmstadt 1980, S. 40.

2 Vgl. z.B. E. K. CHAMBERS, The Boy Bishop, in: The Medieval Stage, Oxford [6]1967, 2 Bde., hier Bd. 1, S. 336-371, hier S. 368; K. YOUNG, The Drama of the Medieval Church, Oxford 1962, 2 Bde., hier Bd. 1, S. 104-111. T. WARTON, History of the English Poetry from the Twelfth to the Close of the Sixteenth Century, hg. von W. C. HAZLITT, London 1871 (ND Hildesheim 1968), 4 Bde., hier Bd. 3, S. 293.

3 Vgl. YOUNG, The Drama (wie Anm. 2), S. 110.

4 M. B. DU TILLIOT, Mémoires pour servir à l'histoire de la Fête des Foux, Lausanne/Genève 1751, S. 21: "La chose etoit assez ridicule: ce bel évêque se placoit dans le Siège Episcopal durant l'office de ce jour-là, & avoit autour de lui ses officiers. Les chanoniers leur quittoient leurs places, & faisoient dans le Choeur toutes les fonctions qui sont destinées à ces enfants. On sonnoit les cloches en quarillion, & d'abord que le dernier coup des Vêpres & de la Messe etoit sonné, les enfants de Choeur alloient quérir en Procession l'évêque en la Maison de la Maîtrise: ils l'amenoient dans l'église avec le même cérémoniel. Certainement c'étoit une espèce de Jonglerie qui n'aprevoit qu' à rire[…]."

zeitgenössische Bewertungen einiger prominenter regulativer und normativer Quellen wie der Proklamation Heinrichs VIII. aus dem Jahre 1451, der Beschlüsse der Konzilien von Salzburg 1274 und Baseler Konzils aus dem Jahre 1435 sowie dem Brief der Pariser Theologischen Fakultät aus dem Jahre 1244 zurückführen, welche das Fest als eine Variante des Narrenfestes darstellen und seinen lächerlichen, ja exzessiven Charakter betonen.[5] Im Brief der Pariser Theologen wird der Hergang des Festes drastisch wie folgt geschildert:

> *Videbat populus sacerdotes & clericos divini officii tempore larvatos, montrosos vultibus aut in vestibus mulierum aut Lenonum vel histrionum choreas ducere, in choro cantilenas inhonestas cantare, offas pingues supra cornu altaris juxta celebrantem missam comedere, ludum taxillorum exarare, Thurificare de fumo foetido ex Corio veterum sotulaium, et per totam Ecclesiam currere.*[6]

Die zweite Hauptthese im Sinne einer Erholungs- und Ventilfunktion des Kinderbischofsfestes wurde durch LEACH vorgetragen.[7] Beide Thesen argumentieren zuungunsten einer Interpretation als ernst zu nehmendes liturgisches Fest mit religiöser Fundierung. Diesen vergleichsweise neueren Ansatz vertreten u. a. Richard DEMOLEN[8] und

---

5 Die Proklamation Heinrichs VIII. ist abgedruckt unter dem Titel: A decree for observing the feasts of S. Luke, S. Mark, and S. Mary Magdalene, etc., in: Concilia Magnae Britanniae et Hiberniae ab anno MCCCL ad annum MDXLV, ed. D. WILKINS, 4 Bde., hier Bd. 3, S. 860. Einen Auszug des 17. Kanon des Konzils von Salzburg zitiert F. A. DÜRR, Commentatio de Historia de Episcopo puerorum vulgo vom Schulbischoff, Mainz 1755, S. 33. Die 21. Sektion des Basler Konzils vom 9. Juni 1435 trägt den Titel De spectaculis in Ecclesia non faciendis, in: J. D. MANSI (Hg.), Sacrorum conciliorum nova et amplissima collectio. Unveränd. Nachdruck, Paris/Leipzig 1901 – 1927, Bd. 30, Sp. 108. Zum Brief der Pariser Theologischen Fakultät vgl. Copia cuiusdam Epistolae a venerabili Facultate theologiae studii Parisiensis, praelatis et capitulis ecclesiarum regni Franciae transmisse, ad detestandum, condemnandum, et onmio abolendum quemdam superstitiosum et scandalosum ritum, quem quidam festum Fatuorum vocant, qui a ritu paganorum et infidelium idololatrum initium et originem sumpsit, ed. J.-P. MIGNE (Patrologia Latina 212), Paris 1969, Sp. 1169-1176.

6 Vgl. MIGNE, (wie Anm. 5), Sp. 1171.

7 Vgl. A. F. LEACH, The Schoolboy's Feast, in: The Fortnightly Review, N.S. 59 (1896), S. 128-141, hier S. 129, 140. Auch F. FALK, Die Schul- und Kinderfeste im Mittelalter, in: Frankfurter zeitgemäße Broschüren 3/8 (1880), S. 229-248.

8 Vgl. R. DEMOLEN, Pueri Christi Imitatio. The Festival of the Boy-bishop in Tudor England, in: Moreana 12 (1975), S. 17-29.

Hubertus LUTTERBACH.[9] Der vorliegende Aufsatz schließt in seiner Interpretation an die Thesen DEMOLENs und LUTTERBACHs an und soll versuchen, das Kinderbischofsfest in England zunächst auf einer ersten deskriptiven Ebene hinsichtlich seines Zeitpunktes, seiner Länge und Verbreitung, dem damit verbundenen Wahlzeremoniell sowie den liturgischen Funktionen und der materiellen Versorgung darzustellen. Anschließend werden im zweiten Teil drei Hauptursprünge beleuchtet, welche zugleich die Hauptstränge der Forschungsinterpretation darstellen: das römische Saturnalienfest, der Nikolauskult und die Verehrung der Unschuldigen Kinder.

Bezug nehmend auf die oben genannten Aspekte sollen drei Forschungsfragen geklärt werden. Zunächst soll gefragt werden, wodurch die Autorität des Kinderbischofs konstituiert wurde. Davon ausgehend soll zu der Frage Stellung bezogen werden, ob es sich beim Kinderbischofsfest um eine ‘echte Statusumkehr’ oder lediglich um einen spielerischen Akt mit Ventilfunktion handelte. Und letztlich soll versucht werden, die theologischen Begründungsmuster für eine eventuelle temporäre Statusumkehr zu identifizieren.

Am Schluss der Analyse steht die Entwicklung einiger Thesen, welche die Interpretation der Wahl mittelalterlicher Kinderbischöfe als ein theologisch fundiertes, ernsthaftes liturgisches Ereignis vorschlagen, welches mit einer Aufwertung der Rolle des Kindes ebenso wie mit einer temporären Autoritätszuschreibung einhergeht und gewissermaßen einen geistigen Tabubruch darstellt.

I. Deskription

Das Kinderbischofsfest ist in den Kontext der Klerikerfeste am Jahresende einzuordnen und fand europaweite Verbreitung in den

---

[9] Vgl. den Beitrag des Autors in diesem Band, H. LUTTERBACH, Die Mönche – besondere Gotteskinder?, sowie DERS., Gotteskindschaft. Kultur- und Sozialgeschichte eines christlichen Ideals, Freiburg/Basel/Wien 2003. Eine frühe Ausnahme im Hinblick auf die Interpretation des Festes in diesem Sinn stellt die sehr ergiebige Studie C. H. EVELYN WHITES dar, welche bereits 1905 im Journal of the British Archaeological Association, NS Vol XI, S. 30-48 und S. 231-256 erscheinen ist.

Kathedralen, Pfarrkirchen und Klöstern Englands, dem Gebiet des heutigen Deutschlands, in Frankreich sowie Italien und Spanien.[10] Es gehört zeitlich in den Kontext der dem Weihnachtsfest folgenden drei *tipudia*, welche durch Johannes Belethus 1189 erstmals systematisch beschrieben wurden.[11] Demnach gehen dem Kinderbischofsfest am 28. Dezember das Fest des heiligen Stephan, welches durch die Diakone am 26. Dezember gefeiert wurde, und das durch die Priester gefeierte Fest des Hl. Johannes des Evangelisten am darauf folgenden Tag voraus. Das eigentliche Narrenfest, mit welchem die genannten Feste häufig assoziiert wurden, fand zwischen dem Neujahrstag und dem Epiphaniasfest statt und wurde von den Subdiakonen begangen.

In Bezug auf den Zeitpunkt und die Dauer der Amtszeit geben die Quellen unterschiedliche Auskunft. In der Kathedrale von Paris, im Eton College oder am King's College in Cambridge fand das Fest zu Ehren des Heiligen Nikolaus an dessen Festtag, dem 6. Dezember, statt[12]; an vielen anderen Orten wurde das Fest am Tage der Unschuldigen Kinder, dem genannten 28. Dezember gefeiert.[13] Vielerorts kann von einer Fusion beider Festtage ausgegangen werden, so dass die Amtszeit des Kinderbischofs sich auch über den gesamten

10 Zur Verbreitung des Festes in Deutschland siehe: G. BLAICHER, Der Kinderbischof in Eichstätt und anderswo, in: Sammelblatt des Historischen Vereins Eichstätt 90 (1997), S. 41-56, sowie F. A. DÜRR, Commentatio Historica de Episcopo Puerorum, vulgo vom Schul-Bischoff, Mainz 1755; zu Frankreich vgl. A. CHEREST, Nouvelles recherches sur la fête des innocents et des fous, qui se faisent autrefois dans plusieurs églises, et notamment dans l'église de Sens, in: Bulletin de la Société des Sciences Historiques et Naturelles de l'Yonne 2 (1853), S. 7-82; A. GASTÉ, Les Drames liturgiques de la Chathédrale de Rouen - contribution à l'histoire des origines du théâtre en France, Evreux 1893; zum spanischen Raum siehe J. P. WICKERSHAM-CRAWFORD, A Note on the Boy Bishop in Spain, in: Romanic Review 12 (1921), S. 146-164.

11 Vgl. Johannes Belethus, De quadam libertate Decembris (1182-90) in: Ders., Rationale Divinorum Officium, Kap. 72, ed. J.-P. MIGNE (Patrologia Latina 202), Paris 1975, Sp. 120-123.

12 Vgl. CHAMBERS, The Medieval Stage (wie Anm. 2), Bd. 1, S. 363, 365.

13 Für die Kathedrale von Canterbury wurde der Zeitraum des Festes 1279 durch Erzbischof John Pecham beispielsweise genau festgelegt: *Puerilia autem solemnia, quae in festo solent fieri Innocentum post vesperas S. Iohannis, tantum inchoari permittimus, et in castrino in ipsa die Innocentum totaliter terminentur.* Vgl. Concilia, ed. WILKINS (wie Anm. 5), Bd. 2, S. 38.

Zeitraum zwischen diesen beiden Festtagen erstrecken konnte, wie im Falle der Kirche von Sarum.[14]

Allein die den Quellen zu entnehmende Vielfalt an Bezeichnungen für den Kinderbischof wie *episcopellus, episcopus puerorum, episcopus puerilis/parvulus, scholarium episcopus, episcopus innocentium, barne-bishop, Apfel-Bischoff, episcopus Sancti Nicolai/Nicholatensis, episcopus iuvenum, episcopus choristarum* verweist auf die verschiedenartigen Zuordungsmöglichkeiten und Assoziationen des Festes hinsichtlich seines Ursprungs und des Alters des jeweiligen Kandidaten. Letzteres anhand der Quellen zu rekonstruieren dürfte sich als sehr schwierig erweisen, da in keinem mir bisher bekannten Fall das Alter eines Kinderbischofs genannt wird, so dass lediglich ungenaue Spekulationen möglich sind. Sulamith SHAHAR hat das Alter der Chorknaben, aus deren Reihen der Kinderbischof gewählt wurde, mit sechs bis zehn Jahren, das der Domschüler mit acht bis sechzehn Jahren angegeben,[15] eine Einschätzung die angesichts der variierenden Angaben mittelalterlicher Lebensaltermodelle in Bezug auf die *pueritia* oder *adolescentia* ungenau bleiben muss. Die Wahl des Kinderbischofs erfolgte durch die Chorknaben selbst, was ein allerdings nicht umgesetzter Regulierungsversuch Nicholas Uptons, des Präzentors der Kathedrale von Salisbury, aus dem Jahre 1448 zu ändern versuchte, laut dem eine Nominierung dreier Knaben durch das Kapitel der Wahl durch die Chorknaben vorausgehen sollte.[16] Zu den mit einer solchen Wahl verbundenen Qualifikationen eines Kandidaten finden sich Angaben in einem Kapitelregister aus York von 1367, das denjenigen Knaben als am geeignetsten beschreibt, welcher am längsten der Kirche gedient und sich dabei als nützlich erwiesen habe, darüber hinaus sollte dieser auch äußerlich von schöner Gestalt sein, sonst sei die Wahl ungültig.[17] Einige Jahre später, nämlich 1390, wurde diese Bestimmung ergänzt durch den Hinweis [...] *nisi habuerit claram vocem puerilem.*[18]

---

14 Hier werden auch die Einflüsse dieser beiden Festtraditionen deutlich, auf die im zweiten Teil des Aufsatzes noch einzugehen ist.

15 Vgl. SHAHAR, The Boy Bishop's Feast. A Case-Study in Church Attitudes towards Children in the High and Late Middle Ages, in: Studies in Church History 31 (1994), S. 243-260, hier S. 248f.

16 Vgl. CHAMBERS, The Medieval Stage (wie Anm. 2), Bd. 1, S. 353.

17 Zit. in T. WARTON, The History of the English Poetry (wie Anm. 2), hier Bd. 4, S. 224, Anm. 1: *Ioannes de Quixly confirmatur Episcopus Puerorum, et Capitulum ordinavit, quod electio Episcopi Puerorum in Ecclesia Eboracensi de cetero fieret de eo, qui diutius et magis*

I. 1. Die liturgischen Funktionen des Kinderbischofs

Die liturgischen Funktionen, welche dem Kinderbischof an den Festtagen zwischen dem 6. und 28. Dezember zukamen, lassen sich anhand liturgischer Regelwerke, wie z.B. dem Sarum Office aus dem 11. Jahrhundert rekonstruieren. Die darin enthaltene minutiöse Beschreibung des Ablaufes der zu feiernden Messen verdeutlicht die bedeutungsvolle Rolle, welche dem gewähltem Chorknaben eine eindeutige Leitungsfunktion zuweist und mit einer ungewöhnlichen Autoritätszuschreibung verbunden ist, wie im Folgenden dargestellt werden soll. Demnach begann in der Kathedrale von Sarum das Fest des Kinderbischofs am Vorabend des 28. Dezember mit einer feierlichen Prozession der singenden Chorknaben zum Altar der Unschuldigen Kinder, respektive der heiligen Dreifaltigkeit oder Allerheiligen. Die in seidene Gewänder gekleideten, mit angezündeten Kerzen und Fackeln versehenen Knaben wurden angeführt durch den Kinderbischof, welcher *ponificalibus induto*, also im vollen bischöflichen Ornat, erschien.[19] Daraufhin intonierte allein der Kinderbischof den Gesang *Centum quadraginta,* auf welchen ihm drei Knaben antworteten. Nach der Weiterführung der Gesänge durch den Chor, wobei man das *Gloria Patri* ausdrücklich nicht singen durfte, erfolgte die Beweihräucherung des Altars durch den Kinderbischof: *Ad hanc processionem non dicatur Gloria Patri sed dum prosa cantitur tunc Episcopus Puerorum thurificet altare: deinde ymaginem Sancte Trinitatis.*[20] Danach sprach er folgendes Gebet: *Deus, cuius hodierna die preconium innocentes martires non loquendo sed moriendo confessi sunt: omnia in nobis vitiorum mala mortifica, ut fidem tuam, quam lingua nostra loquitur, eciam moribus vita fateatur. Qui cum Deo Patre.* Der Präzentor der Knaben hatte daraufhin das Responsorium der Hl. Maria anzustimmen. Die Prozession der Chorknaben begab sich währenddessen durch das

---

in dicta ecclesia laboraverit, et magis idoneus repertus fuerit, dum tamen competenter sit corpore formosus, et quod aliter facta electio non valebit.

18 Vgl. ebd., S. 237.

19 *In die sancti Johannis: Ad vesperas, post memoriam de S. Stephano eat procession Puerorum ad altare Innocentium, vel Sancte Trinitatis et Omnium Sancorum quod dicitur Salve, in capis sericis, cum cereis illuminates et ardentibus in minibus, cantando, Episcopo Puerorum pontificalibus induto (executore officij, sive Episcopo presente) incipiente hoc resonsorium.* Vgl. hierzu das Sarum Office abgedruckt bei CHAMBERS, The Medieval Stage (wie Anm. 2), Appendix M, Bd. 2, S. 282-287.

20 Vgl. ebd., S. 283.

Westtor der Kirche zum Chor, wo alle Chorknaben die erhöhten Plätze des Dekans und der Chorherren einnahmen, *et ab hac hora usque post processionem diei proximi succentis nullus clericorum solet gradum superiorem ascendere, quiuscumque condicionis fuerit.* Diese eindeutige und zunächst räumlich vollzogene temporäre Statusumkehr wurde komplettiert durch die niederen Aufgaben des Tragens des Weihrauchfasses, der Bücher und der Kerzen, welche den ansonsten höhergestellten Klerikern an dieser Stelle zugewiesen wurden: *Ad istam processionem pro disposicione puerorum scribuntur canonici, ad ministrandum eisdem, maiores ad thuribulandum, et ad librum referendum, minores ad candelabra deferenda.*[21] Nach dem Sprechen eines weiteren Gebetes zu Ehren Christi und der Jungfrau Maria bestieg der Kinderbischof den Bischofsthron und segnete alle Anwesenden.[22] Daraufhin nahm der *crucificerarius* den Bischofstab, wandte sich an die Anwesenden, sang ein weiteres Antiphon und sprach zu ihnen: *Cum mansuetudine et caritate, humilitate vos ad benediccionem.* Dieser Aufforderung zur Verneigung folgte die erneute Übergabe des Stabes an den Kinderbischof, welcher sich daraufhin den Klerikern und den anderen Versammelten zuwandte, wobei er weitere Segnungen aussprach. Gleiches ereignete sich am Festtag der Unschuldigen Kinder, wobei den gesamten Tag über alle Messen durch den Kinderbischof geleitet wurden. Dass das Kinderbischofsfest nicht nur in England in dieser Weise mit der außergewöhnlichen Zuschreibung liturgischer Funktionen und damit Autorität an seinen Protagonisten einherging, beweisen auch nichtenglische Quellen, wie beispielsweise das Officium Infantum von Rouen aus dem 11. Jahrhundert, das Offizium von Bayeux oder ein Offizium aus Padua aus dem 13. Jahrhundert.[23] Die hier beschriebene Statusumkehr und zeitgleiche Aufwertung basierte somit zum einen auf der äußeren Repräsentation des Kinderbischofs in seiner Kleidung und Ausstattung, d.h. dem Mantel, der Mitra, dem Bischofsstab und dem Ring, zum anderen in der räumlichen Aufwertung durch seine Platzierung auf dem höchsten Stuhl innerhalb des Chores. Vor allem

---

21 Vgl. ebd., S. 284.

22 Ebd.: *Tunc episcopus intret stallum suum, et in sede sua, benedicat populum.*

23 Vgl. hierzu: das *Officium infantum* aus Rouen, ed. GASTÉ, Les drames liturgiques de la Cathedrale de Rouen (wie Anm. 10), S. 35f.; auf dieses Dokument sowie auf eine deutsche Handschrift aus dem 16. Jh. weist auch H. LUTTERBACH im vorliegenden Band hin. Das italienische Messbuch, welches zugleich als ein wichtiger Beweis für die Existenz des Kinderbischofsfestes in Italien gewertet werden kann, findet sich angedruckt bei YOUNG, The Drama (wie Anm. 2), Bd. 1, S. 106-109.

jedoch – und dies erscheint bemerkenswert – wurde die Statusveränderung des Kindes herbeigeführt durch den Akt der Segnung, der Beweihräucherung des Altares sowie durch das Anstimmen der Hymnen und Responsorien. Symbolische Funktionen und Darstellungsweisen sowie die materielle Ausstattung bilden hier eine Einheit, welche an der Ernsthaftigkeit eines solchen Festes kaum Zweifel erlaubt.

Im folgenden Abschnitt soll dieses Ergebnis durch weitere Quellenfunde noch ergänzt werden, welche über die rein liturgischen Funktionen hinaus und zeitlich gewissermaßen an diese anschließend, weltliche Funktionen und materielle Aspekte des kindlichen Amtsträgers beschreiben.

I. 2. Weltliche Funktionen und materielle Ausstattung

Aussagen über die materielle Ausstattung englischer Kinderbischöfe lassen sich diversen Inventaren und Abrechungen einzelner Kathedralschulen und Klöster entnehmen. Aus einem Inventar der Abtei von Westminster von 1388 geht hervor, dass der Amtsträger, hier *Seynt Nicholas bysshoppe* genannt, mit einer reich verzierten Mitra ausgestattet wurde, welche mit dem Spruch *Ora pro nobis Sancte Nicholai* bestickt war.[24] Weitere Belege finden sich in einer Abrechung des *custos* Nicholaus de Newerk von York des Jahres 1396.[25] Der York *compotus* bietet neben der Auflistung der durch den Kinderbischof gesammelten Gelder und Gaben auch Informationen hinsichtlich der von ihm und seiner Entourage vollzogenen Visitationsreise, welche sich bis in den Februar

---

24 Vgl. J. WICKHAM LEGG, On an inventory of the Vestry in Westminster Abbey. Taken in 1388, in: Archaeologia. Or Miscellaneous Tracts Relating to Antiquity 52 (1890), S. 195-286, hier S. 220f. Daraus: *The vj myter of Seynt Nicholas bysshoppe, the grounde therof of whyte sylk, garnysshed complete with ffloures, gret and small, of sylver and gylte, and stones complete in them, with the scripture, Ora pro nobis Sancte Nicholai, embroidered thereon in perll, the sides sylver and gylt, and the toppys of sylver and gylt, and enamelyd with ij labelles of the same, and garnysshed in lyk maner, and with viij long bells of sylver and gylt, weying together xxiij unces.*

25 Dieser *compotus* wurde erstmals durch E. F. RIMBAULT als Appendix abgedruckt im Kontext der Edition zweier Kinderbischofspredigten in: The Camden Miscellany 7 (1875), S. 31; ein zweiter Abdruck fand in CHAMBERS, The Medieval Stage (wie Anm. 2), Bd. 2, S. 287ff. statt.

1397 erstreckte. Der Kinderbischof nahm in dieser Zeit Geldgeschenke im Wert von insgesamt 8 Pfund, 15 Shillings und 5 Pence ein, wovon er Ausgaben für Kleidung, Verpflegung während der Reise, die Ausstattung der Pferde und die Entlohnung seiner Dienerschaft[26] in Höhe von 6 Pfund, 14 Shillings und 10 Pence tätigte. Der Rest des Geldes verblieb in seinen Händen, *ad usum Episcopi*.[27] Interessant erscheint hierbei die örtliche Abfolge bzw. der Aktionsradius des Kinderbischofs, welcher sich weit über die *clausura* (dort erhielt er Gaben des Präzentors, des Kanzlers, des Schatzmeisters, des Erzdiakons und einiger *magistri*) und die *villa* hinaus auf die gesamte Diözese und keineswegs nur auf geistliche Haushalte erstreckte. Während seiner Reise durch die so genannte *patria* wurden ihm Gaben und Geschenke verschiedener Äbte und Prioren[28] zuteil, aber auch einige weltliche Herrscher überließen ihm kostbare Gaben, wie die Gräfin von Northumbrien, die ihm 20 Shillings und einen goldenen Ring schenkte. Unter die Ausgaben fällt auch das vom Kinderbischof ausgerichtete *convivium*, welches 15 Shillings und 6 Pence kostete. Die Buchführung über diese Visitationsreise kann als ein weiteres Indiz für die relative Aufwendigkeit der Festorganisation gewertet werden, dessen Verlauf und Finanzierung in den Händen seiner Leitfigur, dem Kinderbischof, lag und welche durch großzügige Gaben seitens geistlicher und weltlicher Autoritäten unterstützt wurde. Auch königliche Förderung erfuhr der Kinderbischof beispielsweise im Jahre 1299 durch König Edward I., welcher kostbare Geschenke verteilte, als dieser in Heton, nahe Newcastle-upon-Tyne, predigte. 1310 erhielt der Kinderbischof von St. Mary's Church in Nottingham 10 Shillings durch Edward II. am Tag der Unschuldigen Kinder.[29] Folglich geschah die

---

26 Unter diesen waren der *tenor* Nicholas de Newsome, welcher gleichzeitig das Pferd des Kinderbischofs führte, der Seneschall Robert Dawtry, ein *cantor* namens Johannes Baynton, ein Marschall und ein Diener für die Pferde. Weitere Gaben erhielten die Ministranden des Kinderbischofs, der Subkanzler, die Kammerkleriker und der Sakristar. Zu Verlauf und Bedeutung der Visitationsreise vgl. Y. DAHHAOUI, Voyages d'un prélat festif. Un 'évêque des Innocents' dans son évêché, in: Revue historique 639 (2006), S. 677-694.

27 Vgl. CHAMBERS, The Medieval Stage (wie Anm. 2), Bd. 2, S. 289.

28 Die visitierten Klöster waren: Kirkham, Bridlington, Watton, Bainton, Melsa, Feriby, Drax, Selby, Pontefracte, Monkbretton, Newburgh sowie Bellalandi. Hier erhielt der Kinderbischof Geldgeschenke zwischen 20 Pence und 6 Shillings.

29 Vgl. M. J. FLETCHER, The Boy-Bishop at Salisbury and elsewhere. A Lecture, Salisbury 1921, S. 19.

Autoritätszuschreibung an den Kinderbischof nicht nur auf liturgischer Ebene, sondern erstreckte sich auch über den zeitlich begrenzten Festakt innerhalb der Kirche hinaus auf die Ebene praktischer Pflichten und weltlicher Verantwortung eines realen Bischofs. Diese Vermutung wird gestützt durch die Tatsache, dass der Kinderbischof in einigen Diözesen, wie Mainz, Cambrai oder Beauvais, während seiner Amtszeit sogar über die Neuvergabe frei werdender Pfründen entscheiden konnte bzw. diese temporär an ihn fielen.[30] Des weiteren ließe sich das Münzprägerecht des Kinderbischofs anführen, auf welches z.B. Münzfunde in Bury St. Edmunds schließen lassen; ebenso existiert eine Reihe französischer Münzen aus dem Spätmittelalter, welche eindeutig Darstellungen von Kinderbischöfen bzw. des Hl. Nikolaus zeigen.[31]

II. Subtexte und Kontexte: zu den Ursprüngen des Kinderbischofsfestes

Nachdem im vorangegangenen Abschnitt eine Darstellung der aus einigen Quellen zur rekonstruierenden Aspekte hinsichtlich der Funktionen des Kinderbischofs versucht wurde, soll im zweiten Abschnitt die Kontextualisierung des Festes in Auseinandersetzung mit drei möglichen Ursprüngen erfolgen.

II. 1. Das römische Saturnalienfest

Das römische Saturnalienfest gilt als das populärste Fest im alten Rom, welches jedes Jahr beginnend am 17. Dezember über mehrere Tage hinweg[32] zu Ehren Saturns, des Gottes des Ackerbaus und im Gedenken

---

30 Vgl. dazu DÜRR, Commentatio (wie Anm. 10), S. 39.

31 Vgl. hierzu die Studie von M. J. RIGOLLOT, Monnaies inconnues des Evêques des Innocents, des Fous, et de quelque autres Associations singulières du même Temps. Avec une introduction par C. LEBER, 2 tômes, Paris 1837. Im zweiten Band sind zahlreiche Abbildungen der Münzen enthalten.

32 Die Dauer dieses Festes variierte zwischen sieben Tagen zur Zeit Ciceros, drei Tagen unter Augustus, während Caligula sie wieder auf fünf Tage ausdehnte. Vgl. hierzu M. FUHRMANN, Fastnacht als Utopie: Vom Saturnalienfest im alten Rom, in:

an das goldene Zeitalter, die *Saturnia regna*, gefeiert wurde. Im Verlauf dieses Festes, welches um den Tempel des Saturn am Fuße des Kapitols stattfand, wurden symbolisch die Bänder an den Füßen der Statue Saturns losgebunden, womit eine Zeit der Ausgelassenheit und Freude begann, während der man sich mit den so genannten *sigillaria* (kleinen Tonfiguren) beschenkte, ein öffentliches Opfer darbrachte und ein *convivium publicum* abhielt. Auch ein *saturnicalicus princeps* wurde gewählt. Das für die vorliegende Untersuchung wesentliche Merkmal des Saturnalienfestes jedoch ist das exzeptionelle Gleichheitsprinzip, welches sich dadurch ausdrückte, dass höhergestellte Römer in dieser Zeit die Toga als Standeszeichen gegen informellere Kleidung eintauschten, wohingegen die Sklaven zu dieser Zeit am Tisch des Herrn Platz nehmen durften und von diesen sogar bedient wurden. Eine sehr illustrative Beschreibung gibt der assyrisch-römische Rhetoriker und Satiriker Lucian von Samosata (120-180 n. Chr.) in seinem Stück *Saturnalia*[33], in welchem er Chronos in einem Dialog mit einem Priester selbst die Worte sagen lässt:

> Die ganze Herrlichkeit dauert nicht länger als sieben Tage; sind diese vorbei, so bin ich wieder ein Privatmann wie ein anderer und verliere mich unter dem großen Haufen. Aber auch in diesen sieben Tagen ist mir nicht erlaubt, irgend etwas Ernsthaftes und Wichtiges zu verrichten: mich betrinken, jauchzen, spielen, würfeln, Festkönige bestellen, die Sklaven gastieren, nackend singen und tanzen, auch wohl gar mir das Gesicht mit Ruß beschmieren und mich in kaltes Wasser werfen lassen, das alles kann und darf ich, soviel mir's beliebt: allein, was Reichtum, Gold und andere Dinge von dieser Wichtigkeit betrifft, diese gibt Jupiter, wem er wohl will.[34]

Die Beschreibung dieses ausgelassenen Ausnahmezustandes wird noch ergänzt durch den ausdrücklichen Hinweis auf die Gleichheit aller Beteiligten und die Anordnung, alle Geschäfte ruhen zu lassen, mithin auf die Außerkraftsetzung aller statusgenerierenden Tätigkeiten:

H. Bausinger / U. Jeggle / M. Scharfe / B. J. Warneken (Hgg.), Narrenfreiheit. Beiträge zur Fastnachtsforschung, Tübingen 1980, S. 29-42.

33 Vgl. Lukian, Saturnalische Verhandlungen, in: Ders., Werke in drei Bänden, ed. J. Werner / H. Greiner-Mai, übersetzt von Christoph Martin Wieland, Berlin/Weimar ²1981, hier Bd. 2, S. 5-28.

34 Vgl. ebd., S. 6.

> Niemand unterstehe sich, während des Festes weder öffentlich noch zu Hause etwas anderes zu treiben, als was auf Spiel, Wohlleben und Fröhlichkeit hinausläuft: denn Köche und Kuchenbäcker allein sollen an diesen Tagen arbeiten. Knechte und Freie, Arme und Reiche sollen auf gleichem Fuße sein. Zornig zu werden, böser Laune zu sein oder einem anderen zu drohen, ist jedermann ohne Unterschied verboten! Niemand soll, solange das Fest dauert, sein Geld oder seine Kleider zählen; alles Schreiben und alle gymnastischen Übungen sollen untersagt sein; auch ist es verboten, andere Reden auszuarbeiten oder zu halten als solche, wobei es bloß auf Kurzweil, Scherz und Belustigung abgesehen ist.[35]

In dieser Umkehr der Normen, welche zweifelsohne auch parodistische Züge trug, wird jedoch ein klarer Rollenwechsel zugunsten der Herstellung einer ‘verkehrten Welt’ vollzogen, welcher wiederum dazu beigetragen hat, sowohl das Kinderbischofsfest als auch das Narrenfest im Sinne dieser Festtradition zu interpretieren.[36] Dieses Ritual wurde im 4. Jahrhundert nach Christus allmählich im christlichen Sinne umgedeutet und in den Zyklus der Festtage um das Weihnachtsfest integriert. Es handelt sich hierbei um eine nicht mehr nachzuvollziehende Verschmelzung christlicher mit antiken Festtraditionen.

II. 2. Die Verehrung der Unschuldigen Kinder

Die zentrale Stelle der heiligen Schrift, welche für die Verehrung der Unschuldigen Kinder als Märtyrer die schmale schriftliche Basis bietet, ist Mt. 2,16: “Als Herodes nun sah, daß er von den Weisen betrogen war, wurde er sehr zornig und schickte aus und ließ alle Kinder in Bethlehem töten und in der ganzen Gegend, die zweijährig und darunter waren, nach der Zeit, die er von den Weisen genau erkundet hatte.” Der dort auf Geheiß des römischen Stadthalters Herodes beschriebene Mord an

---

35 Vgl. ebd., S. 13.

36 Vgl. u.a. F. SNELL, The customs of old England, London 1911, S. 39-51, hier S. 39f.; CHAMBERS, The Medieval Stage (wie Anm. 2), Bd. 1, S. 370; FLETCHER, The Boy Bishop at Salisbury (wie Anm. 29), S. 4f.; LEACH, The Schoolboy's Feast (wie Anm. 7), S. 141; N. MACKENZIE, Boy into Bishop, in: History Today 37 (1987), S. 10-16, hier S. 11.

allen Kindern unter zwei Jahren in Bethlehem begründete das Andenken an diese anstelle Christi gestorbenen Sonder-Märtyrer,[37] welches wiederum eine Säule des Kinderbischofsfestes darstellt. Daran anschließend finden sich Belege mittelalterlicher Theologen wie Johannes Belethus, welcher im 70. Kapitel seines *Rationale Divinorum Officiorum* den Ursprung des Festes am 28. Dezember wie folgt beschreibt: [...] *et pueri in ipso festo Innocentium, quia innocentes pro Christo occisi sunt,* [...] *in festo itaque Innocentium penitus subticentur cantita laetitoae, quoniam ii ad infernos descenderunt.*[38] Ein noch früheres Beispiel vom Ende des 11. Jahrhunderts ist dem Werk *De Officiis Ecclesiasticis* des Johannes Abrincensis zu entnehmen, welcher an derselben Stelle auch das Verbot des Singens des *Te Deum*, des *Gloria in excelsis* sowie des *Alleluia* als unmodern verurteilt: *Licet, ut in morte Domini, Te Deum et Gloria in excelsis et Alleluia in aliquod ecclesiis, ex morte antiquo, ommittantur; quia ut Christus occideretur tot parvuli occidi iubentur ; et illis occidis fit mors Christi secundum aestimationem Herodis; tamen quia placuit modernis, placet et nobis ut cantentur.*[39]

Auf den direkten Zusammenhang zwischen dem Kinderbischofsfest und der Verehrung der Unschuldigen Kinder weist auch Hubertus LUTTERBACH hin: "Wenn zum rituellen Gedenken an dieses Ereignis auch die Wahl eines Kinderabtes gehörte, dann liegt dies gewiß mit darin begründet, dass der liturgische Inhalt des Festes insgesamt als 'Besinnung auf die vier Begriffe *heilig*, *unschuldig*, *Märtyrer* und *Kinder* angesehen' werden kann."[40] Die Reinheit und Unschuld als direkt von den heiligen Märtyrer-Kindern abzuleitende typisch kindliche Eigenschaft legitimiert in diesem Zusammenhang die Autorität des Kinderbischofs.

---

[37] Zu den Unschuldigen Kindern vgl. J. HENNIG, Zur liturgischen Lehre von den unschuldigen Kindern, in: Archiv für Literaturwissenschaft 9/1 (1965), S. 72-85; H. HERTER, Das Unschuldige Kind, in: Jahrbuch für Antike und Christentum 4 (1961), S. 146-162.

[38] Vgl. Rationale Divinorum Officiorum Auctore Joanne Beletho Theologo Parisiensi, c. 70: De festis Nativitatem sequentibus, ed. J.-P. MIGNE (Patrologia Latina 202), Paris 1975, Sp. 77f.

[39] Vgl. Johannes Abrincensis, De Officiis Ecclesiasticis, ed. J.-P. MIGNE (Patrologia Latina 147), Paris 1966, S. 42.

[40] Vgl. H. LUTTERBACH, Gotteskindschaft (wie Anm. 9), S. 159.

II. 3. Der Nikolauskult

Zu der oben geschilderten theologischen Legitimationsgrundlage kommt eine zweite Säule, auf welche sich die Tradition des Kinderbischofsfestes zurückführen lässt. Dies spiegelt sich, wie schon erwähnt, im variierenden Zeitpunkt des Festes wider, welches in einigen Kathedralen, Klöstern und Kirchen bereits am Tage des Heiligen Nikolaus gefeiert wurde oder begann. Im Nikolauskult[41] verbinden sich die Viten zweier Heiliger, wobei die Basis der Legende die Vita des Bischofs Nikolaus von Myra bildet, dessen Todestag mit dem 6. Dezember 342 oder 347 angegeben wird. Mit der frühesten Legende (*praxis de stratelatis*) aus dem 6. Jahrhundert vermischte sich die Legende des Archimandriten Nikolaus von Sion, dem Bischof von Pinara in Lykien (†564); seither existiert der Grabeskult in Myra, welcher den Heiligen Nikolaus zum Hauptwundertäter neben der Gottesmutter in der Ostkirche aufsteigen ließ. Das Zentrum des Kultes dort war Konstantinopel, bis im Jahre 1087 die Translation der Gebeine des Heiligen nach Bari erfolgte, wo die neu gebaute Kultstätte von Urban II. 1089 eingeweiht wurde. Von dort aus verbreitete sich der Kult im Abendland durch die Gründung von mehr als 2000 Kultstätten bis in das Jahr 1500. In Rom wurde der Festtag seit dem 11. Jh. begangen, die Konzilien von Soisson (1125) und Toulouse (1129) zählten den 6. Dezember zu den Festtagen und das Konzil von Oxford aus dem Jahre 1222 beschloss die Aufnahme des Festes in die Liturgie der Bettelorden und Benediktiner und erhob es somit endgültig zum Festtag ersten Ranges. Eine relativ späte,[42] wenn ungleich berühmte Vita des Heiligen stammt von Jacobus von Voragine

---

41 Vgl. hierzu beispielsweise D.-R. MOSER, Bräuche und Feste im christlichen Jahresverlauf, Graz/Wien/Köln 1993, Kap. 3, S. 37-60; des weiteren die klassische Darstellung von K. MEISEN, Nikolauskult und -brauch im Abendland, Düsseldorf 1931, sowie D. TSCHIZEWSKIJ, Der Hl. Nikolaus (Ikonen 4), Recklinghausen 1957; L. HEISER, Nikolaus von Myra. Heiliger der ungeteilten Christenheit (Sophia. Quellen der östlichen Liturgie 18) Trier 1978; W. MEZGER, Nikolaus von Myra. Ein Heiliger im Kulturprozeß, in: U. MÜLLER / W. WUNDERLICH (Hgg.), Herrscher, Helden, Heilige (Mittelalter Mythen 1), St. Gallen 1996, S. 607-628.

42 Die Grundlage für die abendländische Rezeption des Nikolauskultes bildet die Vita des Simeon Metaphrastes aus dem 9. Jahrhundert. Die erste lateinische Lebensbeschreibung, die Vita s. Nicolai episcopi, verfasste Johannes Diaconus um 880; daneben sind die anglonormannische Legendensammlung von Robert Wace aus dem 12. Jahrhundert sowie ein Nikolausspiel von Jean Bodel aus Arras um 1200 zu nennen. Vgl. dazu auch MEZGER, Nikolaus von Myra (wie Anm. 41), S. 607ff.

in seiner Vitensammlung *Legenda Aurea.* In dieser wird die exemplarische Heiligkeit des Kindes Nikolaus schon im Säuglingsalter herausgestellt:

> Des ersten Tages, da man Sanct Nicolaus das Kindlein baden sollte, da stund es aufrecht in dem Becken, und wollte auch am Mittwoch und Freitag nicht mehr denn einmal saugen seiner Mutter Brust. Als das Kind zu Jahren kam, schied es sich von den Freuden der anderen Jünglinge und suchte die Kirchen mit Andacht; und was er da verstand von der heiligen Schrift, das behielt er mit Ernst in seinem Sinne. Als sein Vater und seine Mutter tot waren, begann er zu betrachten, wie er den großen Reichtum verzehre in Gottes Lob und nicht zu der Ehre der Menschen.[43]

Die Heiligmäßigkeit des Nikolaus, welche sich typischerweise schon im Kindesalter andeutete, erfährt ihre Ausformung in einer Vielzahl von Wundertaten, welche den Heiligen als Universalpatron[44] prädestinieren. Eine dieser Wundererzählungen, welche vermutlich im nordfranzösischen Raum entstand, beschreibt die Rettung und Wiederbelebung dreier von einem Wirt und dessen Frau ermordeten und eingepökelten Schulknaben durch Nikolaus, welche zuerst im 12. Jahrhundert durch die Hildesheimer Handschrift *Liber sacti Godehardi* überliefert wurde.[45] In ihr liegt der Grundstein für das Patronat Nikolaus' über die Kinder und Schüler. Nikolaus fungiert somit nicht nur als Heiliger *par excellence*, er bietet durch seine Funktionen als Patron der Kinder und Schüler sowie als Bischof ideale Anknüpfungsmöglichkeiten für das Kinderbischofsfest.

---

43 Jakobus de Voragine, Legenda Aurea, aus dem Lateinischen übersetzt von R. BENZ, Darmstadt/Gerlingen [12]1997, S. 26.

44 Nikolaus gilt als Patron der Alpgenossen, Angestellten, Bergleute, Drechsler, Färber, Flussschiffer, Händler, Holzsäger, Kalkbrenner, Küster, Schneider, Schreiber, Schuhmacher, Senner, Weber, Diebe und Mörder sowie der Liebenden, vgl. MOSER (wie Anm. 41), S. 40f.

45 Die Genese dieser Legende, welche übrigens nicht in die *Leganda Aurea* einging, beschreibt ausführlich MEISEN (wie Anm. 41), S. 289-306. Dieser fasst den Inhalt des hier zugrunde liegenden Mirakelspiels wie folgt zusammen: „Drei wandernde Schüler nehmen in einem einsam gelegenen Hause Herberge. Der Wirt, der bei den Schülern Schätze vermutet, ermordet sie mit Hilfe seiner Frau in der Nacht. Da kommt der Hl. Nikolaus in der Gestalt eines Bettlers, bittet um Unterkunft und überführt die Schuldigen unter dem Vorwande, frisches Fleisch haben zu wollen, ihres Verbrechens. Auf ein Gebet des Heiligen erscheint ein Engel und verkündigt, dass die drei Schüler zum Leben zurückgekehrt seien." (vgl. ebd., S. 289).

III. Der Kinderbischof als Prediger

Anschließend an die rituell-liturgischen Funktionen mittelalterlicher Kinderbischöfe erscheinen die drei hier vorzustellenden englischen Kinderbischofspredigten als ein weiteres Indiz für die Zuschreibung von Autorität an den Kinderbischof. Diese Predigten des ausgehenden 15. und frühen 16. Jahrhunderts, welche durch den gewählten Amtsträger vorgetragen wurden, vermitteln den Eindruck der Vorbildhaftigkeit des Kindes und tragen dem Statut John Colets zufolge normativen Charakter. Der Gründer der St. Paul's school legte 1512 fest, dass *alle these Chyldren shall every Chyldermasse day come to paulis Church and here the Chylde Bisshoppis sermon, and after be at hye masse, and eche of them offer a I d. to the Childe Bisshopp; and with theme the Maisters and surveyours of the scole.*[46] Diese Forderung erhält umso mehr Gewicht, da sie aus einer Zeit stammt, in welcher der Status und die Existenz des katholischen Festes im Zuge der Reformation bereits in Frage gestellt worden war. Die Proklamation Heinrichs VIII. aus den Jahre 1541 verurteilte die Feste zu Ehren des Hl. Nikolaus, der Hl. Katharina, des Hl. Clemens sowie der *Holye Innocentes* als unchristlichen Hohn (*derision*) und Aberglauben (*superstition)* und schuf neben einer Reihe von Konzilsbeschlüssen eine weitere Grundlage für die überwiegend negative Bewertung des Festes.[47] Das Fest wurde nach dem Tode Heinrichs VIII. 1547 durch Mary 1554 wieder eingeführt und schließlich unter Elizabeth I. offiziell abgeschafft.

---

46 Vgl. J. H. LUPTON, A Life of John Colet. Dean of St. Paul's, and founder of St. Paul's school, London 1887 (ND New York 1974), App. A, S. 278.

47 Die entsprechende Textstelle lautet: *And whereas heretofore dyverse and many superstitious and childysshe observations have been usid, and yet to this day are observed and kept in many and sondry parties of this realm, as upon sainte Nicolas, sainte Catheryne, sainte Clemet, the holye Innocentes, and such like; children be strangelye decked and apperelid to counterfaite priestes, bysshopps, and women; and so leddewith songes and daunces from house to house, bleasing the people, and gatherynge of money; and boyes doo singe masse, and preache in the pulpit, with suche other unfittinge and inconvenient usages, rather to the derision than to any true glory of God, or honour of his saints; the kyng's majestie therefore mynding nothing so moche, as to avaunce the true glorye of God without vayne superstition, willith and commaundeth, that from henceforth all suche superstitions be loste and clyerlye extinguished throughowte all this his realms and dominions, foreasmoche as the same doo resemble rather the unlawfull superstition of gentilitie, than the pure and sincere religion of Christe.* Vgl. Concilia, ed. WILKINS (wie Anm. 5), Bd. 3, S. 860.

III. 1. John Alcock: In die Innocencium sermo pro episcopo puerorum (1495)

Die älteste dieser überlieferten Predigten wurde für den Kinderbischof der Kathedrale von St. Paul's um 1495 von John Alcock, dem damaligen Bischof von Ely, verfasst.[48] Ausgehend von der Annahme der Reinheit des jungen Kindes (*infantum*) beschreibt der Autor zwei weitere Lebensphasen: das zweite Alter, die *adolescentia*, in welchem der Knabe dem Einfluss des Guten und Schlechten ausgeliefert ist[49] sowie das Mannesalter, in dem sich der Mensch selbst zu korrigieren hat.[50] Im Gegensatz zur fehlenden geistigen Reife und mangelnden Vernunft wird in dieser Predigt jedoch die besondere Stellung der Kinder in den Augen Gottes herausgestellt: *Tho children thenne the whiche lacke dyscrecyon, use of reason, and parfyght cognycyon, and yet attayne to the ende that is prepared for mannes blysse, as thyse blessyd Innocentes whoos solempnyte we halowe this daye.*[51] Aus der erneuten Berufung auf die herausragende Stellung der Unschuldigen Kinder sowie auf das Exemplum Daniels leitet der Autor der Predigt die Autorität des Kinderbischofs her.[52] Diese nutzt er sogleich, um seinen Lehrern spöttisch den Weg nach Tyburn, dem öffentlichen Galgenplatz Londons, zu wünschen.[53]

---

48 Diese wurde zusammen mit der Predigt der Gloucester Cathedral von 1558 erstmals von Wynkyn de Worde um 1498/99 gedruckt, danach von RIMBAULT 1875 ediert (vgl. Anm. 25); beide liegen mittlerweile in einer neuen Edition vor. Vgl. A sermon for a Boy Bishop by John Alcock, Bishop of Ely (1430-1486-1500), ed. A. WARD, in: Ephemerides Liturgicae 112 (1998), S. 58-81 sowie Richard Ramsey's Sermon for a Boy Bishop (1558), ed. A. WARD, in: Ephemerides Liturgicae 111 (1997), S. 476-505.

49 Zum ersten Lebensabschnitt: *And soo verely the Infant age of a childe is ryght neyther dysposed to vertue neyther to vyce, as the Phylosophre syth, Tanquam tabula nuda in qua nichil depingitur. But the seconde age is called Adolescencia, and hath two lynes, aright and a crokyd, sygnefyenge the dysposycion that hath thenne to vyce and thenne to virtue.* Vgl. WARD (wie Anm. 48), S. 63.

50 Vgl. ebd., S. 69.

51 Vgl. ebd., S. 63.

52 *In the begynnynge thenne of this symple exhortacyon, that I a chylde, wantynge the habyte of connynge, maby dyrected by hym that gave to that childe Danyell Sermonem rectum et Spiritum Deorum, somwhat to say to his laude and praysynge, and to alle pure chylderne that bene here present edifyenge, we shall ate thus tyme devoutly make our prayers.* Vgl. ebd. S. 64

53 Vgl. ebd., S. 65.

Im folgenden Teil der Predigt erfolgt nun endlich der Verweis auf Mt 18: *Nisi conversi fueritis, et efficiamini sicut parvuli, non intrabis in regnum caelorum,* welchem wir auch in den zwei anderen Predigten begegnen. Die Betonung der Reinheit und Unschuld als Grundlage für den Eintritt ins Himmelreich erfährt eine immer wiederkehrende Betonung innerhalb der Predigten, woraus sich die Aufforderung an alle Anwesenden ergibt, vorbildhafte Kindlichkeit in eben jenem Sinne anzustreben.[54]

III. 2. Richard Ramsey: Sermon of the Child Bishop pronownsyd by John Stubs, Querester (1558)

Auf genau diese Tugenden nimmt noch deutlicher und ausführlicher Richard Ramsey in seiner für den Kinderbischof von Gloucester vom 28. Dezember 1558 verfassten Predigt Bezug. Auch der Name des erwählten *queresters* wird genannt: John Stubbs. Gleich zu Beginn steht das Zitat aus Mt 18 der Predigt als Ausgangspunkt voran; der Autor führt aus, dass durch die Taufe als Moment der Wiedergeburt alle Christen in den Zustand der Kinder zurückkehren, demnach alle als Gotteskinder bezeichnet werden können.[55] Der Erläuterung der spirituellen Kindschaft folgt der Satz: *love litill ones therfor and learn of them how you may have an entre in to the kyngdom of heavyn.*[56] Hierauf werden die natürlichen Stärken der Kinder, darunter vor allem ihre natürliche Demut, im Vergleich zu dem oft vergeblichen Streben der Erwachsenen nach Tugendhaftigkeit herausgestellt: *...but thanks be vnto God litill ones have by nature what the elder have by wrestlyng and stryving with ther own affections. Thei have humilitie of mynd and sprite, which vertue the lower it goeth the nerer it approchet to the kingdom of heavyn, and other like virtues the childer have which are degrees to the kingdom.*[57] Auch die klare Referenz an das Andenken der

54 Vgl. ebd., S. 66: *And in this fourme alle maner of people and al maner of ages in clennesse of lyf to be pure as childerne* [...].

55 [...] *that ther was a birth spirituall in water and in the holy goost which now is dayly usyd of the churche in the Sacrament of baptisme, after the birth it is possible for all ages both yong and old to be born again anew, and so to gain an entre into the kingdom of heaven.* Vgl. A. WARD, Richard Ramsey's sermon (wie Anm. 48), S. 481.

56 Vgl. ebd., S. 482.

57 Vgl. ebd.

Unschuldigen Kinder erfolgt, wobei ihre Stellung als Sonder-Märtyrer, welche ihr Leben im Verständnis des Autors direkt für die Person Christus gaben, nochmals betont wird.[58] Im zweiten Teil der Predigt wandte sich der Kinderbischof nun an alle Anwesenden mit dem Aufruf alle schändlichen Verhaltensweisen abzulegen, *which are dissonant & disagreable with the incorrupt maners of childer.* Dass Kindlichkeit hier im Sinne Paulus' 1 Cor. 14 nicht als Kindlichkeit im Verstehen, sondern im Abstandnehmen von Sünde und Bosheit, als Kindsein in Reinheit, verstanden werden soll, hatte der Kinderbischof den Anwesenden zu erläutern:

> *Considre well the nature of innocent childer, & yow shall perceive in them no maner of malice, no envy, no disdayn, no hurtfullness, so synfull affection, no pride, no ambition, no singularitie, no desire of honor, of riches, of carnalitie, of revenginge, or quitting evill for evyll but all the affections quiet in all pacience, in all simplicitie, in all puritie, in all tractableness, in all obedience, in all humilitie, & in all innocency, & no such synfull affections reigning in them as commynly rageth in men & women of years.*[59]

Die natürliche Tugendhaftigkeit der Kinder könne bis zum vierzehnten Lebensjahr bewahrt werden, was jedoch, so der Autor der Predigt, bei den meisten der Kinder schon sehr früh nicht mehr der Fall sei. Hier wendet er sich direkt an die anwesenden Kinder mit der Frage: *Tell me, yow boys, yow childer, yow litill ones? are yow not ashamyd of you partes that yow are so sone corruptyd, so sone ripe, & so sone rottyn, so late innocentes, & so sonme lewd lads deservyng nother love nor prayse of any honest person?* Die Gründe hierfür seien der frühzeitige schlechte Einfluss in der Stadt, welcher zu Blasphemie und Frühreife führe, jedoch seien die Knaben auch nicht in den Schulen hiervor gefeit, was den Autor/Prediger schließlich dazu führt, Eltern und Lehrer für die Verdorbenheit der Kinder verantwortlich zu machen. Diese ließen es an Strenge und Züchtigung

---

58 Vgl. ebd., S. 484: [...] *these innocentes dyd shed ther bloud, not only in the quarell of Christ but also in the person of Christ, which was a prerogative aboute all other martyres* [...]*;* dergleichen auf S. 485: *Thus much I have said of the virtue of Innocency, for the honor of these blessyd Innocentes & Innocent childer, which are remembryd in the churches this day, which day, as it is commynly tremyd Chyldermas day, so is it celebrate and solempnisyd by the preferment of childer in all great cathedral churches, which gyve the childer the prerogative this day above men, in tokyn that the Innocent childer which shed ther bloud for the person of the most pure Innocent child Jesus had a prerogative above all men in ther kind of martyrdom, as I said before.*

59 Vgl. ebd.

fehlen; fehlerhaft schätzt er auch die Einstellung gegenüber ihren Kindern ein, die in zu großer Weichheit und falscher Angst, den Kindern Schaden zuzufügen, bestehe. Somit sei es an den Lehrern - als *tertios parentes* - die Kinder nicht nur beim Lernen zu korrigieren, sondern auch ihre Sitten zu prägen und ihre Seelen zu erziehen.[60] Ausgehend von der Bewahrung kindlicher Unschuld und Reinheit werden durch den Kinderbischof an dieser Stelle konkrete Anweisungen und Appelle zur Erziehung erteilt. Ihm wird gleichsam selbst die Rolle eines Erziehers und damit erneut Autorität zugewiesen, welche sich nunmehr nicht nur spirituell im Vollzug liturgischer Handlungen, sondern ganz lebensnah präsentiert. Ein letzter Blick auf den Entstehungszeitpunkt dieser Predigt sei erlaubt: Mit dem Tode Marys I. am 17. November 1558 und dem Regierungsantritt Elizabeths entstand die Predigt Richard Ramseys sozusagen kurz vor dem endgültigen Verbot des Kinderbischofsfestes. Diesem Umstand trägt die Predigt in polemisierender Weise Rechnung, indem sie im Zusammenhang mit kindlicher Wankelmütigkeit und Mangel an Verstand diejenigen anklagt, welche sich aus diesem Grunde von der alten Religion abwenden und der unsteten Lehre des Protestantismus hingeben würden.[61]

III. 3. Erasmus von Rotterdam: *Concio de puero Iesu* (1511)

In vielerlei Hinsicht knüpft die Predigt Erasmus von Rotterdams aus der Zeit um 1511 an das bisher Gesagte an, sie geht jedoch auch in einigen Punkten darüber hinaus. Die in enger Anbindung an die Vorstellungen John Colets und vermutlich in gemeinsamer Arbeit mit ihm entstandene[62] *Concio de puero Iesu* wurde schon kurz nach ihrer

60 Vgl. ebd., S. 492ff.

61 Vgl. ebd., S. 487f.: *Let us not be still as childer that be waveryng & wilbe caried hyder & thyder with every blast of doctrine by the wylynes & craftynes of men which lay way to deceive us, yf we note thes wordes of S. Pawl well, yow shall perceive that he takes it to be a childish point for any Christian man to waver in his faith, & that it is for lak of witt if he be caried from the doctrine of his awncient religion in to a new fanglyd doctrine, which hath no suretie in it but it is inconstant as the wynd.*

62 Vgl. zum Verhältnis des Erasmus und John Colet: LUPTON, A Life of John Colet (wie Anm. 46) sowie die Einleitung E. KEARNS' zu Erasmus, Concio de puero Iesu,

Entstehung in das Studienprogramm der Schule *De copia* und die darin enthaltene Schrift *De ratione studii* aufgenommen und erstmals von Robert de Keysere 1511 gedruckt. Darauf folgten die Editionen Bades 1512 und Matthias Schürers in Straßburg 1514. Zwei Jahre später wurde das Werk ins Spanische, 1540 ins Englische und 1607 ins Niederländische übersetzt, wovon man auf seine große Popularität schließen kann. Bis in das Jahr 1563 wurde die Predigt 37 Mal gedruckt.

Auch Erasmus betont die Wiedergeburt aller durch die Taufe, ebenso sah er die Tugendhaftigkeit der Kinder in ihrer *simplicitas* and *puritas,* so wie es das Vorbild des Knaben Jesus gebietet. Schon im Prolog führt er Jesus als Vorbildfigur ein, lobt die gottgegebene Eloquenz der Kinder und sogar Säuglinge[63] und ruft die kindlichen Zuhörer zum Enthusiasmus auf, welcher aus drei Motiven entspringt: der Verehrung Christi, der Liebe zu Christus und der Belohnung in Form des Eingangs in das Himmelreich.[64] Im ersten Teil erfolgt die Erläuterung der Größe Christi, woraufhin der Autor das besondere Verhältnis Jesu zu den Kindern als *puerorum princeps* beschreibt und hierbei Bezug nimmt auf Mt 19,13, und Mt 18,2-3.[65] Darüber hinaus beschreibt er deutlich ein Ideal des gottgefälligen Kindseins, welches mit dem Motiv des *puer senex* genauestens übereinstimmt: *Tantu demus operam, ut eius modi simus pueri cuius modi diligit Jesus, id est innocentuos, pures, dociles, simplices, at illud interim meminerimus hanc deo gratia pueritia non in annis esse sita sed animis, non in temporibus sed in moribus.* [...] *Est igitur novu quod a pueritiae genus quod a christo approbatur, pueritia citra puerilitate & senilis quaedam pueritia, quae non annorum numero constat, sed innocentia, sed ingenii simplicitate.*[66] Jesus liebt demnach die unschuldigen, lenkbaren und einfachen Kinder. Das Kindsein besteht nicht in Jahren oder Alter, sondern in Gesinnung und Verhalten. Dieses gealterte Kindsein (*senilis pueritia*) beschreibt das Ideal einer Alterstranszendenz, in welcher jeder durch eigenes Bestreben und

---

ed. E. FANTHAM / E. RUMMEL, in: Collected Works of Erasmus, Bd. 29, Toronto/Buffalo/London 1989, S. 52-55.

63 Vgl. Erasmi Roterdami, Concio de puero Iesu in schola Coletica Londini instituta pronunciandi, in: Ders., De ratione studii, ed. M. SCHÜRER, Straßburg 1514, S. 195.

64 Vgl. ebd., S. 196.

65 Vgl. ebd.

66 Vgl. ebd., S. 199.

Tugendhaftigkeit vermag, sein natürliches Lebensalter zu überwinden.[67] Die gängigen auch von frühchristlichen Autoren in diesem Zusammenhang angeführten biblischen Exempla der *pueri senes* nennt auch Erasmus: Daniel, Salomon, Nikolaus, Benedikt aber auch Beispiele für die weniger häufigen *puellae senes*: die Hl. Agnes und Cecilia.[68] Auch der zwölfjährige Jesus im Tempel wird als ein Beispiel für den altersweisen Knaben angeführt.[69] Die moralische Zielsetzung der Predigt an die Schüler von St. Paul's school formuliert Erasmus gegen Ende des zweiten Teils folgendermaßen: *sui (Iesum) similis evadere, hoc est, castos, puros, incontaminatos, mites, simplices, tractabiles, expertes fuci, ignaros doli, nescios invidiae, parentibus morigeros, preceptoribus dicto audientes, mundi contemptores, rebus divinis addictos, literis intentos, nobis ipsia cotidie meliores, probatos superis, gratos hominibus, odore bonae famae et plurimos ad Christum allicientes.*[70] Der Kinderbischof, welcher sich an seine *commilitones* wendet, dient hier als Organ zur eindringlichen Vermittlung der Vorbildhaftigkeit des Jesusknaben und zur Aufforderung diesem durch Gehorsam und Lernen gerecht zu werden.

Lässt man die Erkenntnisse, welche sich aus den Predigten ergeben, nochmals Revue passieren, so bleibt anzumerken, dass dem Kinderbischof in allen drei Predigten eine eindeutige Autoritätsposition schon allein durch den formalen Akt der Predigt, jedoch viel mehr noch durch die darin vermittelten Inhalte zukommt. Er tritt als Mahner der Kinder wie Erwachsenen auf, verweist auf die Gottesnähe der Kinder in Bezug auf deren Unschuld und Reinheit, und preist neben der Taufe als Wiedergeburt vor allem bei Erasmus den altersweisen Knaben als christliches Ideal, welcher nicht aufgrund von Jahren, sondern durch moralische Haltung und Sittlichkeit das natürliche Lebensalter zu transzendieren vermag.

---

67 Zum Motiv des *puer senex* und zum christlichen Ideal der Alterstranszendenz vgl. C. GNILKA, Aetas spiritalis. Die Überwindung der natürlichen Altersstufen als Ideal frühchristlichen Lebens, Bonn 1972.

68 Vgl. Erasmus, Concio de puero Iesu, ed. SCHÜRER (wie Anm. 63), S. 201.

69 Vgl. ebd., S. 205. *Cum puer ille coelestis sapientia die patris in medio doctorum sedeat, audiens vicissim ac respondens, sed ita respondens ut omnes sapientiam admirentur.*

70 Vgl. ebd., S. 206.

IV. Thesen und Ausblick

Fasst man die hier vorgestellten Aspekte abschließend unter der Fragestellung zusammen, ob und wie eine Autoritätszuschreibung an den Kinderbischof stattfand und ob es sich somit beim Kinderbischofsfest um einen spielerischen Akt mit Ventilfunktion oder eine echte Statusumkehr handelte, so bleibt festzuhalten, dass sowohl die liturgischen Funktionen als auch die materielle Ausstattung sowie die Rolle des Kinderbischofs als Prediger eindeutig auf eine Autoritätszuschreibung und tatsächliche Statusumkehr mit "wirklichkeitsverändernder Wirkung"[71] hinweisen. Als Begründung für die "performative Magie" der Investitur des Kinderbischofs schreibt Velten:

> Denn zum einen verändert sie die Vorstellung, welche die Akteure von der Person haben, und damit auch deren Verhalten ihr gegenüber. Das bezieht sich sowohl auf die sprachlichen Zuweisungen (Ehrentitel, Aussprechen des Titels) als auch auf die mit der Referenz verbundenen Gesten (Körperhaltung, Anordnung im Raum) sowie auf die äußeren Kennzeichen der Position (Insignien, Kleidung).[72]

Konkret manifestiert sich diese in den bischöflichen Insignien, der kostbaren Kleidung, der räumlichen Positionierung des Bischofs an höchster Position im Chor, liturgischer Akte wie Segnung und Beweihräucherung, ebenso wie im Visitations- und Münzprägerecht. In diesem Fall, so könnte man schlussfolgern, schafft der sakrale Raum der Kathedrale oder Kirche die Voraussetzungen für den Grad der Ernsthaftigkeit des Rituals, in welcher "gerade die Ritualdynamik und ihre performativen Aspekte einer Analogiebildung [zu offiziellen Einsetzungsritualen, Anm. der Autorin] zuträglich sind."[73] Spielerische Elemente des Festes deuten sich vor allem außerhalb der Kirche,

---

71 Vgl. H. R. VELTEN, Einsetzungsrituale als Rituale der Statusumkehr. Narrenbischöfe und Narrenkönige in den mittelalterlichen Klerikerfesten (1200-1500), in: M. STEINICKE / S. WEINFURTER (Hgg.), Investitur- und Krönungsrituale. Herrschaftseinsetzungen im kulturellen Vergleich, Köln/Weimar/Wien 2005, S. 201-221, hier S. 215.

72 Vgl. ebd.

73 Vgl. ebd., S. 205.

beispielsweise bei Umzügen durch die Stadt oder dem *convivium,* an. Daneben haben vor allem regulative Quellen kirchlicher Autoritäten und Berichte über Ausschreitungen und Exzesse[74] das negative Bild der Klerikerfeste nach Weihnachten, und damit die bisherige unzureichende Forschungsmeinung, weitestgehend geprägt. Bei der Suche nach den Ursprüngen des Kinderbischofsfestes wurde bisher vor allem die Rückführung auf antik-heidnische Festtraditionen vorgenommen, welche die Statusumkehr und den Ausnahmecharakter des Festes betonen. Dennoch erscheint es elementar, das Fest als ein theologisch fundiertes ernsthaftes Ereignis zu betrachten, welches sich in Anlehnung an den Festtag des Hl. Nikolaus, insbesondere jedoch im Andenken an die Unschuldigen Kinder, die Aufforderung Jesu zur kindlichen Unschuld und Reinheit (Mt 18) zurückzukehren und dem Streben nach einem geistigen Kindsein, entwickelte.

[74] Ein solcher Bericht über einen Mord im Zusammenhang mit dem Kinderbischofsfest stammt aus Paris im Jahre 1367 und trägt den Titel: Occasione ludi episcopalis nocte S. Nicolai conflictus cruentus inter scholares Paris. et servientes et milites gueti subortus est. Causa coram Parlamento delata servientes punitur, in: Cartularium Universitatis Parisiensis, ed. H. DENIFLE, Paris 1889-1897, 4 Bde., hier Bd. 3, S. 166-175.

FATHERS AND SONS IN THE CLOISTER.

Ecclesiastical Dynasties in the Early Irish Church

ANNETTE KEHNEL

Abstract: The paper investigates into the question why "fathers and sons" in leading positions of the Western Christian Church became an obviously "unwanted" constellation in the course of the first millennium. The New Testament does not make any provisions against this constellation. However, the absence of sons of those in higher clerical orders features as the natural outcome of celibacy which in turn became the most usual realization of sexual chastity in the Western European church. Arnold ANGENENDT argued that this development had its roots in the general religious need for ritual purity, the claim for "pure hands" of those who serve and approach the deity rooted in the classical Greek, Roman and Jewish Religions.[1] He describes the development towards celibacy in the medieval church as a victory of popular religious needs for ritual purity over Christendom. The paper attempts to highlight an interesting move in the course of this development (in fact a cul-de-sac): the Medieval Irish Church prior to the Irish church reform of the 12th century, ruled over by monastic dynasties. It is suggested that the historical developments in the Irish monastic church gave shape to a potential alternative: The need for ritual purity of those in higher orders who participate in religious rituals was here seemingly separated from the need for clerical and monastic celibacy. Quite obviously Irish abbots, bishops and even the leaders of the spiritual communities within the monastic churches produced offspring and installed their sons in leading offices in their churches. The general tendency to read the state of the Early Irish Church as one in need of reform might have to be turned upside down: The Irish monastic Church, with the concept of fathers and sons in leading positions, could also be read as a chapter in the history of the Medieval Western Christian Church which offers a glimpse at how ecclesiastical life might have been organized on a high spiritual

---

1 K. GROSS, Menschenhand und Gotteshand in Antike und Christentum, aus dem Nachlass hrsg.v. Wolfgang SPEYER, Stuttgart 1985.

level and with high ascetic standards but without the priestly obligation for celibacy.

Introduction

"Fathers and sons" are very prominent right in the centre of the Jewish-Christian narrative: Noah and his sons Shem, Ham and Japheth fathered the new human race after the Flood, Abraham and his son Isaac founded the dynasty of the chosen ones, the sons of Jacob became the ancestors of the twelve tribes, David and Salomon built up the powerful kingdom of Israel and, of course, it was God the Father and God the Son, who jointly undertook the work of redemption. There is, however, a certain irritation inherent to the latter story, since the father-son constellation in this case is strangely varied in the threefold fatherhood of Joseph, God father and the holy spirit, all three somehow involved in the conception, the procreation and the education of Jesus the son.[2]

This slight irritation might be read as an indication for a most significant change which took place in the Christian Church, more precisely in the Western Christian Church in the course of the first twelve hundred years or so of its existence: A development towards what one might call an "anti-natural-father tendency" in spiritual and temporal leadership within the Western Christian Church. Fatherhood, more precisely natural fatherhood, was something which might happen to a leading man in the Christian Church, but it was rarely regarded a great merit. In fact, quite the opposite was the case, if we think of the famous examples like St. Augustin and his son Adeodatus or of Abelard and Astrolabius. Fatherhood was the stigma of the unbridled past prior to celibacy.

---

2 P. BROWN, Die Keuschheit der Engel. Sexuelle Entsage, Askese und Körperlichkeit am Anfang des Christentums, München 1991; A. KOSCHORKE, Die Heilige Familie und ihre Folgen, Frankfurt/M. 2000; J. GOODY, Die Entwicklung von Ehe und Familie in Europa, Frankfurt/M. 1989; G. SIGNORI, Die verlorene Ehre des heiligen Joseph oder Männlichkeit im Spannungsfeld spätmittelalterlicher Altersstereotypen, in: K. SCHREINER/G. SCHWERHOFF (eds.), Verletzte Ehre. Ehrkonflikte in Gesellschaften des Mittelalters und der Frühen Neuzeit, Köln/Weimar/Wien 1995, pp. 183-213; B.-P. MCGUIRE, Patterns of male affectivity in the late Middle Ages: the case of Jean Gerson, in: S. KARANT-NUNN (ed.), Varieties of devotion in the Middle Ages and Renaissance, Turnhout 2003, pp. 163-178.

Of course, one might argue that the discourse on clerical celibacy from the times of St. Paul and his letter to the Corinthians marginalized fathers holding leading positions in the Christian Church from the very beginning. Fatherhood was 'unwanted', since whoever wanted to get somewhere within the church would have to be – like St. Paul – celibate. We all remember his self-confident "I wish everybody was like me" – namely celibate – at the end of a lesson to the Corinthians about marriage as the lesser evil (1 Cor 7, 1–7 and 32–34).

No fathers in the church? No fathers in leading positions in the Christian Church? And, vice versa of course, no sons of leading ecclesiastical figures in the church since their potential fathers were all engaged in the work of the Lord in a way that excluded earthly obligations like marriage, wives, families and sons (and of course daughters). Those in higher orders in the Western Christian Church were celibate – thus excluding the existence of the "father-son" constellation at least in leading positions of the Church.

In my paper I want first briefly to recapitulate the history of asceticism and celibacy as the most obvious precondition for the absence of fathers and sons in leading positions within the ecclesiastical hierarchy. In the second part I suggest looking at a particular historical example which seems to suggest historical alternatives: the case of the Irish Church where patterns of ecclesiastical leadership in favour of fathers and sons prevailed at least until the twelfth century. The argument brought forth here is that the early Irish model of ecclesiastical leadership combined procreation, asceticism and celibacy in a particularly successful way. In the third part potential explanations for the victory of celibacy and the decision against fathers and sons in lead of the Western Christian Church will be revisited. The interpretations presented follow the arguments worked out by Arnold ANGENENDT and Hubertus LUTTERBACH.

1. History of asceticism and celibacy

1. 1 Historical context: fathers and sons in the early church

As it is well known, married priests and bishops in the early church are a rather common feature. In fact they were the norm. One of the best-known examples is Gregory of Nazianz, the son of a priest. Apparently his father, Gregory the elder, conceived him when already a priest, around the year 326, with his mother being rather advanced in age. The father Gregory the elder was promoted to a bishopric soon after the birth of Gregory the younger and later in life encouraged his son to take clerical vows since he urgently needed support for the care of souls in his bishopric. Eventually in 361, Gregory the younger (then around 35) was ordained to the priesthood by his father and later he took over his fathers bishopric.[3]

Here we have a perfect example for hereditary succession in ecclesiastical office. The case of the Gregory of Nazianz is of course no exception at all. Clerical dynasties were a constant feature of the early church down to the 5th century.

Stefan HEID, who most carefully reconstructs evidence to prove the genuine apostolic roots of clerical celibacy, takes into account that the early church apparently knew but married clergy. His study dedicates a whole chapter to clerical dynasties and he makes the point that chastity became an obligation only *after* the taking of vows. There are the well-known examples of Bishop Polycrates of Ephesus, who had seven members of his family in episcopal order, amongst them Eustathius and Eulalius of Sebaste, Pope Damasus, Chrysanthus, and Markianus, again father and son, the latter following his father in the office as bishop of Novatia. Or we have Julian, son of a south Italian bishop, who at the occasion of his marriage to Titia, daughter of a neighbouring bishop, was praised for his chastity combined with the wish the couple might be blessed with many virgins and priests and thus become the founders of a righteous and priestly dynasty (Paulinus von Nola). Julian took clerical

---

3 S. HEID, Zölibat in der frühen Kirche. Die Anfänge einer Enthaltsamkeitspflicht für Kleriker in Ost und West, Paderborn/München/Wien/Zürich 1997, pp. 167f.

vows himself and was later promoted to the sea of Eclanum near Benevent.

This pattern that obviously allows for priestly and episcopal offspring is clearly in favour of fathers and sons in the church. The principle of clerical dynasties might not necessarily offend against the principal of clerical chastity. Basically the argument runs: first you do your duty in order to supply the successor generation of priests, then you take clerical vows and live chaste in future.

1. 2 Gradually growing opposition against fathers and sons

However, this altogether plausible idea of clerical chastity – this kind of serial chastity which allows for procreation in an early stage of life, guaranteeing spiritual purity within the bounds of marriage after the consecration – this understanding of clerical chastity – as is well known – did not survive the high Middle Ages.

The first disciplinary measure against sexual activity amongst the clergy is generally dated to the year 306 at the synod of Elvira, now Granada in Spain. Canon 33 of this synod decrees in general (*in totum*) for bishops, presbyters, deacons and other clerics (*vel omnibus clericis positis in ministerio*) not to come together with their wives and not to beget children. Contravention is punished with suspension. The proper reading of this canon is not quite agreed on and it was suggested that it actually agrees on married clergy, but demands abstinence only for the time before mass. However, the synod of Elvira is generally read as the earliest legislation on celibacy. The council of Nicea in 324/325 decrees in canon 3 that bishops, priests, deacons etc. should not have women around them, with the exception of their mothers, sisters, aunts etc. This idea met with opposition, as the famous plea of bishop Paphnutius – himself an unstained and dedicated celibate – makes apparent. The story tells how the bishop, who had lost an eye in the times of persecution, and who was much loved by the emperor, insisted on the respectability of marriage and bespoke his colleagues to consider the heavy burden imposed on the clergy by such a disproportionate rigor. He even spoke of cohabitation with the legitimate wife as a form of chasteness. The story is transmitted in the church history of Socrates († after 439). According to him the whole congregation agreed with his wise speech and no decision was taken on the council of Nicea.[4] Of course the historicity of this story has been doubted, but it reflects an attitude towards celibacy in the fourth century A.D. In fact, it reflects the reservations towards clerical celibacy. This idea eventually succeeded in the Eastern Church. The Council of Constantinople in the year 692 (also called the II. Trullan Synod) decreed for the Eastern Church that bishops, deacons, priests and other clerics are not allowed to marry. However, marriages dating prior to taking vows should be continued with the obligation to chastity at the days of mass. It was even forbidden to divorce a wife for alleged reasons of piety (*pietatis praetextu*). The synods held in the Western Church, in the Merovingian and Carolingian realm, likewise dealt with the sexual behaviour of the clergy. Marriage was not a hindrance for a career as a priest, however, the concept of cultic purity increasingly enforced *continentia* on the priest. The synods imposed separation of bed and house on the couple and forbid them to return to the conjugal bed (*ad conjugale thorum*).[5]

1. 3 The victory of celibacy in the 11th and 12th centuries

A severe change took place in the 11th century. Measures against married clergy were gradually tightened. Local councils, bishops, popes and emperors enforced legislation in favour of celibacy. Under the Salian king and Emperor Henry II, who himself was married but is said to have led a chaste and abstinent marriage (*Josephsehe*). He not only enforced marriage restrictions with a vigour hitherto unknown, but also fought against married priests with rather rude methods.[6] His enforcement of clerical celibacy in the German realm became one of the main assets of the Gregorian Reform movement under the leadership of the German popes Leo IX and Gregory VII. A most vivid account of the severe

---

4 Sokrates, Kirchengeschichte. Historia ecclesiastica, ed. G. C. HANSEN (Die griechischen christlichen Schriftsteller der ersten Jahrhunderte N.F. 1), Berlin 1995, cap. 1, 11, here cit. after HEID, Zölibat in der frühen Kirche (note 3 above), pp. 14f.

5 Cf. H. LUTTERBACH, Sexualität im Mittelalter (Beihefte zum Archiv für Kulturgeschichte 43), Köln/Weimar/Wien 1999, pp. 220-223, 233-239.

6 S. WEINFURTER, Heinrich II (1002-1024), in: B. SCHNEIDMÜLLER/S. WEINFURTER (eds.), Die deutschen Herrscher des Mittelalters, historische Portraits von Heinrich I. bis Maximilian I. (919-1519), München 2003, pp. 97-118.

conflicts is given by Lampert of Hersfeld in his annals. He describes how in 1074 at a synod in Mainz the archbishop read out a letter from the pope, which left it to the priests and bishops either to give up their wives or their offices. According to Lampert's report, the entire clergy present decided that the pope was a heretic and his teaching ludicrous. Unanimously they declared rather to give up priesthood than their wives. And in this case, they threatened the pope, who expected the leaders of the church to live like angels, to find his angels elsewhere. Lampert takes up the story once more; this time the archbishop of Mainz tried to enforce papal legislation once more in the year 1075. However, he met with such aggressive opposition that he feared for his life and decided for the future not to tackle the issue anymore, but to leave it to the pope.[7] It seems that basically every cleric in the second half of the 11th century was married or lived with a woman, at least, all those present at the two councils were apparently – if we belief Lampert's report – entirely upset by the papal idea that a priest should live celibate. Some twenty years later, at the Synod of Clermont-Ferrand in 1095 it was decided that the sons born out of concubinage were to be excluded from ecclesiastical offices. Eventually the second Lateran Council in 1139 at the latest did away with clerical marriages, declaring every sort of clerical marriage illegal according to canon law, moreover, declaring clerical offspring illegitimate, thus overruling the hereditary principle within the church altogether, which means overruling the principle of hereditary ecclesiastical dynasties in general. It was argued that the history of clerical celibacy only started in 1139 because here for the first time married clergy was disavowed in general according to canon law.[8] In the context of these developments the measures taken against sons and daughters of the clergy in the medieval church played an important role as a means in the struggle for the ultimate enforcement of celibacy.[9]

---

7 Lamperti Monachi Hersefeldensis, Annales. Lampert von Hersfeld, Annalen, ed. O. HOLDER-EGGER, transl. A. SCHMIDT (Ausgewählte Quellen zur Deutschen Geschichte des Mittelalters 13), Darmstadt 1957, pp. 256-261, 302f.

8 E.g. E. SCHILLEBEECKX, Der Amtszölibat. Eine kritische Besinnung, Düsseldorf 1967.

9 B. SCHIMMELPFENNIG, Zölibat und Lage der "Priestersöhne" vom 11. bis zum 14. Jahrhundert, in: HZ 227 (1978), pp. 1-44, here 16.

2. Fathers and sons in ecclesiastical leadership: The case of the Irish Church

I will highlight this development in the case of Clonmacnoise, an example of an Irish monastic church that I studied in some detail in the course of my doctoral thesis. Clonmacnoise was founded by St. Ciarán († 545) sometime around the year 532. It was one of the leading monastic centres in Ireland for half a millennium, from the 6th to the 12th century. The Irish hereditary mode of succession in ecclesiastical offices might possible highlight models of ecclesiastical leadership that in the long run did no succeed (at least not within the church).

2. 1 Sources and methodological problems

The following reconstruction of hereditary dynasties in the Irish monastic settlement of Clonmacnoise is generally based on the information gathered from the Irish Annals and from hagiographical and saga material of the time. The now extant early Irish annalistic compilations can be generally divided into two main bodies, one represented by the Annals of Ulster, the other by the 'Clonmacnoise group of annals', the latter including the Annals of Tigernach, the Chronicon Scotorum, the Annals of Clonmacnoise, the Annals of Innisfalen and the Annals of Roscrea. Only in the early 10th century (more precisely in the year 911) the two groups of annals start to diverge considerably and it seems that from the 10th century onwards chronicles were first kept independently in Clonmacnoise.[10]

As regards the hagiographical sources it should suffice to point out here that there are four main versions of the Life of St. Ciarán, three in Latin, one in Irish. All four versions came down to us in the major Irish

---

10 T. M. CHARLES-EDWARDS, The Chronicle of Ireland, Liverpool 2006; K. HUGHES, Early Christian Ireland: Introduction to the sources, London 1972, pp. 101, 117-119; cf. G. MAC NIOCAILL, The medieval Irish annals, Dublin 1975, pp. 22f.; D. DUMVILLE/K. GRABOWSKI, Chronicles and annals of mediaeval Ireland and Wales. The Clonmacnoise-group of Texts, Woodbridge 1984, pp. 53-56.

hagiographical collections, in versions that are clearly 13th and 14th century revisions of earlier material.[11]

For our reconstruction of monastic dynasties in Clonmacnoise two methodological problems have to be kept in mind:

1. From the early 10th century onwards patronymic surnames came into use in Ireland. Ferdomnach Ua Maonaigh, abbot of Clonmacnoise, who died in 952, is one of the earliest examples in the Clonmacnoise annals. (Incidentially this particular surname indicates descent from a *manaig*, that is from an ecclesiastical tenant, who lived and worked on the church land). This means that prior to the 10th century it is quite difficult to identify members of one and the same family.

2. From the 10th century onward, independent chronicles were kept in Clonmacnoise. That means that scribes and chroniclers at work in Clonmacnoise had an active part in the writing and revising of history according to the respective needs of their times. One has to take into account that later additions and information about presumed ancestry might have found entry into to chronicles of the early times with hindsight.[12]

2. 2 Early monastic dynasties

Not surprisingly therefore, the earliest evidence for monastic dynasties in leading positions in Clonmacnoise dates from the 10th century. Amongst the eldest dynasties to be identified the above-mentioned Ua Maonaigh might be counted. According to the annals, Ferdomnach Ua Maonaigh, abbot of Clonmacnoise, died in 952. Later entries also associate him with the monastery of Glendalough. A certain Rechtabra mac Maonaigh was

---

11 The Latin and Irish Lives of St. Ciarán, ed. R. A. S. MACALISTER, London 1921; cf. R. SHARPE, Medieval Irish Saints' Lives, Oxford 1991, pp. 93-119, 227-246, 247-273.

12 Thus the 8th century figure Flann Sinna died according to the Annals of Ulster as abbot of Clonmacnoise in 732. The annals of Tigernach (at the time kept in Clonmacnoise) add that he was of the Ui Chremthainn, an Airgiallan tribe settled in the East, in the wider vicinity of the monastery of Louth; A. KEHNEL, Clonmacnois – the Church and lands of St. Ciarán: change and continuity in an Irish monastic foundation (6th to 16th century) (Vita regularis 8), Münster 1997, pp. 249f., 256.

possibly the abbot's brother, or may have been his father. He died as a priest in Clonmacnoise in the year 948. One Muiredach Ua Maonaigh died as an abbot in the nearby Roscrea two generations later, in 1006.[13]

Another of the early families is the Conaillech-Clan, that again is said to have roots in the Eastern parts of Ireland, South-Ulster. They supplied abbots, scribes and priests mainly in the 10th and 11th centuries (926–1044). Colmán son of Ailill died 926 as abbot and bishop of Clonmacnoise and the neighbouring monastery in Clonard. He might be called a second founder of Clonmacnoise. Under him the relation with the Clann Cholmáin kings of Meath (Flann Sina) were highly intensified: a stone church was built, independent chronicle keeping was begun in Clonmacnoise, and the famous Highcross in Clonmacnoise, the Cross of the Scriptures, was erected. An inscription commemorates Abbot Colmán for having made the cross for the contemporary king of Meath. The carvings on the cross show two men holding a pole, which is traditionally interpreted to show Ciarán and king Diarmait mac Cerbaill, the ultimate ancestor of the Clann Cholmán kings of Meath. According to the Chronicon Scotorum Colmán was of the Conaille Muirthemne seated in what is now county Louth, a little north of the monastery of Louth. The family was surnamed Conaillech after their tribal origin (Connaille Muirthemne) and remained active in Clonmacnoise in the 10th century. Máel Tuile, son of Colmán, died as scribe (ferleiginn) of Clonmacnoise in 923; one Diarmait Conaillech died as a scribe in the year 1000. Bresal Conaillech was abbot (comarba) of Clonmacnoise in the early 11th century († 1030). A certain Ailill, son of Bresal, died as resident priest in Clonmacnoise in 1044.[14]

2. 3 The Meic Cuinn na mBocht

The most prominent lay ecclesiastical dynasty was known as the Meic Cuinn na mBocht, the sons of Conn na mBocht. The family traces its origins back to Airgialla, near Louth in the North-eastern parts of Ireland. The family is said to be of the Mugdorna Maigen. Twenty-five members of the family are mentioned by name in the sources for the

---

13 KEHNEL, Clonmacnois, (note 12 above), pp. 259f.

14 Ibid., pp. 257f.

time between the 8th and the 12th century (758–1180). In fact, the annals – that were of course written in Clonmacnoise – provide an impressively detailed pedigree of the family. According to the Annals of Tigernach, a certain Gormán, the ultimate ancestor of the Meic Cuinn na mBocht was scribe and abbot in the monastery of Louth. He came to live for a year as an anchorite on the waters of the well in Clonmacnoise, and he is said to have died there in 758. His son Torbach was abbot of Armagh, his grandson Áedacán (son of Torbach, son of Gormán) followed his grandfather in the abbacy of Louth. He also ended his life on pilgrimage in Clonmacnoise in 835. Sometimes this monastic dynasty is alternatively named after its two seventh-century founders, namely "Muintir Gormán" or "Cinél Torbaig".

The grandson of Torbach called Éogan was again an anchorite in Clonmacnoise; he fathered Luchairén who took over the leadership in the scriptorium in Clonmacnoise as scribe or lector. Luchairén died in 865 and his son Ecertach took over the office as head of the Little Church (Eglais Beg) that was then probably the mortuary Chapel in Clonmacnoise. Ecertach had two sons, Óenacán and Dúnadach, who are said to have been fostered in Louth by bishop Caínchomrac. Apparently the family ties with Louth were still kept up in the 10th century. Óenacán later followed his father in the office as head of the Little Church and he is also mentioned as a bishop in his obituary from the year 949. His brother Dúnadach died as bishop of Clonmacnoise in the year 955.

The two brothers both had children: Bishop Dúnadach, son of Ecertach, fathered Dúnchad who held the position of the lector in Clonmacnoise and was also anchorite. He died in 1006 and is praised in the Annals of the Four Masters as head of the rule and history of Clonmacnoise. Bishop Óenacan († 949) in turn is mentioned in the Chronicon Scotorum to have been the grandfather (*germanus atavi*) of Conn na mBocht.

With this Conn na mBocht (= Conn of the Poor) we finally meat with the eponymous family member of the Meic Cuinn na mBocht. He is called Conn of the Poor; according to the Annals the reason why he was called Conn of the Poor was the number of poor that he used to feed habitually. In fact, this man must have enjoyed considerable wealth if we believe the Four Masters who twice insist on Conn's hospitality and generosity. He is said to have invited the poor in the year 1031 and he presented them with twenty cows of his own. The official title styles him head of the Céili Dé and the anchorites in Clonmacnoise.[15] Brian Ó CUIV suggested that the term 'Poor' (Irish: boicht) in this case refers to a new group of monastic dwellers that was either identical or closely associated with the Céili Dé, an older Irish reform movement, dating from the 8th century.[16] The two groups together formed the actual spiritual community within the monastic settlement.

When Conn died in 1060, he left a grand family behind. Five of his sons are individually named in the annals: Céilechair, who died as bishop in 1067; Máel Chiráin, who according to the Four Masters was abbot of Clonmacnoise and undertook major roadworks in the monastic settlement. Then there are Máel Finnén († 1056), Gilla Chríst – who died according to the Annals of the Four Masters as the best ecclesiastical student in Ireland in 1085 – and finally Máel Íosa († 1103). The latter's greatest merit was seemingly the quality of being a son of Conn na mBocht.

In the eleventh generation the family provided another abbot of Clonmacnoise with Cormac, son of Máel Finnén, grandson of Conn na mBocht, who died as vice-abbot in Clonmacnoise in 1103. His cousin Máel Muire, the son of bishop Céilechair mac Cuinn na mBocht, must surely be counted amongst the most famous of the Irish medieval scribes or writers, at least since he was identified as the reviser of the Book of the Dun Cow, the Lebor na hUidre.[17] Abbot Cormac had a son, named after grandfather Céilechair of the Meic Cuinn na mBocht. He died in 1134 and is commemorated as a most learned senior, as head of the council and fountain of wisdom and history. Finally, the death of another member of the family, Máel Muire, senior and wise man, is recorded in the Annals of the Four Masters for the year 1180.

To sum up: We have here a monastic dynasty that can be retraced in Clonmacnoise over four centuries and over more than twelve generations. Altogether, the Meic Cuinn na mBocht provided seven anchorites, three lectors, three 'heads' of the Little Church in

---

15 B. Ó CUÍV, Miscellanea 1. "Boicht" Chorcaige, in: Celtica 18 (1986), pp. 105-111.

16 Ibid.; see also P. O'DWYER, Celtic monks and the Culdee Reform, in: J. MACKEY (ed.), An introduction to Celtic Christianity, Edingburgh 1989, pp. 140-171.

17 T. Ó CONCHEANAINN, The reviser of Leabhar na hUidhre, in: Éigse 15 (1974) pp. 277-288.

Clonmacnoise, five bishops, one priest, two learned seniors and two 'heads of the Céili Dé'.

This example of the rise of a monastic dynasty is certainly quite extraordinary: In the 8th century, they started a family tradition as pious anchorites in Clonmacnoise. Then they took over leading offices and supplied bishops, scribes, seniors and wise men in the monastic settlement. In the 11th century – under Conn na mBocht – the dynasty asserted leadership and exercised authority as leading members of the Reform Community of the Poor and the Céili Dé in Clonmacnoise which were based in an appurtenance of Clonmacnoise, called Íseal Chiaráin. Finally, in the late 11th century, the family managed gradually to take over the church and holdings in Íseal Chiaráin as a family property.

One might argue that such examples simply highlight the desolate state of the Irish church as a whole, and especially in the eleventh century. One might go further and argue that members of Meic Cuinn na mBocht family were in leading positions in the monastic scriptorium of Clonmacnoise, and thus in charge of chronicle keeping in the monastery. Quite obviously it was very easy for them to stabilize their position by supplying the family with a decent pedigree, basically legitimizing the families' claims to leadership in Clonmacnoise by proof of a respectable past as a dynasty of pious anchorites, a tradition handed down over the generations from father to son in regular hereditary succession.

2. 4 Monastic dynasties in times of the church reform of the 12th century.

However, even if this might be so, the case is quite obvious: it can always be argued that this was exactly the situation to be abolished in the course of the Irish Church reform of the 12th century. And in fact, the Meic Cuinn na mBocht did disappear from leadership or at least from the annals of Clonmacnoise in the course of the reform movement of the 12th century. 1134 and 1180 are the only entries for members of the Meic Cuinn na mBocht in the 12th century and one might reckon here to encounter an immediate success of the activities of the Irish Reformers. However, there were successors in the leadership of the reform movement of the Céili Dé: One Uareirge Ua Nechtain died in this position in 1132. A certain Máel Mórda, son of Uareirge Ua Nechtain, succeeded his father in office and died in 1170, in the month of November. Uareirge, son of Máel Mórda, son of Uareirge Ua Nechtain died as 'one of the noble sages of Clonmacnoise' in succession of his father and grandfather in the year 1200. Here we have a clear case where one ecclesiastical dynasty displaced the other. The Ua Nechtain, a family from Connacht, took over the leading position of the Céili Dé Reform Community in Clonmacnoise and handed the office down in father-to-son succession over three generations throughout the 12th century.

In another sector of the monasteries' life the Ua Conghaile took over. This was a family from Tethba, northeast from Clonmacnoise that supplied masters of the guesthouse in Clonmacnoise throughout the 12th century (1093-1166). Áed Ua Conghaile († 1093), Ceinnéittigh Ua Conghaile († 1128), Céilechair Ua Conghaile († 1166) all died as masters of the guesthouse in Clonmacnoise.

A similar occurrence can be recognized in the office of the vice-abbacy in Clonmacnoise. In the eleventh century, members of the Uí Maelduin dominated this position. The family claimed common ancestry with the Clann Cholmáin kings of Meath. They supplied vice abbots in Clonmacnoise over three generations from 1021 to 1106: Longarg Ua Máeldúin died as vice-abbot in 1021; Conchobar, son of Fogartach Ua Máeldúin, died as his successor in 1089; Muiredach Ua Máeldúin held the same office until the year 1106. Another member of the family, Cormac Ua Máeldúin, was in charge of the school in Clonmacnoise and died as lector in 1073.[18]

One might again suggest that here the wind changed with the advent of the 12th century church reform. And in fact, both the Ua Conghaile as well as the Uí Maelduin disappeared from the scene.

However, again the needs of the reformers would not be bound up with the obligation of celibacy. Quite the opposite was the case: The dominance of the Uí Máeldúin in the vice-abbacy in Clonmacnoise was quite obviously broken, but only in order to give room to the rise of a rival dynasty: the Uí Máeleoin. This family could claim common ancestry with the Uí Conchobair kings of Connacht, neighbours of the monastery to the West. They rose to power in Clonmacnoise with the advent of the

18 KEHNEL, Clonmacnois, (note 12 above), p. 40.

reform and supplied its abbots throughout the 12th and 13th century (1127–1263). Gilla Chríst Ua Máeleoin died in 1127 as most famous abbot of the churches in Ireland, and is praised in the annals for his extensive renovations in the monastery. One Áed Ua Máeleoin was his successor and died in 1153, followed in office by Tigernach Ua Máeleoin who died in 1172. The Annals of Ulster record the death of Gilla Chríst, son of the abbot of Clonmacnoise, in the same year. In the year 1230 (according to the Annals of Clonmacnoise), Máel Muire Ua Máeleoin is praised as the 'happiness and prosperity of the superiors of the churches of Ireland'. Máel Chiaráin Ua Máeleoin died in 1263 and is the last abbot of Clonmacnoise who finds mention in the annals. Members of this Connacht family then took over the bishopric: Cathal Ua Máeleoin died as bishop of Clonmacnoise in 1208; Áed Ua Máeleoin, bishop of Clonmacnoise, drowned in the year 1220, his namesake and successor in the office retired in the Cistercian house of Kilbeggan in the year 1236.

2. 5 Hereditary succession, fathers and sons in lead of the church – a telltale sign of decay?

The most familiar explanatory scheme for these very obvious findings is that of decay and reform. The argument might be summarized as follows: The Irish Church was originally founded and then lead by ascetic monks, abbots and bishops who from the time of the arrival of St Patrick in the mid 5th to the 7th century established coherent ecclesiastical structures based on high asceticism and spiritual standards. Then suddenly, in the 8th century, the winds turned "when a break with traditional values can be seen."[19] The Golden Age of Irish Saints and Scholars came to an end. Increasing secularization, wealth and lay-patronage superseded Arcadian asceticism and cleared the way for decay, marked by the churches' assimilation to secular society, by the contract between church and laity and by changing goals and guiding concepts, namely power and influence instead of asceticism and spirituality. Within

---

19 J. LYDON, The making of Ireland. From ancient times to the present, London 1998, pp. 17f.

this process the rise of monastic dynasties has to be understood as an obvious sign of decay.[20]

Of course such a truncated version of the often told and retold "course of Irish History and Irish Church" cannot do justice to the many great achievements and research results in the field. However, ecclesiastical dynasties in this scheme of explanation clearly figure as a symptom of decline. This seems to me at least arguable. In fact, many of the formidable great achievements of Irish monks and nuns strangely coincide with the time 'after' the Golden Age. The dating of the Book of Kells to the 8th century is generally agreed about. Many other great artistic achievements in the Irish Church – it might suffice here to remind of the Cross of the Scriptures in Clonmacnoise made in the 9th century – date from the time from the 8th century onward. The same applies to the Irish ascetic tradition. Although there is no doubt that Ireland brought forth the oldest *libri paenientiales* in the 6th and 7th centuries, we have to bear in mind that many of the Irish Penitentials pass down to us in manuscripts from the 8th century and later.[21] In any case one should at least consider the possibility that the Irish Church brought forth both at the same time: extreme asceticism on a high spiritual level as well as ecclesiastical dynasties in leadership.

To sum up: The explanatory power of historical theories that equal hereditary succession in the leading offices of the church with "decay" – and consequently equal the abolition of this feature with "reform" – is at least doubtful. In fact, the evidence we have from Clonmacnoise seems to indicate that the reform movements of the eleventh and twelfth centuries were actually borne by the leading monastic dynasties. Thus we have the Meic Cuinn na mBocht in the 11th century in lead of the Ceili

---

20 D. O'CORÁINN, Ireland c. 800. Aspects of Society, in: D. Ó CRÓINÍN (ed.), A New History of Ireland, vol 1: Prehistoric and Early Ireland, Oxford 2005, pp. 549-608, here 584-600.

21 Cf. The Irish Penitentials, ed. L. BIELER (Scriptores Latini Hiberniae 5), Dublin 1963, pp. 1-11. Note also that not all of the 'late' compilations can be attributed to reform movements such as the Ceili Dé with its centre in Tallaght, near Dublin (see D. Binchy, Penitential Texts in Old Irish, in: The Irish Penitentials, ed. BIELER [see above] pp. 47-51); cf. J. KENNEY, Sources for the Early History of Ireland, vol. 1: Ecclesiastical, New York 1929; L. KÖRNTGEN, Studien zu den Quellen der frühmittelalterlichen Bußbücher, Sigmaringen 1993.

Dei movement and we have the Uí Máeleoin rising to leadership in the early 12th century, coeval with the advent of the Church reform.

One might look at the findings from a different angle and briefly recall the advantages of dynastic succession and family based organisation and management. First of all, there is the obvious advantage of 'familiarity'. The future elites are brought up within the community and therefore most familiar with its social and cultural contexts as well as with the natural surroundings of the estates they are expected to run themselves in a later state of their lives. Thus the guest master's son would always know how to run a guesthouse; a boy brought up in the household of the Head of the Culdees would certainly have little problems to take over a leading position in the monastic school. We might also take into account that family ties amongst the leading elite might increase individual motivation and commitment, since the promotion of business interest would at the same time promote family interest.

3. Why did history decide against fathers and sons in the monastery?

I suggest interpreting the Irish case presented above as an example that might show that dynastic principles in leadership of the church functioned very well – at least the case of Clonmacnoise in the times from the late 9th to the 12th century seems to show a functioning and rather successful model of ecclesiastical organisation based on dynastic principles. However, these hereditary principles did not succeed in the long run – they fell prey to the ever-growing call for clerical celibacy. Sons of priests and other clerics were increasingly marginalised in the Christian tradition and eventually declared illegal. The concept of clerical celibacy gained the victory over the idea of married clergy. The natural consequences of chastity, namely the lack of offspring, favoured celibate bachelors instead of 'fathers and sons' in lead of the Western Christian Church.

The question why this was the case has been answered from many different angles. We might briefly recapitulate here the most common arguments brought forth.[22] It has been suggested that the call for celibacy goes back to the times of the apostles. Renouncing wives and children

---

22 G. DENZLER, Die Geschichte des Zölibats, Freiburg 1993, pp. 60-121.

for the sake of discipleship was the proper way to serve God in the days of the New Testament. Especially those immediately involved in the Christian Cult would have been required to abstain from intercourse with women. The historical developments toward clerical celibacy till the final breakthrough in the 12th century would thus be a gradual return to the roots of Christian life according to the New Testament.[23] A cultural anthropologist might argue that times of abstinence or even lifelong abstinence are well known in many different cultures and are prescribed for priests and all those professionally engaged in religious rituals. Moreover, ascetic practices and the repression of basic bodily impulses form a stable implement in the education of future elites and their training for excellence and highest performance in many different fields, be it sports, the arts, classical learning or leadership. Also from a sociological point of view these formative aspects of celibacy might be called a mode to produce elites in societies dominated by family structures. Celibacy is in this case a mode to renounce mingling with the world at large for the benefit of a greater good, be it God, be it learning, be it the care of souls. Finally one might argue with economic interests. An institution in possession of economic goods, which far outruns the size of a family business, needs to find ways not to dilapidate these goods in order to avoid impoverishment. Just think of a local priest bound to life from the income of his parish: if he has to feed a wife and children, the parishioners would soon be overstressed. Moreover, if his sons and daughters lay claim to their inheritance the church might eventually dissolve into innumerable tiny little units. This was one of the important points at the opening of the Council in Pavia in 1022 where Pope Benedict VIII clearly named the married clergy as the one responsible for the impoverishment of the church by splitting up its possessions amongst their offspring.[24]

All these theories share the conviction that the 'rational' argument behind the ever-growing demand for clerical celibacy can be found in its

---

23 Here summarized after HEID, Zölibat in der frühen Kirche (note 3 above). He cites Christian COCHINI, Origines apostoliques du célibat sacerdotal, Paris 1981; R. CHOLIJ, Clerical Celibacy in East and West, Worcester 1989; A. M. STICKLER, Der Klerikerzölibat. Seine Entwicklungsgeschichte und seine theologischen Grundlagen, Abensberg 1993; H. KRUSE, Eheverzicht im Neuen Testament und in der Frühkirche, in: Forum für katholische Kirche 1 (1985), pp. 94-116.

24 DENZLER, Geschichte des Zölibats (note 22 above), pp. 96f.

functional and practical aspects for the process of institutionalization of the Medieval Church.

There are other concepts that argue with more 'external' reasons: Conrad LEYSER stressed the political dimension and the power of asceticism and celibacy. In his book on authority and asceticism he examines the formation of the Christian ascetic tradition in the Western Roman Empire during the period of the barbarian invasions in the 5th and 6th centuries. He found out that in an aggressively competitive political context one of the most articulate claims to power was made, paradoxically, by men who had renounced 'the world' committing them to a life of spiritual discipline in the hope of gaining entry to an otherworldly kingdom. Often dismissed as mere fanaticism or open hypocrisy, the language of ascetic authority was, as Conrad LEYSER shows, both carefully honed and well understood in the late Roman and early medieval Mediterranean. LEYSER charts the development of this new moral rhetoric by abbots, teachers, and bishops from the time of Augustine of Hippo to that of St Benedict and Gregory the Great.[25] Albrecht DIEM undertook an examination of asceticism and sexual chastity as an essential organizational principle in early medieval monastic communities.[26] From within the monastic world the call for asceticism and celibacy eventually spread amongst the clergy. Arnold ANGENENDT and others investigated the roots of chastity and celibacy outside the confines of Christian traditions in general religious concepts, namely in the need for cultic purity.[27] According to this theory, Christian priests and clerics were originally married and within their marriage sexually active. The decisive change took place not so much in the Churches' attitude towards sexuality, but rather in the understanding of the mass and the service to the lord. The Christian rite gradually gained a meaning as a ritual sacrifice. These were not in the first place genuine Christian ideas, but rather common religious ideas about cultic purity.

---

25 C. LEYSER, Authority and Asceticism from Augustine to Gregory the Great, Oxford 2000.

26 A. DIEM, Das monastische Experiment. Die Rolle der Keuschheit bei der Entstehung des westlichen Klosterwesens (Vita Regularis 24), Münster 2005.

27 A. ANGENENDT, Geschichte der Religiosität im Mittelalter, Darmstadt 1997, pp. 453-462, 570-572; LUTTERBACH, Sexualität (note 5 above) pp. 234f.; P. GERLITZ, Keuschheit (Religionsgeschichtlich), in: Theologische Realenzyklopädie 18 (1989), pp. 113-119; BROWN, Keuschheit der Engel, (note 2 above), p. 40.

Thus, it came that both in the Western and Eastern Church priests and laity would refrain from intercourse at the days of mass. The developments in the 4th century, when daily mass for priests became obligatory, lead necessarily to constant abstinence and therefore to celibate and childless clergy. The demand to approach the deity with pure hands forms part of the purity-prescriptions of many pagan antique religions.

"No fathers and sons in leading positions in the Christian Church" might in this context appear as merely a by-product, an unintended consequence of the implementation of general religious concepts concerning the need for ritual purity within the very heart of the cult.

4. No fathers and sons in ecclesiastical leadership!?

Of course it is a well-known fact that despite the splendid 'normative' victory of clerical celibacy – generally dated to the 12th century – deacons, priests, and bishops continued to have wives and sons and daughters all through the Middle Ages and beyond.[28] It might be argued that the general religious requirements for ritual purity could not stand up to their transformation in a religious practice which made purity a "life-time" rather than a momentary "obligation" confined to certain times of the year or to special days. Bernhard SCHIMMELPFENNIG's study on celibacy and illegitimate sons of priest is still most instructive from evidence in late medieval papal registers concerning cases mostly from Southern Germany and France. He cites the examples such as a local priest in Schwäbisch Hall who in the late 14th century had himself, his wife (Pfarrmaid) and his children portrayed in the choir of the parish church. Or else there is the story of sons who minister their father as altar boys. SCHIMMELPFENNIG reconstructs what in Ireland would be called 'clerical dynasties' from the papal letters of dispensation: a priest asks dispensation as the son of a monk and a priest's daughter; the monk in question is himself the son of a priest and a priest's daughter, his mother's mother in turn was the daughter of a priest and his cook. Finally he brought forth evidence that the education of clerical offspring was well organized on a local level. In some cases the local communities

---

28 SCHIMMELPFENNIG, Zölibat, (note 9 above), pp. 1-46.

apparently paid for the education of the sons of their parish clergy; in another case there seems to have been an official agreement between the bishop and the local parish priests to exchange their children temporarily in order to guarantee for their education.[29] The evidence brought to light by SCHIMMELPFENNIG initialised series of research in this field, altogether making quite clear that 'clerical families' were a rather well-established feature in the medieval church, be it insular or continental.

Obviously it was not the lack of clerical offspring, which overruled father-to-son succession in leading ecclesiastical positions. The decisive point was the lack of legal rights for the sons of the clergy. The status 'son of priest' might do no harm to a person in the local context, the person in question might even profit from it, gain access to circles, offices and authority, closed to others. However, the status of a son of a priest would never suffice to claim hereditary rights in conflict situations.

So back to the introductory question: what is wrong with fathers and sons in the medieval Church? The answer lies close at hand and was obvious from the very start: the ascetic obligation for clerical celibacy – the result of the victory of general religious concepts of ritual purity over genuine Christian ideas – necessarily leads to a lack of offspring in the priestly class. However, the 'side-effects' of these developments are manifold: 1. a break with the dynastic principles, prevailing in medieval society; 2. the elaboration of compensatory subsystems of kinship, i.e. concepts of spiritual fathership and spiritual kinship; 3. a constant 'thorn in the flesh of the medieval church', a structural point of weakness in the ecclesiastical claims to power.

The church deliberately renounced the worldly – that is dynastic – principles of leadership and power. Instead, systems of spiritual kinship evolved in the ecclesiastical and monastic context, they replaced the principles of secular leadership. However, and here we come to the point where further investigations might be worthwhile, the obligation for celibacy made the clerical elite 'vulnerable'. No fathers and sons in the medieval church from the 12th century onward has been a repeated demand but never a fact. This demand made the clergy vulnerable, it confined the claims to power of the literate clerical elite and thus made it compatible with secular society in the long turn. The standard critique against the lustful priest and his many sons and daughters wanders

---

29 Ibid., pp. 29-32.

throughout the Middle Ages in the topic formulations of the anti-clerical traditions and it might be regarded as a necessary prerequisite for the enduring existence of the church as an institution. Elites in order to survive in the longue durée need structural points of vulnerability. We might embed these ideas in a broader concept of what I call the 'powers of weakness'. It is suggested here that the obligation to celibacy made the clerical elite vulnerable. This obligation had the function of the 'thorn in the flesh' of the legitimising moral claims of the clerical elite. Vulnerability in turn might be an indispensable prerequisite for the enduring exercise of power. Achilles' heel was both at the same time: limiting and enabling the hero's power.

Let me conclude the paper with an exemplary case from the Irish sources. The annals of Ulster record in the year 1498 the death of Cathal Og MacManus, archdeacon of Clogher, who himself compiled a great part of the annals and who entered the births of his children in the annals as they occurred. Some of his children became clerics. His obituary reads as a long eulogy, most likely composed by his son Tomás, who succeeded his father in the archdeaconry. The deceased archdeacon is praised as chest of wisdom, as fount of charity and mildness and meekness, as dove for purity of heart and as "turtle-dove for chastity" [*turtuir ar endca*].[30] This praise seems to express an otherwise rarely traceable knowledge about the close alliance between power and weakness, the alliance of the 'powers of dynastic succession' combined with the 'weakness of ascetic renunciation'.

---

30 Annals of Ulster, ed. with translation by B. Mac CARTHY, Dublin 1895, here s. a. 1498, vol. III, p. 428f. Cf. A. Gwynn, Cathal Og Mac Maghnusa and the Annals of Ulster, ed. by N. O Muraile, Enniskillen 1998 (first published in Clogher Record 2/2 [1958], pp. 230-243; 2/3 [1959], pp. 370-384). See also N. O MURAILE, Cathal Og Mac Maghnusa: His Time, Life and Legacy, in: Clogher Record 16/2 (1998), pp. 45-64 and K. SIMMS, Cathal Og Mac Maghnusa (1439-1498) in: Oxford Dictionary of National Bibliography, Oxford 2004.

GENERATIONENKONFLIKTE IM KLOSTER?

Gedanken zum Mit- und Nebeneinander von Jung und Alt in spätmittelalterlichen Frauenkonventen

GABRIELA SIGNORI

Bekanntermaßen kann der Begriff Generation zwei unterschiedliche Sachverhalte bedeuten: Zum einen lässt er sich – sehr unspezifisch – als Gegensatz zwischen jung und alt begreifen. In diesem Fall spricht die Sozialforschung, der Begriff scheint mir etwas unglücklich gewählt, von einem 'biologisch-genealogischen' Generationenverständnis.[1] Zum andern bezeichnet der Generationenbegriff aber auch Altersgruppen, die durch eine gemeinsame, in der Geschichte verankerte Erfahrung miteinander verbunden sind. In diesem Fall ist weniger das Alter, denn der gemeinsame Erfahrungshintergrund das generationenkonstituierende Kriterium. Bezeichnet wird dieses Generationenverständnis komplementär zum 'biologisch-genealogischen' als ein 'historisch-genealogisches'. Der Begriff ist nicht minder unglücklich.

Eng mit dem 'historisch-genealogischen' Generationenbegriff verknüpft scheinen die zumal im 20. Jahrhundert regelmäßig aufbrechenden Generationenkonflikte. Ob sie wirklich ein Kind der Moderne sind, darüber lässt sich streiten. Nach August NITSCHKE kannten den Generationenkonflikt, wenngleich in anderer Gestalt, schon die mittelalterlichen Gesellschaften.[2] Als paradigmatisch begreift er die seit

---

1 Zum Generationenbegriff vgl. H. JAEGER, Generationen in der Geschichte, in: Geschichte und Gesellschaft 3 (1977), S. 429-452; T. K. HAREVEN, Aging and Generational Relations: A Historical and Life Course Perspective, in: Annual Review of Sociology 20 (1994), S. 437-461; U. JUREIT (Hg.), Generationen. Zur Relevanz eines wissenschaftlichen Grundbegriffs, Hamburg 2005.

2 A. NITSCHKE, Junge Rebellen. Mittelalter, Neuzeit, Gegenwart: Kinder verändern die Welt, München 1985, S. 75; vgl. J. A. SCHULTZ, Medieval Adolescence. The Claims of History and the Silence of German Narrative, in: Speculum 66 (1991), S. 519-539; DERS., The Knowledge of Childhood in the German Middle Ages, 1100-1350, Philadelphia 1995, S. 165f.

der Spätantike überlieferten Konversionsberichte, die bemerkenswert oft von jungen Menschen handeln.[3] Auch Bernard GUENÉE geht von der Existenz spezifisch mittelalterlicher Generationenkonflikte aus. Was im Konfliktfall allerdings genau mit jung und alt gemeint ist, ist selten augenfällig.[4] Die prosopographischen Befunde decken sich keineswegs immer mit der von den Zeitgenossen gewählten Begrifflichkeit (jung oder alt). Noch schwieriger als Alterskohorten scheint es, beim Gewicht, das die mittelalterlichen Gesellschaften der Tradition beimessen, unterschiedliche Erfahrungshintergründe zu erfassen. Das gilt nicht nur für die Bereiche Politik und Bildung, mit denen sich GUENÉE auseinandergesetzt hat, sondern auch für die spätmittelalterliche Klosterwelt, mit der ich mich im Folgenden beschäftigen will. Der erste Teil meiner Ausführungen ist der Altersfrage gewidmet; der zweite dem 'Generationenkonflikt'. Ich beschränke mich auf Frauenklöster, vornehmlich aus dem Dominikanerorden.

Seit den 80er Jahren ist in Auseinandersetzung mit Philippe ARIÈS provokativen Thesen sehr viel über die Kindheit im Mittelalter geforscht

---

[3] H. GRUNDMANN, Adelsbekehrungen im Hochmittelalter. *Conversi* und *nutriti* im Kloster, in: J. FLECKENSTEIN / K. SCHMID (Hgg.), Adel und Kirche. Gerd Tellenbach zum 65. Geburtstag dargebracht von Freunden und Schülern, Freiburg/Basel/Wien 1968, S. 325-345; J. EHLERS, Adlige Stiftungen und persönliche Konversion. Zur Sozialgeschichte früher Prämonstratenserkonvente, in: H. BEUMANN (Hg.), Geschichte und Verfassungsgefüge, Frankfurter Festgabe für Walter Schlesinger (Frankfurter Historische Abhandlungen 5), Wiesbaden 1973, S. 32-55; G. R. EVANS, A Change of Mind in Some Scholars of the Eleventh and Early Twelfth Centuries, in: D. BAKER (Hg.), Religious Motivation. Biographical and Sociological Problems for the Church Historian, Oxford 1978, S. 27-38; E. TREMP, Laien im Kloster. Das hochmittelalterliche Reformmönchtum unter dem Ansturm der Adelskonversionen, in: E. C. LUTZ / E. TREMP (Hgg.), Pfaffen und Laien. Ein mittelalterlicher Antagonismus? (Scrinium Friburgense 10), Freiburg 1999, S. 33-56; J. MULDOON (Hg.), Varieties of Religious Conversion in the Middle Ages, Gainesville/Tallahassee 1997.

[4] Die Schwierigkeiten, in vormodernen Gesellschaften Generationenkonflikte zu "diagnostizieren", zeigen sich u.a. bei B. GUENÉE, *Scandalum inter antiquos et juvenes theologos*. Un conflit de générations à la Faculté de théologie de Paris au début du XVe siècle? in: Le couple, l'ami et le prochain (Histoire et société. Mélanges offerts à Georges Duby 1), Aix-en-Provence 1992, S. 147-155 ; DERS., L'âge des personnes authentiques. Ceux qui comptent dans la société médiévale sont-ils jeunes ou vieux?, in: F. AUTRAND (Hg.), Prosopographie et genèse de l'État moderne, Paris 1986, S. 249-279.

worden[5], auch über die Kindheit im Kloster (Oblaten, Donaten, Klosterschüler und -schülerinnen und ähnliches mehr). Nahtlos ließ sich dabei an die ältere Ordensforschung anschließen, blicken wir unter anderem auf die Studien der Benediktiner Ursmer BERLIÈRE (1861-1932) und Jean LECLERCQ (1911-1993) zurück.[6] Das Ordensideal war über die Jahrhunderte hindurch – für Ulrich von Cluny († 1093) genauso wie für Pater BERLIÈRE – die *vocation murie*, die Berufung des reifen Mannes.[7] Die Praxis, kleine Kinder im Kloster aufzunehmen, reicht weit zurück[8],

---

5 P. ARIES, L'enfant et la vie familiale sous l'Ancien Régime, Paris 1960. Vgl. B. A. HANAWALT, Medievalists and the Study of Childhood, in : Speculum 7 (2002), S. 440-460.

6 J. LECLERCQ, Deux opuscules sur la formation des jeunes moines, in: Revue d'ascétique et de mystique 132 (1957), S. 387-399; DERS., Pédagogie et formation spirituelle du VIe au IXe siècle, in: La scuola nell'Occidente latino dell'alto medioevo (Settimane di studio del centro italiano di studi sull'alto medioevo 19), Spoleto 1972, S. 255-290; DERS., Textes sur la vocation et formation des moines au moyen âge, in: Corona gratiarum. Miscellanea patristica, historica et liturgica Eligio Dekkers oblata (Instrumenta patristica 11), 2 Bde., Brügge/Gravenhage 1975, S. 169-194.

7 U. BERLIÈRE, Le recrutement dans les monastères bénédictins aux XIIIe et XIVe siècles (Académie Royale de Belgique. Classe des lettres. Mémoires 18, 6), Brüssel 1923, S. 5.

8 D. ILLMER, Formen der Erziehung und Wissensvermittlung im frühen Mittelalter. Quellenstudien zur Frage der Kontinuität des abendländischen Erziehungswesens (Münchener Beiträge zur Mediävistik und Renaissance-Forschung 7), München 1971; M. M. MCLAUGHLIN, Survivors and Surrogates: Children and Parents from the Ninth to the Thirteenth Centuries, in: L. DE MAUSE (Hg.), The History of Childhood, New York 1974, S. 101-181; P. RICHE, L'enfant dans la société monastique au XIIe siècle, in: Pierre Abélard, Pierre le Vénérable. Les courants philosophiques, littéraires et artistiques en occident au milieu du XIIe siècle (Colloques internationaux du Centre National de la Recherche scientifique 546), Paris 1975, S. 689-701; K. SCHREINER, Hirsau, Urban II. und Johannes Trithemius. Ein gefälschtes Papstprivileg als Quelle für das Geschichts-, Reform- und Rechtsbewußtsein des Klosters Hirsau im 12. Jahrhundert, in: Deutsches Archiv 43 (1987), S. 469-530, hier S. 484-489; P. A. QUINN, Better than the Sons of Kings – Boys and Monks in the Early Middle Ages (Studies in History and Culture 2), New York/Bern/Frankfurt am Main 1989; M. LAHAYE-GEUSEN, Das Opfer der Kinder. Ein Beitrag zur Liturgie- und Sozialgeschichte des Mönchtums im Hohen Mittelalter (Münsteraner theologische Abhandlungen 13), Altenberge 1991; M. DE JONG, In Samuel's Image. Child Oblation in the Early Medieval West (Brill's Studies in Intellectual History 12), Leiden/New York/Köln 1996; DIES., Growing Up in a Carolongian Monastery. Magister Hildemar and his Oblates, in: Journal of Medieval History 9 (1983), S. 99-128; J. DORAN, Oblation or Obligation? A Canonical

ebenso weit aber auch die entsprechenden Verbote, wie die 'Jungfrauenregel' des Caesarius von Arles († 542) zeigt.[9] Früh auch wird das Verhältnis zwischen Jung und Alt im Kloster als eines der Über- bzw. Unterordnung definiert. Die Alten stehen über den Jungen, leiten sie, kontrollieren sie, erziehen sie.[10] Zwar mögen Teilbereiche weiterhin sehr unscharfe Konturen aufweisen;[11] dennoch sind wir, was die wissenschaftliche Durchdringung des Gegenstandes anbelangt, ungleich besser über die Jungen als über die alten Menschen im Kloster informiert.[12] Ebenso wenig Beachtung gefunden hat, klammern wir die Bereiche Bildung und Erziehung aus, das Mit- oder Nebeneinander von jung und alt und damit auch das Mit- oder Nebeneinander unterschiedlicher Erfahrungshorizonte.

Die normative Literatur der Jungfrauenspiegel verschluckt tendenziell jede Art von Differenzerfahrung. Dazu gehören die den Klosteralltag bestimmenden und regulierenden Altersunterschiede. Dem *Speculum virginum* (12. Jahrhundert) zufolge sind alle 'Jungfrauen', egal wie alt, gleichermaßen Bräute Christi und werden dementsprechend als junge Frauen imaginiert.[13] Dies scheint, vorsichtig formuliert, zugleich Teil

---

Ambiguity, in: D. WOOD (Hg.), The Church and Childhood (Studies in Church History 31), Oxford 1994, S. 127-141; I. COCHELIN, Enfants, jeunes et vieux au monastère. La perception du cycle de vie dans les sources clunisiennes (909-1156), Montréal 1996; H. LUTTERBACH, Gotteskindschaft, Kultur- und Sozialgeschichte eines christlichen Ideals, Freiburg/Basel/Wien 2003.

9 Césaire d'Arles, Règle des vierges, ed. A. DE VOGÜE / J. COURREAU, in: Œuvres monastiques. Œuvres pour les moniales (Sources chrétienne 345), Paris 1988, Bd. 1, S. 187.

10 Caesarius von Arles zufolge sollten alte Nonnen die jungen überwachen (ebd., 182f.) ; vgl. I. COCHELIN, *In senectute bona*: pour une typologie de la vieillesse dans l'hagiographie monastique des XIIe et XIIIe siècles, in: H. DUBOIS / M. ZINK (Hgg.), Les âges de la vie au moyen âge (Cultures et civilisations médiévales 7), Paris 1992, S. 119-138, hier S. 132ff.

11 I. COCHELIN, Peut-on parler de noviciat à Cluny pour les Xe-XIe siècles?, in: Revue Mabillon, NS 9 (1998), S. 17-52.

12 Zu den *seniores* vgl. CHOCHELIN, *In senectute bona* (wie Anm. 10), passim, sowie G. CONSTABLE, *Seniores* et *pueri* à Cluny au Xe, XIe siècles, in: Le moine, le clerc et le prince (Histoire et société. Mélanges offerts à Georges Duby 3), Aix-en-Provence 1992, S. 17-24.

13 Speculum virginum. Jungfrauenspiegel, ed. J. SEYFARTH (Fontes Christiani 30), 4 Bde., Freiburg/Basel/Wien 2001, hier Bd. 3, S. 564-646; vgl. M. BERNARDS, *Speculum virginum*. Geistigkeit und Seelenleben der Frau im Hochmittelalter (Beihefte

ihres Selbstverständnisses als Klosterjungfrauen gewesen zu sein.[14] Unter die Jungfrauen mischen sich aber auch zahlreiche Ehefrauen und Witwen. Das *Speculum virginum* übernimmt die spätantike Vorstellung von den unterschiedlich großen Verdiensten der drei Stände.[15] Etwas anders gewichtet der pseudo-bernhardinische *Liber de modo bene vivendi.*[16] Ihm folgt zwei Jahrhunderte später Nikolaus von Kues († 1464). Die Waldschwestern von Halltal mahnt Cusanus nachdrücklich, nicht allein Jungfrauen aufzunehmen, sondern auch Witwen und Ehefrauen, *dann auch oft Wittib Gott strenger und mit größerer Begird dienen, nachdem sie unter den Trübsalen und Kummernus diser Welt versuecht haben.*[17]

Wo immer uns die Quellenlage Einblick in die Altersstruktur eines Frauenklosters gewährt, ergibt sich über die Jahrhunderte hinweg ein bemerkenswert heterogenes Bild. Neben Kindern, die dem Kloster geweiht oder dem Kloster zur Erziehung anvertraut worden sind, begegnen wir jungen Frauen, aber, wie angedeutet, auch zahlreichen Witwen und Ehefrauen (z. T. als *conversae* bezeichnet).[18] Letztere bilden,

---

zum Archiv für Kulturgeschichte 16), Köln/Wien ²1982, S. 186; J. BUGGE, *Virginitas.* An Essay in the History of a Medieval Ideal (Archives internationales d'histoire des idées 17), Den Hague 1975; K. COYNE KELLY, Performing Virginity and Testing Chastity in the Middle Ages, London/New York 2000.

14 P. D. JOHNSON, *Mulier et Monialis.* The Medieval Nun's Self-Image, in: Thought 64 (1989), S. 242-253.

15 Speculum virginum, ed. SEYFARTH (wie Anm. 13), ebd.; BERNARDS, *Speculum virginum* (wie Anm. 13), S. 40-72.

16 Ebd., S. 51.

17 G. FUßENEGGER, Nikolaus von Kues und die Waldschwestern von Halltal, in: N. GRASS (Hg.), Cusanus Gedächtnisschrift (Forschungen zur Rechts- und Kulturgeschichte), Innsbruck 1970, S. 381-456, hier S. 421.

18 Vgl. u. a. E. PERSOONS, Lebensverhältnisse in den Frauenklöstern der Windesheimer Kongregation in Belgien und in den Niederlanden, in: Klösterliche Sachkultur des Spätmittelalters (Österreichische Akademie der Wissenschaften. Phil.-Hist. Klasse 367. Veröffentlichungen des Instituts für mittelalterliche Realienkunde Österreichs 3), Wien 1980, S. 73-111; P. D. JOHNSON, Equal in Monastic Profession. Religious Women in medieval France, Chicago/London 1991, S. 27-34; J. WALMSLEY, The Early Abbesses, Nuns and Female Tenants of the Abbey of Holy Trinity, Caen, in: Journal of Ecclesiastical History 48 (1997), S. 425-444; K. BRUNNER, *Quae est ista, quae ascendit per desertum.* Aspekte des Selbstverständnisses geistlicher Frauen im 12. Jahrhundert, in: Mitteilungen des Instituts für Österreichische Geschichtsforschung 107 (1999), S. 271-310; J.

auf das spätere Mittelalter bezogen, ein weitgehend unbearbeitetes Forschungsfeld, obschon es an Beispielen nicht mangelt.[19]

Nicht nur die Altersstruktur, auch das Spektrum unterschiedlicher Lebensformen innerhalb des Klosters ist bemerkenswert breit[20]: Für viele Klosterschülerinnen ist das Klosterleben bloß eine Phase; andere legen später die Profess ab; noch andere, vorwiegend ältere Frauen, erstehen sich eine Pfründe und ziehen sich in kleine Häuschen in unmittelbarer Klosternähe zurück.[21] Noch andere leben im klostereigenen Kranken- oder Siechenhaus. Auch diejenigen, die das Bett nicht mehr verlassen können, sind fester Bestandteil der Klostergemeinschaft.[22] Das ist bekannt. Systematisch erfasst sind die beiden Paralleleinrichtungen aber

---

RÖHRKASTEN, The Mendicant Houses of Medieval London 1221-1539 (Vita regularis 21), Münster 2004, S. 89-102.

19 Zur Konversion der Gisela von Umkirch notiert die Priorin Anna von Munzingen (1316-1317 u. 1319-1327), die Verfasserin des Adelhausener Schwesternbuchs, drei Jahre lang habe sie auf ihren Mann einwirken müssen: *Darnach halff ir Gott, dz er sich schied vnd für zem Tütschen huse mit eim sune vnd für si gen Adelhusen mit einre dochter.* Die Chronik der Anna von Munzingen, ed. J. KÖNIG, in: Freiburger Diözesan-Archiv 13 (1880), S. 129-236, hier S. 164; vgl. U. DENNE, Die Frauenklöster im spätmittelalterlichen Freiburg im Breisgau, ihre Einbindung in den Orden und in die städtische Kommunität (Forschungen zur oberdeutschen Landesgeschichte 39), München 1997, S. 249. Zum hohen Mittelalter vgl. R. BIRKMEYER, Ehetrennung und monastische Konversion im Hochmittelalter, Berlin 1998, sowie M. M. WILKINSON, The Juridical Position of *Conversae* in the Late Eleventh and Early Twelfth Centuries: The Nuns of Fontevrault and Marcigny, in: N. BOUTER (Hg.), Les Religieuses dans le cloître et dans le monde des origines á nos jours. Actes du Deuxième Colloque International du C.E.R.C.O.R, St. Etienne 1994, S. 713-730.

20 Breit erschlossen ist vor allem die Gruppe der Laienbrüder bzw. Konversen (wobei der Begriff *conversus/conversa* mehrdeutig ist), vgl. u. a. E. TREMP, Laien im Kloster (wie Anm. 3); J. WOLLASCH, A propos des *fratres barbati* de Hirsau, in: Le moine, le clerc et le prince (Histoire et société. Mélanges offerts à Georges Duby 3), Aix-en-Provence 1992, S. 37-48; M. TÖPFER, Die Konversen der Zisterzienser. Untersuchungen über ihren Beitrag zur mittelalterlichen Blüte des Ordens (Berliner historische Studien 10, Ordensstudien 4), Berlin 1983; B. FRANK, Konversen und Laien in benediktinischen Reformklöstern des 15. Jahrhunderts, in: K. ELM (Hg.), Beiträge zur Geschichte der Konversen im Mittelalter (Berliner Historische Studien 2, Ordensstudien 1), Berlin 1980, S. 49-66.

21 M. OLIVA, The Convent and the Community in Late Medieval England. Female Monasteries in the Diocese of Norwich, 1350-1540 (Studies in the history of medieval religion 12), Woodbridge 1998, S. 45-48.

22 FUßENEGGER, Nikolaus von Kues (wie Anm. 17), S. 412-414.

nicht.[23] Noch andere schließlich wählen das schwierige Dasein als Laienschwester. Auch von Laienbrüdern (in Frauenkonventen) ist verschiedentlich die Rede.[24]

Das Alter der Nonnen zu bestimmen ist gewöhnlich unmöglich. Dazu fehlen uns zumeist unverzichtbare Instrumente wie Professbücher oder Konventslisten.[25] Auch der Witwenstatus erlaubt keinen Rückschluss auf das Alter; er verrät allein, im Vergleich zu den Mädchen und den jungen Frauen, die im Kloster aufgewachsen sind, einen anderen, einen weltlichen Erfahrungshintergrund. Das gilt gleichermaßen für die Ehefrauen.[26] Thematisiert wird diese Erfahrung jedoch selten; so sie überhaupt Erwähnung findet, wird sie rhetorisch als Antithese benutzt.[27]

Etwas gesprächiger erweisen sich im Hinblick auf die Altersfrage neben den Viten allein die Schwesternbücher, eine vor allem für die Darstellung mystischer und paramystischer Erlebnisse bekannte Literaturform.[28] Meist werden die Klosterfrauen darin allerdings sehr unspezifisch

---

23 Fast jede Klostermonographie nennt solche Pfründner und Pfründnerinnen, ein systematischer Überblick liegt aber nicht vor. Zur Frühzeit vgl. G. JORDAN, "Nichts als Nahrung und Kleidung". Laien und Kleriker als Wohngäste bei den Mönchen von St. Gallen und Redon (8. und 9. Jahrhundert) (Europa im Mittelalter. Band 9), Berlin 2007.

24 Der Nonnen von Engelthal Büchlein von der genaden uberlast, ed. K. SCHRÖDER (Bibliothek des litterarischen Vereins Stuttgart 108), Stuttgart/Tübingen 1871, S. 10: *Einew kom her zu uns, die hiezze Reichilt von Gemmershaim, mit irm elichen wirt, der wart ein convers*; bei Alheit von Herspruk heißt es: *die kom mit irm ewirt her zu unserer geselleschaft. Er hiez Heinrich, und der legt dem covent groz gut an den baw* (ebd., S. 15), vgl. JOHNSON, Equal in Monastic Profession (wie Anm. 18), S. 29f.

25 A. MÜLLER, Studien zur Besitz- und Sozialgeschichte des Dominikanerklosters St. Katharinental bei Dießenhofen, Villingen 1971, S. 26f. (Fragmente eines Professbuches). Mehrere Konventslisten müssen sich aus Frauenklöstern der Windesheimer Kongregation erhalten haben. Auf Altersfragen hin untersucht sind sie aber nicht. Vgl. PERSOONS, Lebensverhältnisse (wie Anm. 18), S. 84f.

26 In den Kurzviten werden diese Erfahrungen zumeist ausgeblendet oder als literarische Kontrastfolie verwendet, um der Konversion plastischere Gestalt zu verleihen.

27 Zu den Vorurteilen alten Frauen gegenüber vgl. J. M. ZIOLKOWSKI, The Obscenities of Old Women. Vetularity and Vernacularity, in: DERS. (Hg.), Obscenity. Social Control and Artistic Creation in the European Middle Ages (Cultures, Beliefs and Traditions 4), Leiden/Boston/Köln 1998, S. 73-89.

28 Vgl. u.a. O. LANGER, Christliche Mystik im Mittelalter. Mystik und Rationalisierung – Stationen eines Konflikts, Darmstadt 2004; S. BÜRKLE, Literatur im Kloster.

einfach als jung oder als alt bezeichnet, mit Ausnahme besonders junger und besonders alter Frauen. Letztere verkörpern sozusagen leibhaftige Archive der Klostergeschichte. Sie sind eine wichtige Informationsquelle für die Schreiberinnen der Schwesternbücher.[29]

Zahlreich belegt sind Mädchen, die zwischen fünf und zehn Jahren ins Kloster kamen.[30] Vereinzelt ist aber auch von jüngeren Kindern die Rede. Bei Willi von Konstanz heißt es, sie sei drei gewesen, als man sie dem Kloster Töß übergeben habe. Da aber sei sie gar *ellend*, d. h. einsam, auf sich selbst gestellt gewesen und habe "von niemandem Trost empfangen".[31] Im Alter erkrankte sie und wurde geistig verwirrt. An Gott aber habe sie sich noch erinnern können und stets aufmerksam gelauscht, wenn sein Name fiel. Schwester Christina hingegen war schon zwölf Jahre alt, als ihre Mutter sie dem Kloster Kirchberg übergab. Es sei

---

Historische Funktion und rhetorische Legitimation frauenmystischer Texte des 14. Jahrhunderts (Bibliotheca Germanica 38), Tübingen/Basel 1999; L. P. HINDSLEY, The Mystics on Engelthal. Writings from a Medieval Monastery, Houndmills 1998; B. W. ACKLIN ZIMMERMANN, Gott im Denken berühren. Die theologischen Implikationen der Nonnenviten (Dokimion 14), Freiburg 1993; U. PETERS, *Vita religiosa* und spirituelles Erleben. Frauenmystik und frauenmystische Literatur im 13. und 14. Jahrhundert, in: G. BRINKER-GABLER (Hg.), Deutsche Literatur von Frauen, München 1988, 2 Bde., hier Bd. 1, S. 88-113; S. RINGLER, Viten- und Offenbarungsliteratur in Frauenklöstern des Mittelalters. Quellen und Studien (Münchener Texte und Untersuchungen zur deutschen Literatur des Mittelalters 72), München 1980.

29 Das Leben der Schwestern von Töß beschrieben von Elsbeth Stagel, ed. F. VETTER (Deutsche Texte des Mittelalters 6), Berlin 1906, S. 90: *und sy sait der schwester die dis schraib, das wol uff xxx jar was, das* [...].

30 I.-C. RIGGERT, Ausbildung und Aufnahmeriten der Nonnen in den Lüneburger Klöstern während des Spätmittelalters, in: Jahrbuch der Gesellschaft für niedersächsische Kirchengeschichte 92 (1994), S. 17-42, hier S. 18.

31 Das Leben der Schwestern von Töß, ed. VETTER (wie Anm. 29), S. 48; Deutsches Nonnenleben, ed. M. WEINHANDL (Katholikon 2), München 1921, S. 185. Zum Kloster Töß vgl. M.-C. DÄNIKER-GYSIN, Geschichte des Dominikanerinnenklosters Töß 1233-1525 (289. Neujahrsblatt der Stadtbibliothek Winterthur), Winterthur 1957; E. EUGSTER, Adlige Territorialpolitik in der Ostschweiz. Kirchliche Stiftungen im Spannungsfeld früher landesherrlicher Verdrängungspolitik, Zürich 1991; H. SULZER / J. R. RAHN, Die Geschichte des Dominikanerinnenklosters Töß, in: Mitteilungen der antiquarischen Gesellschaft in Zürich 26 (1903/4); zum Schwesternbuch K. GRUBMÜLLER, Die Viten der Schwestern von Töß und Elsbeth Stagel (Überlieferung und literarische Einheit), in: Zeitschrift für deutsches Altertum und deutsche Literatur 98 (1969), S. 171-204.

ein ernsthaftes Kind gewesen, das am liebsten im Chor verweilte. Eines Tages sei sie vor den Altar getreten und habe sich bei Christus beschwert, dass ihre Mutter sie seit drei Jahren nicht mehr besucht habe. Auch Boten hätte sie ihr nicht geschickt, *und des kom es gen got in ein gar jamerig weinen, da es sein ellende also herczenlich betrachtet.*[32]

Nicht nur von Kindern, auch von sehr alten Frauen berichten die Schwesternbücher überraschend häufig. Hohes Alter bedeutet aus ihrer Sicht zumeist Krankheit und körperliche Behinderung. Nahezu biblische hundert Jahre alt sollen Schwester Metzi von Waltershofen und Adelheid von Lindau geworden sein;[33] letztere war gegen Ende ihres Lebens blind und ans Bett gefesselt;[34] von der um die neunzig Jahre alten Schwester Elsbeth von Cellinkon heißt es, sie habe gegen Ende ihres Lebens einem Kind von drei Jahren geglichen. Aus Altersschwäche vermochte sie weder reden, noch gehen; auch gesehen habe sie nicht mehr viel.[35] Ähnlich beschwerlich war das Leben für Schwester Elsa von Neuenstadt geworden, die siebzig Jahre lang im Kloster Adelhausen verbracht hatte. *Vor alter vnd vor siechtagen* sei sie am Ende ihrer Tage des Lebens gar überdrüssig geworden.[36] Bei Schwester Irmgart von Eichstätt waren es die Mitschwestern, die sie pflegten, die Gott darum baten, er möge die

---

32 F. W. E. ROTH, Aufzeichnungen über das mystische Leben der Nonnen von Kirchberg bei Sulz Predigerordens während des XIV. und XV. Jahrhunderts, in: Alemannia. Zeitschrift für Sprache, Kunst und Altertum besonders des alemannisch-schwäbischen Gebiets 21 (1893), S. 103-148, hier S. 141. Ähnliche Klagen sind aus Briefen von Kindern bzw. Mädchen bekannt, die klösterlichen Einrichtung zur Erziehung übergegeben wurden. Gerade für die Kleinen, die ohne Mutter und/oder ohne Schwestern ins Kloster gelangten, konnten, wenn der Besuch ausfiel, die ersten Klosterjahre eine Qual sein, vgl. dazu G. SIGNORI, Wanderer zwischen den 'Welten'. Besucher, Briefe, Vermächtnisse und Geschenke als Kommunikationsmedien im Austausch zwischen Kloster und Welt, in: Krone und Schleier: Kunst aus mittelalterlichen Frauenklöstern, Ausstellungskatalog, Bonn/Essen 2005, S. 130-141, hier S. 133.

33 Die Chronik der Anna von Munzingen, ed. KÖNIG (wie Anm. 19), S. 176; vgl. DENNE, Die Frauenklöster im spätmittelalterlichen Freiburg (wie Anm. 19), S. 250.

34 Das Leben der Schwestern von Töß, ed. VETTER (wie Anm. 29), S. 85f.; Deutsches Nonnenleben, ed. WEINHANDL (wie Anm. 31), S. 245f.

35 Das Leben der Schwestern von Töß, ed. VETTER (wie Anm. 29), S. 90-95; Deutsches Nonnenleben, ed. WEINHANDL (wie Anm. 31), S. 258.

36 Die Chronik der Anna von Munzingen, ed. KÖNIG (wie Anm. 19), S. 177; vgl. DENNE, Die Frauenklöster im spätmittelalterlichen Freiburg (wie Anm. 19), S. 250.

alte Frau erlösen. Langes Liegen hatte zu einem offenen Dekubitus geführt.[37] Schwester Kunigunde von Vilsek wurde, obschon sie die meiste Zeit ihres Lebens im klösterlichen Krankenhaus verbracht hatte, achtzig Jahre alt.[38] Achtzig Jahre waren es, trotz strenger Askese, auch bei Schwester Willbirch von Offeningen. Davon hatte sie mehr als sechzig im Kloster Kirchberg verbracht.[39]

Mehr als sechsundsechzig Jahre lang hatte auch Diemut Ebnerin im Kloster Engelthal gelebt. Eingetreten sei sie, heißt es sehr vage, in jungen Jahren.[40] Früh schon habe sie dank Visionen und Erscheinungen göttlichen Trost erfahren. Auch im Paradies verweilte sie während ihrer Entrückungen verschiedentlich. Der Schreiber des Schwesternbuchs interessiert sich nicht für Diemuts äußeres Leben, allein ihr inneres, spirituelles Erleben hält er fest. Ähnlich verfährt das Schwesternbuch von Kirchberg. Mehr als 53 Jahre habe Adelheid von Haiterbach unserem Herrn gedient. Ihr langes Leben war ganz der *Imitatio Christi* ergeben.[41] Bei Schwester Mechthild von Waldeck, die im Alter von acht Jahren ins Kloster gekommen war, waren es bloß 34 Jahre. Aber was heißt hier schon bloß? Mechthild starb 1305 im Alter von nur 42 Jahren.[42] Ihr Eintrag ist einer der wenigen, der mit einem Datum versehen ist. Die irdische Zeit spielt in den Schwesternbüchern meist eine untergeordnete Rolle, eben weil das innere, das spirituelle Erleben der Klosterfrauen gewöhnlich im Vordergrund steht. Im Schwesternbuch von Katharinenthal ist dieser Zug noch ausgeprägter als in Adelhausen, Engelthal, Kirchberg und in Töß.

Trotz ihrer Begnadung stehen die Schwestern nicht für sich selbst, sondern stehen bzw. verstehen sich als Teil der klösterlichen Gemeinschaft. Untereinander verbunden sind sie bald freundschaftlich,

---

37 Vgl. Der Nonnen von Engelthal Büchlein, ed. SCHRÖDER (wie Anm. 24), S. 20; Deutsches Nonnenleben, ed. WEINHANDL (wie Anm. 31), S. 291.

38 Vgl. Der Nonnen von Engelthal Büchlein, ed. SCHRÖDER (wie Anm. 24), S. 38f.; Deutsches Nonnenleben, ed. WEINHANDL (wie Anm. 31), S. 317.

39 Vgl. ROTH, Aufzeichnungen über das mystische Leben der Nonnen von Kirchberg (wie Anm. 32), S. 112f.

40 Vgl. Der Nonnen von Engelthal Büchlein, ed. SCHRÖDER (wie Anm. 24), S. 32; Deutsches Nonnenleben, ed. WEINHANDL (wie Anm. 31), S. 308.

41 Vgl. ROTH, Aufzeichnungen über das mystische Leben der Nonnen von Kirchberg (wie Anm. 32), S. 110f.

42 Vgl. ebd., S. 118.

bald durch Verwandtschaft. Kleine 'Familien', die sich aus Geschwisterpaaren oder aus Klostermutter und Klostertochter bzw. -töchtern (so auch die 'amtliche' Bezeichnung) zusammensetzen, bilden sich, die häufig in denselben Räumlichkeiten wohnen.[43] Zum Teil sind es die eigenen Töchter, welche die Frauen mit ins Kloster brachten; in anderen Fällen handelt es sich um Tante und Nichte, in noch anderen Fällen sind es zum Teil ständeübergreifende 'Wahlverwandtschaften'.[44]

Nach Max WEBER (1864-1920) bricht das Christentum radikal mit den Sippenbanden, in dem es deren religiöse Bedeutung verneint.[45] Diskutiert wird die Unvereinbarkeit der beiden Wertesysteme u. a. im Kontext immer strengerer Klausurbestimmungen.[46] Dennoch bzw. trotzdem ist Verwandtschaft, bald im leiblichen, bald im künstlichen, bald im metaphorisch-spirituellen Sinn, auch in der abendländischen Klostergeschichte allgegenwärtig, etwa in Gestalt der Geschwisterkonversionen. Bekannt ist das Phänomen dank prominenter Stifterfiguren wie Bernhard von Clairvaux († 1153) oder Gottfried von Cappenberg († 1127).[47] Dazu gesellen sich weniger 'berühmte' Beispiele wie die Gebrüder Heinrich, Paulus, Konrad, Johannes und Nikolaus von

---

43 Die wie weltliches Gut von einer Generation an die nächste vererbet werden, vgl. Iohannes Meyer Ord. Praed. Buch der Reformacio Predigerordens VI und V Buch, ed. B. M. REICHERT (Quellen und Forschungen zur Geschichte des Dominikanerordens in Deutschland 2), Leipzig 1908, S. 85: *die stübli und cellen, die sy von andren frowen in dem closter ererbet hattent, als denn söliches laider an sorgklich bös gewonhait ist in sölichen clöstern.*

44 G. SIGNORI, Leere Seiten: Zur Memorialkultur eines nicht regulierten Augustiner-Chorfrauenstifts im ausgehenden 15. Jahrhundert, in: DIES. (Hg.) Lesen, Schreiben, Sticken und Erinnern. Beiträge zur Kultur- und Sozialgeschichte mittelalterlicher Frauenklöster (Religion in der Geschichte 7), Bielefeld 2000, S. 151-186, hier S. 162-173; I. EBERL, Stiftisches Leben in Klöstern. Zur Regeltreue im klösterlichen Alltag des Spätmittelalters und der frühen Neuzeit, in: I. CRUSIUS (Hg.) Studien zum Kanonissenstift (Veröffentlichungen des Max-Planck-Instituts für Geschichte 167, Studien zur Germania Sacra 24), Göttingen 2001, S. 275-315, hier S. 279f.

45 M. WEBER, Wirtschaft und Gesellschaft. Die Wirtschaft und die gesellschaftlichen Ordnungen und Mächte. Nachlass, Teilband 5: Die Stadt, ed. W. NIPPEL (Max Weber Gesamtausgabe 22-5), Tübingen 1999, S. 114, 118f.

46 G. SIGNORI, Wanderer zwischen den 'Welten' (wie Anm. 32), S. 131, 140.

47 Vgl. Anm. 3.

Linz, die 1355 das Chorherrenstift Beerenburg gegründet hatten.[48] Intendiert wird im Fall der Geschwisterkonversion im Sinne von Max WEBER das Erlöschen der Sippe, eines der radikalsten Opfer im mittelalterlichen Wertesystem.

Nicht minder radikal ist der Entschluss, gemeinsam der Welt zu entsagen, bei den Frauen. Denn, was gerne vergessen wird, auch auf ihren Schultern konnte der Fortbestand einer Sippe ruhen. Als Erbtöchter waren sie durchaus befähigt, den Namen ihres Geschlechts an die nächste Generation weiterzugeben. Dante Alighieri (1265-1331) beispielsweise ist ein Träger eines Geschlechternamens, der auf eine Ahnfrau zurückgeht, ebenso Heirich Seuse († 1366).[49] Dennoch sind bei Frauen spektakuläre Gruppenkonversionen vergleichsweise selten.[50] In vielen Fällen hatten sie gar keine Wahl. Vier seiner Töchter habe der Vater der Margret von Hünikon dem Kloster Töß übergeben, dessen 'besonderer Freund' er gewesen sei.[51] Der Ehemann der Rilindis von Bissegg 'opferte' alle seine acht Kinder, seine zwei kleinen Söhne nahm er mit sich, als er dem Deutschorden beitrat, seine sechs Töchter verteilte er auf verschiedene Einrichtungen. Zwei davon begleiteten Rilindis, als sie in das Kloster Unterlinden eintrat.[52]

Geschwisterpaare sind in fast allen spätmittelalterlichen Frauenklöstern zu finden, zuhauf, auch unter den Äbtissinnen und Priorinnen.[53]

---

48 Die Augustiner-Chorherren und die Chorfrauen-Gemeinschaften in der Schweiz, bearbeitet von E. GILOMEN-SCHENKEL u.a. (Helvetia sacra, Abt. IV, 2), Basel 2004, S. 484.

49 O. GUYOTJEANNIN, Les filles, les femmes, le lignage, in: M. BOURIN / J.-M. MARTIN / F. MENANT (Hgg.), L'anthroponymie. Document de l'histoire sociale des moines méditerranées médiévaux, Rom 1996, S. 383-400.

50 Die Augustiner-Chorherren (wie Anm. 48), S. 148f. (sechs Nichten).

51 Das Leben der Schwestern von Töß, ed. VETTER (wie Anm. 29), S. 43f.; Deutsches Nonnenleben, ed. WEINHANDL (wie Anm. 31), S. 179f.

52 Les "Vitae sororum" d'Unterlinden. Édition critique du manuscrit 506 de la Bibliothèque de Colmar, ed. J. ANCELET-HUSTACHE, in: Archives d'histoire doctrinale et littéraire du moyen âge 5 (1930), S. 460f.; vgl. K.-E. GEITH, Zur Textgeschichte der 'Vitae Sororum' (Unterlindener Schwesternbuch) der Katharina von Gueberschwihr, in: Mittellateinisches Jahrbuch 21 (1986), S. 230-238.

53 So teilten sich zum Beispiel Cäcilie und Margarete von Königsegg abwechselnd die Leitung über das Chorfrauenstift Münsterlingen; ihnen folgten später Ursula und Elisabeth von Landenberg in der Stiftsleitung: Die Augustiner-Chorherren (wie Anm. 48), S. 366-373; J.-L. EICHENLAUB, Les grandes lignes de l'histoire du

Dem versuchte manch ein Statutenbuch entgegenzuwirken, zumeist allerdings vergeblich.[54] Die Verwandtschaft war das stärkste Band, das die mittelalterlichen Gesellschaften zusammenhielt, auch innerhalb des Klosters; darauf hat vor Jahren schon Klaus SCHREINER aufmerksam gemacht.[55]

Ebenso häufig belegt ist der gleichzeitige Klostereintritt von Mutter und Tochter. Gemeinsam mit ihren Töchtern trat die Witwe Irmendraut von Hiltegarthausen im Kloster Kirchberg ein.[56] Im Schwesternbuch von Engelthal heißt es: *Eine hiez swester Alheit von Roet, die waz ein witib und braht ein tohterlin mit ir in daz closter, daz hiz Irmelin.* Auch Irmelins Schwester

---

monastère d'Unterlinden des origines au XVIIe siècle, in: Les dominicaines d'Unterlinden, Ausstellungslatalog, Bd. 1, Paris/Colmar 2000, S. 18-63. Dasselbe Phänomen beobachten wir auch in vielen anderen Frauenkonventen und -stiften: M. KUHN-REHFUS, Die soziale Zusammensetzung der Konvente in den oberschwäbischen Frauenzisterzen, in: H.-M. MAURER / F. QUARTHAL (Hgg.), *Speculum Sueviae.* Beiträge zu den historischen Hilfswissenschaften und zur geschichtlichen Landeskunde Südwestdeutschlands. Festschrift für Hansmartin Decker-Hauff zum 65. Geburtstag, Stuttgart 1982, Bd. 2, S. 7-31; JOHNSON, Equal in Monastic Profession (wie Anm. 18), S. 20f.; DENNE, Die Frauenklöster im spätmittelalterlichen Freiburg (wie Anm. 19), S. 246, 254-260, 262; OLIVA, The Convent and the Community (wie Anm. 21), S. 225-227; I.-C. RIGGERT, Die Lüneburger Frauenklöster (Veröffentlichungen der historischen Kommission für Niedersachsen und Bremen 37, Quellen und Untersuchungen zur Geschichte Niedersachsens im Mittelalter 19), Hannover 1996, S. 248; S. URBANSKI, Geschichte des Klosters Harvestehude *In valle virginum.* Annäherung an die wirtschaftliche, soziale und religiöse Entwicklung eines Nonnenklosters bei Hamburg (1245-1530), Münster 2001, S. 70ff.; S. KNACKMUß, "Meine Schwestern sind im Kloster ..." Geschwisterbeziehungen des Nürnberger Patriziergeschlechts zwischen Klausur und Welt, Humanismus und Reformation, in: G. FREITAG (Hg.), Geschwister (im Druck).

54 K. SCHREINER, Consanguinitas. Verwandtschaft als Strukturprinzip religiöser Gemeinschafts- und Verfassungsbildung in Kirche und Mönchtum des Mittelalters, in: I. CRUSIUS (Hg.), Beiträge zu Geschichte und Struktur der mittelalterlichen Germania Sacra (Veröffentlichungen des Max-Planck-Instituts für Geschichte 93), Göttingen 1989, S. 176-305; DERS., 'Versippung' als soziale Kategorie mittelalterlicher Kirchen- und Klostergeschichte, in: N. BULST / J.-P. GENET (Hgg.), Medieval Lives and the Historian, Studies on Medieval Prosopography, Kalamazoo 1986, S. 163-180.

55 SCHREINER, Consanguinitas (wie Anm. 54), S. 179-214.

56 ROTH, Aufzeichnungen über das mystische Leben der Nonnen von Kirchberg (wie Anm. 32), S. 134.

Kunigund lebte im Kloster.[57] Die Beispiele ließen sich mühelos mehren.[58]

Ähnlich eng präsentiert sich der Bezug zwischen Tante und Nichte, wenngleich er sich weniger leicht erschließen lässt wie das Verhältnis zwischen Mutter und Tochter. Gemeinsam mit ihrer Brudertochter lebte Schwester Mechthild von Neitstein im Kloster Engelthal. Die Nichte war von schwacher Konstitution; sie starb vor der Tante.[59] Bei Guta Jünging aus Kloster Weiler bei Esslingen heißt es: *Dise vorgeschribene swester het auch swestertöhter in unserm closter, der hieß eine Irnburch und die ander Katherina, die waren beyde unmessige andehtige menschen.*[60] Tante und Nichte sind wie Mutter und Tochter, nicht nur in der Abgeschiedenheit des Klosters.[61] Enge Verwandtschaftsbanden lassen sich auch zwischen den Frauen und den für sie zuständigen Klerikern erkennen (Bruder und Schwester, Onkel und Nichte, Vater und Tochter), ein weiteres noch weitgehend unbearbeitetes Arbeitsfeld.[62]

Fehlten leibliche Töchter oder Nichten, dann nahmen sich die älteren Schwestern gerne fremder Mädchen an. Je jünger die Mädchen ins Kloster kamen, desto wichtiger scheint es für sie gewesen zu sein, bei einer Ersatzmutter 'Trost' zu finden. Daraus entwickelten sich 'Freundschaften', die über den Tod hinaus wirkten.[63] Eine solche tiefe Freundschaft verband die ehemalige Begine Adelheid von Ingolstadt mit

---

57 Der Nonnen von Engelthal Büchlein, ed. SCHRÖDER (wie Anm. 24), S. 7-9.

58 Les "Vitae sororum" d'Unterlinden, ed. ANCELET-HUSTACHE (wie Anm. 52), S. 350, 452, 456, 461.

59 Der Nonnen von Engelthal Büchlein, ed. SCHRÖDER (wie Anm. 24), S. 25; Deutsches Nonnenleben, ed. WEINHANDL (wie Anm. 31), S. 298.

60 K. BIHLMEYER, Mystisches Leben in dem Dominikanerinnenkloster Weiler bei Esslingen im 13. und 14. Jahrhundert, in: Württembergische Vierteljahrshefte für Landesgeschichte, N. F. 25 (1916), S. 61-93, hier S. 76.

61 G. SIGNORI, Geschwister: Metapher und Wirklichkeit in der spätmittelalterlichen Denk- und Lebenswelt, in: G. FERTIG (Hg.), Geschwister – Eltern – Großeltern. Beiträge der historischen, anthropologischen und demographischen Forschung (Historical Social Research 30), Berlin 2005.

62 Der Nonnen von Engelthal Büchlein, ed. SCHRÖDER (wie Anm. 24), S. 5, S. 38f.; Deutsches Nonnenleben, ed. WEINHANDL (wie Anm. 31), S. 316 (Kunigund v. Vilsek, Tochter des Kaplans); ROTH, Aufzeichnungen über das mystische Leben der Nonnen von Kirchberg (wie Anm. 32), S. 106 (Adelheid, Schwester des Kaplans).

63 SIGNORI, Leere Seiten (wie Anm. 44), S. 179-184.

Mechthild Krumpfin, die in jungen Jahren ins Kloster Engelthal gekommen war.[64] Es werden Begriffe wie Gespielin, Gesellin und Freundin benutzt.

Bislang hat sich die Forschung vornehmlich für die Frage der innerklösterlichen Sozialstruktur interessiert, kaum für die Altersfrage und noch weniger für die Vielfalt unterschiedlicher Lebensformen innerhalb des Klosters.[65] Zweifellos ist die Standesfrage wichtig. Sie kann auch, wie die Briefe aus dem Klarissenkloster Söflingen zeigen, zur Fraktionierung der Klostergemeinschaft führen.[66] Nicht zu unterschätzen ist indessen, auf die Klostertöchter bezogen, die Kraft der für alle gleichen Erziehung. Sie kann sich ständisch durchaus nivellierend auswirken. Fürstenkinder allerdings sind davon auszunehmen. Sie genossen überall Privilegien.

Das Bild, das die Schwesternbücher von dem Miteinander der verschiedenen sozialen Gruppen entwerfen, präsentiert sich ausgesprochen harmonisch. Das dürfte gattungsspezifische Gründe haben. Schwesternbücher sind keine Skandalchroniken klösterlicher Verfehlungen, sondern Erbauungsbücher. Sie erschöpfen sich aber nicht darin. Von Konflikten innerhalb der Klostergemeinschaft ist nämlich auch in anderen Kontexten erstaunlich selten die Rede. Was natürlich nicht besagt es habe keine gegeben, wie auch die diesbezüglichen Mahnungen in den Jungfrauenregeln und die Visitationsprotokolle zeigen.[67]

---

64 Deutsches Nonnenleben, ed. WEINHANDL (wie Anm. 31), S. 287-289. Vgl. G. J. LEWIS, By Women, for Women, about Women. The Sister-Books of Fourteenth-Century Germany (Studies and Texts 13), Toronto 1996, S. 222-225.

65 Kritisch zur Sozialstruktur F. J. FELTEN, Wie adelig waren Kanonissenstifte (und andere weibliche Konvente) im frühen und hohen Mittelalter? in: I. CRUSIUS (Hg.), Studien zum Kanonissenstift (Veröffentlichungen des Max-Planck-Instituts für Geschichte 167, Studien zur Germania Sacra 24), Göttingen 2001, S. 39-128.

66 M. MILLER, Die Söflinger Briefe und das Klarissenkloster Söflingen, Tübingen/Würzburg 1940; M. MÜNTZ, Freundschaften und Feindschaften in einem spätmittelalterlichen Frauenkloster: die sogenannten Söflinger Briefe, in: G. SIGNORI (Hg.), Meine in Gott geliebte Freundin. Freundschaftsdokumente aus klösterlichen und humanistischen Schreibstuben (Religion in der Geschichte 4), Bielefeld ^{2}1998, S. 111-120.

67 Vgl. J. OBERSTE, Die Dokumente der klösterlichen Visitationen (Typologie des sources du moyen âge occidental 80), Turnhout 1999, S. 72.

Das Nebeneinander von jung und alt gehört konstitutiv zum Klosteralltag. Wie aber verhält es sich im Kloster mit dem Problem unterschiedlicher Erfahrungshintergründe? Das heißt, wie verhält es sich im Kloster mit dem Generationenproblem? Für den Historiker sichtbar werden unterschiedliche Erfahrungshorizonte vornehmlich im Konfliktfall, wenn Gruppen mit unterschiedlichen nicht nur Lebenserfahrungen, sondern auch Vorstellungen und Werten aufeinanderstoßen. Aber ist eine solche an Werte und Altergruppen gebundene Fraktionierung der Klostergemeinschaft überhaupt denkbar?

Aus dem Schwesternbuch von Dießenhofen z. B. erfahren wir, dass sich die Nonnen nicht einig gewesen seien, welchem der beiden Heiligen mehr Bedeutung zukäme, Johannes dem Täufer oder Johannes Evangelista.[68] Johannes Meyer († 1485) resümiert:

> *und also denn da zů mal und och dar vor in dem selben closter an sölliche fröwliche gewonhait waz, das an tail swöstren hat liebe zů s. Iohannes Baptisten, an tail zů sant Iohannes evangelysten mit söllich unloblicher andacht, daz vil der swöstren, die ir andacht zů dem ainen sant Iohannes hattent, daz die selben den andren Iohannes etwas warent smechen, und dar umm so namt sich ain tail der swöstren baptisterin, daz ander tail evangelysterin, und hattent wunderliche unrůb under in selbs, also daz sy partyen mit kriegen hielten gegen ain andren von der beden sancte Iohannes wegen.*[69]

Das Schwesternbuch präzisiert, den älteren Klosterfrauen habe der Streit missfallen. Sie hätten die jüngeren Mitschwestern gemahnt, sie sollten beide Heiligen gleichermaßen ehren.[70] Die Ordensregel verlangte es, dass

---

68 Im Nürnberger Klarissenkloster stritten sich die Schwestern wegen Maria Magdalena, vgl. G. PICKEL, Geschichte des Klaraklosters in Nürnberg, in: Beiträge zur bayerischen Kirchengeschichte 19 (1913), S. 158f.

69 Iohannes Meyer Ord. Praed. Buch der Reformacio Predigerordens I, II und III Buch, ed. B. M. REICHERT (Quellen und Forschungen zur Geschichte des Dominikanerordens in Deutschland 2), Leipzig 1909, S. 62. Zum Autor vgl. P. OCHSENBEIN, Art. 'Meyer, Johannes, Dominikaner', in: Biographisch-Bibliographisches Kirchenlexikon, Bd. 5, Herzberg 1993, Sp. 1427-1429, und W. FECHTER, Art. 'Meyer, Johannes OP', in: Die Deutsche Literatur des Mittelalters. Verfasserlexikon, Bd. 6, Berlin/New York ^{2}1987, Sp. 474-489.

70 R. MEYER (Hg.), Das 'St. Katharinentaler Schwesternbuch'. Untersuchung, Edition, Kommentar (Münchener Texte und Untersuchungen zur deutschen Literatur des Mittelalters 104), Tübingen 1995, S. 180. Zum Streit vgl. C. HECK, Rapprochement, antagonisme, ou conformisme dans le culte des saints: Art et dévotion à

die Senioren über die Junioren wachten. So mag die Ausgestaltung der Episode didaktischen Zwecken folgen und nicht Realität abbilden. Dennoch zeigt sich im Streit um die beiden Heiligen, dass Frömmigkeit auch im Frauenkloster einem Wandel unterzogen war, dem zu folgen nicht allen immer gleich leicht fiel.

Auch die in regelmäßigen Abständen wiederkehrende Reformfrage legt nahe, dass der Wertekanon im Kloster zwar feststand, die konkrete Auslegung aber viel Spielraum bot. Schwieriger scheint es indessen, eine Brücke zwischen den Reformanliegen und der Generationenfrage zu schlagen. Reform setzt im mittelalterlichen Verständnis einen Werteverfall voraus, der aber ist nicht automatisch an eine bestimmte Altergruppe gebunden. Trotzdem können sich Generation und Reform im Einzelfall überlagern. Zwischen den Zeilen verrät die Schreiberin des Tösser Schwesternbuchs, dass in den ersten Jahren nach der Klostergründung die Regel noch streng beachtet worden sei. Damals sei die sechsjährige Elsbeth von Cellinkon in das Kloster gekommen, eine *minerin der strengikait und arbeit, des libes armůt und ellend.*[71] Heute zählten diese Werte nur noch wenig, kritisiert die Schreiberin. Schwester Elsbeth wurde, wie wir eingangs erfahren haben, um die neunzig Jahre alt. Über die Jahre hindurch fungierte sie sozusagen als lebendes Mahnmal asketischer, nicht von allen geteilter Regeltreue. Ein ähnlicher Konflikt scheint bei Margret Willin aufgebrochen zu sein, auch sie eine besonders regelkonforme Schwester:

> Ihr genügte nicht die Strenge der Ordensregel, die sie fleißig einhielt: sie plagte sich noch viel gewaltiger, so dass wir gar nicht alles in Worte bringen können. Aller Gesellschaft gab sie einen freiwilligen Abschied. Des Redefensters und aller auswärtigen Menschen achtete sie nicht und sogar gegen ihren eigenen Bruder, den sie in unserem Orden hatte, hielt sie sich fremd. Sie schwieg fast unentweg, so dass sie kaum ein Wort redete. Sie hatte ein Kopfkissen aus Weidengeflecht und eine harte Reisighürde mit einer alten Decke als Lager. Und so viele Steine, als man zu einem Estrich auflegt, waren ihr Bett, worauf sie ruhte. Sie trug ein härenes Hemd mit gräulichen

---

Katharinenthal au quatorzième siècle, in: Viator 21 (1990), S. 229-238, zu Johannes Evangelista J. F. HAMBURGER, St. John the Divine. The Deified Evangelist in Medieval Art and Theology, Berkley 2002.

71 Das Leben der Schwestern von Töß, ed. VETTER (wie Anm. 29), S. 90; Deutsches Nonnenleben, ed. WEINHANDL (wie Anm. 31), S. 253.

> Knöpfen und eine starke eiserne Kette um ihren Leib. Sie nahm zwischen Tag und Nacht drei Bußübungen vor mit einer Geißel, die sie dazu gemacht hatte. Sie aß wenig Speise und trank selten Wein. [...] Sie wachte auch so emsiglich, dass man schätzte, sie schliefe kaum eine Vigil lang.[72]

Margret Willin hatte derart radikal mit der Welt gebrochen, dass sie auch zu keinem Fenster mehr in die Welt hinausblicken wollte. Das war keineswegs allein metaphorisch gemeint. "Zuweilen versuchten sie", leise Kritik wird vernehmbar, "die jungen Schwestern und taten, als ob sie [am Fenster] was Wunder sähen." Doch Margret Willin ließ sich nicht ablenken und "kehrte [...] ihre Augen [nie] dahin."[73]

Auch andernorts gab es mit einzelnen besonders regelkonformen Schwestern Probleme.[74] Damit ließ sich leben. Schwieriger wurde es für den Konvent, wenn sich größere Gruppen zusammentaten; noch schwieriger wurde es im Falle einer Zwangsreform, wenn eine Schar solcher regelkonformen Frauen sozusagen von außen in das Kloster einbrach, und das war bei Zwangsreformen die Regel.[75] Eine Fraktionierung nach Altergruppen beobachtet der Dominikaner Felix Fabri († 1502) in seinem Traktat über die Stadt Ulm beim Benediktinerkloster Urspring. Es seien vor allem die jungen Nonnen gewesen, die Einspruch

---

72 Ebd. (wie Anm. 31), S. 153; ebd. (wie Anm. 29), S. 26: *Ir genůgt nit an des ordens strengi, den sy flisklich hielt: sy arbait sich noch fil groͤsslicher, das wir doch nit alles ze worten kunent bringen. Aller gesellschaft gab sy ain friges urlob; Des redvensters und aller ussrer menschen hat sy kain acht, und joch gen iren aignen brůder, den sy in únsrem orden hat, gen dem hielt sy sich usserlich. Sy schwaig vil nach alwegen, das sy nimer wort geret. Sy hatt ain hobt kússy von velwen und ain hertty hurt under ainem alten strat. Aber als vil stain als so man ainen estrich lait, also was ir bett, da sy růwet. Sy trůg ain herin hemd an mitt grúlichen knoͤpfen und ain starken ysnenen kettenen umb iren lib. Sy nam zwischent tag und nacht dry disciplin mit ainer gaiselen, die sy darzů gefrúmt hat. Sy as wenig spiss und trank selten win; so sy aber etwenn win trank, den vermist sy, das er wenig kraft hatt. Sy wachet och als emsklich das man achtett das sy dik kum ainer vigili lang schlieff.*

73 Ebd.

74 A. BOLLMANN, 'Beeing a Woman on my Own'. Alijt Kae (1415-1455) as Reformer of the Inner Self, in: A. B. MULDER-BAKKER (Hg.), Seeing and Knowing. Women and Learning in Medieval Europe 1200-1550 (Medieval Women. Texts and Contexts 11), Turnhout 2004, S. 67-96.

75 Iohannes Meyer Ord. Praed. Buch der Reformacio Predigerordens VI und V Buch, ed. REICHERT (wie. Anm. 69), S. 46, 52f., 79, 83, 99, 100ff., 108, 113, 117-120, 122, 124, 129f., 136, 146f.

gegen die Reform erhoben hätten, welche die *magistra* einzuführen gedachte.[76] "Da beide Parteien im Konvent ihre jeweilige Verwandtschaft zu Hilfe riefen", ich folge Immo Eberl, "geriet auch diese untereinander in Streit", so dass Mechthild von der Pfalz (1419-1482), die Landesherrin, gezwungen war zu intervenieren.[77] Dafür hatte sie "Nonnen aus dem seit zwei Jahrzehnten reformierten Benediktinerinnenkloster St. Walburg in Eichstätt nach Urspring gerufen."[78] Mit dem Einzug der fremden Schwestern überstürzten sich die Ereignisse. Jung und alt gerieten auch im Benediktinerkloster Geisenfeld aneinander.[79] Dasselbe gilt auch für das Straßburger Dominikanerinnenkloster Sankt Nikolaus-in-undis, dem Bericht des Ordenschronisten Johannes Meyer zufolge. Etliche junge Menschen seien in das Kloster gekommen:

> *die da gaistliche zucht wenig mer achten wolten, und wild und halsstarck begunt werden und etwaz maisterlos; dar umm besorgtent die alten swöstren, daz durch sölich wilde unzucht und ungaistlich swöstren ain schedlicher, böser inbruch möcht werden, da von daz closter in verlümdung möcht komen.*[80]

Johannes Meyer benutzt die Begriffe 'jung' und 'alt' auch bei anderen reformunwilligen Konventen. Nicht immer aber meint er damit wirklich Altergruppen; meist bezeichnet er mit dem Begriff 'alt' die Schwestern, die vor der Reform im Kloster lebten.[81]

In Urspring und Straßburg waren es die jungen Schwestern gewesen, welche die Reform ablehnten; in der Reichsabtei Heggbach hingegen setzte die Äbtissin die Reform gerade mit Hilfe von vier jungen, allerdings konventsfremden Schwestern durch.[82] Gesetzmäßigkeiten in der Rollenverteilung lassen sich, was das Zusammenspiel von Reform

---

76 Bruder Felix Fabris Abhandlung von der Stadt Ulm nach der Ausgabe des litterarischen Vereins in Stuttgart verdeutscht von K. D. HAßLER, Ulm 1909, S. 124; vgl. EBERL, Stiftisches Leben in Klöstern (wie Anm. 44), S. 291.

77 Ebd., S. 292.

78 Ebd., S. 294.

79 J. G. GEISTBECK / M. J. HUFNAGEL, Das Benediktinerinnenkloster Geisenfeld (D'Hopfakirm 5), Pfaffenhofen 1979.

80 Iohannes Meyer Ord. Praed. Buch der Reformacio Predigerordens VI und V Buch, ed. REICHERT (wie Anm. 69), S. 81.

81 Ebd., S. 99, 132.

82 EBERL, Stiftisches Leben in Klöstern (wie Anm. 44), S. 310.

und Generation anbelangt, demnach nicht erkennen. Bald sind es die jungen, bald die alten, die sich gegen die Reform stellen. Homogener erscheint das Bild auf der Ebene der Reaktionen, in den Fällen, in denen der Konvent sich geschlossen gegen die Reformen wendet. Vielerorts ließ der Druck von außen die Generationen einander nähertreten.[83] In diesen Fällen zählte weder das Alter, noch die Herkunft, sondern allein die Gemeinschaft. Gemeinschaft war nicht nur das Ideal, sondern auch die Praxis, wenngleich die reformunwilligen Schwestern ein anderes Gemeinschaftsverständnis pflegten, als die Reformkräfte. Gemeinschaft war für letzere eine von allen geteilte Erfahrung, ein Stück gemeinsamer erlebter Geschichte.

Das Kloster ist in vielen Bereichen weniger homogen, als man auf Anhieb vermutet. Das betrifft nicht nur die verschiedenen Lebensformen, die sich in oder in unmittelbarer Nähe zum Kloster entfalten können, sondern auch die verschiedenen Altersgruppen, die im Kloster seit frühester Zeit zusammenfinden. Wie Jung und Alt sich zueinander zu verhalten hatten, legen Regel und Statutenbücher verbindlich fest. Es geht um Erziehung und Kontrolle. Generationenkonflikte brechen zwar wiederholt auf; doch scheinen sie als solche im Kloster kein Hauptproblem dargestellt zu haben. Wichtiger als die Zugehörigkeit zu der einen oder zu der anderen Altergruppen war es, im Kloster über Beziehungen zu verfügen, Freunde im Kloster zu wissen, die mit einem gute sowie schlechte Erfahrungen teilten. Die gemeinsame Erfahrung stärkte den Zusammenhalt, häufig losgelöst von der Altersfrage.

Verwandtschaft, sowohl leibliche, als auch künstliche, unterteilte die Welt des Klosters in eine Vielzahl kleiner familienähnlicher und in dem Sinne generationenübergreifender Welten. Die daraus resultierenden Probleme waren bekannt. Jede Reformgeneration versuchte von neuem, die Verbindungslinien zu kappen, welche die Verwandtschaft zwischen

---

83 R. WEIS-MÜLLER, Die Reform des Klosters Klingental und ihr Personenkreis, Basel 1956; A. MISCHLEWSKI, Idéal monastique et intérêt de la bourgeoisie. La clôture du couvent des Augustines de la ville libre et impériale de Memmingen, in: Les Religieuses dans le cloître et dans le monde des origines á nos jours, St. Étienne 1994, S. 539-547; S. URBANSKI, *Der begevenen kinder frunde*. Soziale und politische Gründe für das Scheitern eines Reformversuchs am Kloster Harvestehude 1482, in: S. URBANSKI / C. LAMSCHUS / J. ELLERMEYER (Hgg.), Recht und Alltag im Hanseraum, Gerhard Theuerkauf zum 60. Geburtstag (De Sulte 4), Lüneburg 1993, S. 411-428.

Kloster und Welt zog, und sie durch spirituelle Banden zu ersetzen. Am völligen Bruch mit der Welt bzw. mit der Verwandtschaft konnte in der Praxis, anders als in der Theorie, letztlich niemand wirklich interessiert sein. Denn die Verwandtschaft garantierte den Fortbestand des Klosters, sowohl im materiellen wie auch im personellen Sinn. In aller Schärfe brach der Konflikt um die Verwandtschaft nach dem Tridentinum neu auf. Ebenso scharf formulierten fortan aber auch die Reformgegner ihre Wortmeldungen. Sie sprachen im Namen der Verwandtschaft bzw. der Familie gegen die Reform.[84]

---

84 S. EVANGELISTI, "We do not have it, and we do not want it". Women, Power, and Convent Reform in Florence, in: Sixteenth Century Journal 34 (2003), S. 677-700.

THE NOVICE MASTER IN THE CISTERCIAN ORDER*

MIRKO BREITENSTEIN

"An experienced senior shall be assigned to them who is suited for winning souls and watches over them with the utmost care."[1] In his rule, Benedict describes – in these brief words – the character of the person, whose duty it is to introduce the novices to everyday life in a monastery.[2] These are extremely sparse formulations when taking into account that the successful continuation in personnel of a monastery or a religious community in general depended on this man's work to a significant extent.

Benedict's brief description of the duties of a *magister novitiorum* corresponds to a generally striking discretion regarding this office in rule texts handed down to posterity, although it has to be considered one of the most important offices within the *vita religiosa*.[3] Information relating to the novice master has to be rather sought in the customs, constitutions and in similar texts. Their explanations and regulations come closer to the practices of the respective community than can be expected from rules.

---

* The present version of the text corresponds to the paper read at the International Medieval Conference in Leeds 2005 and has only been supplemented with references where necessary. I am very grateful for the services rendered by Olaf Kinne (Dresden) in translating this essay into English.

1 *Et senior eis talis deputetur, qui aptus sit ad lucrandas animas, qui super eos omnino curiose intendat.* (Benedikt von Nursia, Die Benediktsregel. Eine Anleitung zu christlichem Leben, der vollständige Text der Regel lateinisch-deutsch, übersetzt und erklärt von G. HOLZHERR, Zürich [4]1993, cap. 58.6 [p. 269])

2 However, other disciplinary offices that can be structurally compared to those of the novice master are described in the Regula Benedicti (note 1 above) cap. 22.3, 7 (pp. 169f.); 56.3 (p. 265); 66.1 (p. 310).

3 This is emphasised by all authors mentioned in note 4. In addition to this, also comp. V. HERMANS, De novitiatu in ordine Benedictino-Cisterciensi et in iure communi usque ad annum 1335, in: Analecta Sacri Ordinis Cisterciensis 3 (1947), pp. 1-110, here p. 92.

This essay now continues with a brief outline of the position and tasks of the *magister novitiorum* in order to show the importance of the office and its holders for the continuation in religious communities. This task appears all the more necessary in view of the absolutely inadequate research situation, because, compared to the noviciate as such, there are virtually no studies about the novice master.[4] However, the lack of explicit sources concerning the master and his tasks constitutes a major reason for this situation.[5] Here, the Cistercian community is to serve as

---

4 The few texts known to me hardly do justice to the importance of the topic. The first study on the subject, the 1947 dissertation by the redemptorist James Francis LOVER, first of all is – although it was given the title of 'An Historical Synopsis' – an exegesis of the 1917 Corpus Iuris Canonici partially resorting to the Council of Trent (J. F. LOVER, The master of Novices. An historical synopsis and a commentary [The Catholic University of America, Canon law studies 254], Washington 1947). Next, the thesis by the Franciscan Isidor CHMIEL (De magistro novitiorum, Turin 1953), which had been completed at the Pontificial University Antonianum, was published in 1953. Although the historic part of this study allocates about 30 pages to the question of the office's genesis until the middle of the 16th century, it is still limited to a search for possible statements about the master in rules and customs. Nevertheless, the main emphasis of this work definitely lies in dealing with modern canon law. In 1959, the dissertation by the Dominican Franciscus CUBELLI, De magistro novitiorum professorum in veteri legislatione Dominicana [Pistoia 1959], which had also been completed at the Pontificial University Antonianum, was published (yet in excerpts only). In contrast to his predecessors, CUBELLI resorted to a much wider range of sources and considered the decisions of the Dominican general and provincial chapters. All the same, in many aspects this work also remains insufficient as a result of the limitation to one order and the focus on normative texts. The book by the Dominican Émile-Alphonse LANGLAIS, Le père maître des novices et des frères étudiants dans l'Ordre des Frères-Prêcheurs, Brügge 1959, then again addresses the current novice master and his subordinates much more than the historian. Thus, it evolved from a spiritual rather than from a historic-critical impetus.

5 First of all, it is necessary to mention the section dedicated to the novice master in the treatise on offices by the Dominican Humbert de Romanis († 1277) (Humbert de Romanis, Instructiones de officiis ordinis, in: Ders., Opera de vita regulari, ed. J. J. BERTHIER, 2 vols., Rom 1889, vol. 2, pp. 179-371, here cap. 5: *De officio magistri novitiorum* [pp. 213-233]). The only text known to me in addition to this is a short fragment with the title *De officio magistri novitiorum* in the Bayerische Staatsbibliothek München CLM 15312, fol. 93f., which its editor attributed to the Franciscan David von Augsburg († 1272) (E. LEMPP, Analekten, in: Zeitschrift für Kirchengeschichte 19 [1899], pp. 340-360, here pp. 340f.). The Bavarian Franciscan Dagobert STÖCKERL succeeded in proving the existence of further textual evidence of this *opusculum*, cf. D. STÖCKERL, Bruder David von Augsburg. Ein deutscher Mystiker

an exemplary research object, as this community has without doubt a model character within the range of orders in the 12th century. In this, the Cistercians are part of an unfolding *vita religiosa* in as much as they become prototypes and generators of this development themselves. With the help of selected texts, this essay will show the field of activity of the master as well as possible qualifications enabling him to take on this office.

*

The so-called *Ecclesiastica Officia*, the Cistercians' book of customs, provides us with an early and at the same time detailed textual testimony, whose earliest *redactio* handed down to us dates – according to recent studies – from the mid-thirties of the 12th century.[6] In chapter 113[7],

---

aus dem Franziskanerorden (Veröffentlichungen aus dem Kirchenhistorischen Seminar München, 4. Reihe 4), München 1914, pp. 203f.

6 Ecclesiastica officia. Gebräuchebuch der Zisterzienser aus dem 12. Jahrhundert, lateinischer Text nach den Handschriften Dijon 114, Trient 1711, Ljubljana 31, Paris 4346 und Wolfenbüttel Codex Guelferbytanus 1068, nach der lateinisch-französischen Ausgabe von Danièle CHOISSELET und Placide VERNET, übersetzt, bearbeitet und herausgegeben von H. M. HERZOG / J. MÜLLER (Quellen und Studien zur Zisterzienserliteratur 7). This very important text was first edited by Philippe GUIGNARD in the redaction of the manuscript 114 of the Bibliothèque Municipale de Dijon in the year 1878 (Les Monuments primitifs de la règle cistercienne publiés d'après les manuscrits de l'abbaye de Cîteaux, ed. P. GUIGNARD, Dijon 1878, pp. 1-57, pp. 85-403). According to GUIGNARD, this redaction dates from the time between 1175 and 1191. For textually immanent reasons as well as on the basis of comparisons with the Cistercians' statutes, the editors of the critical Latin-French edition of the *Ecclesiastica officia*, Danièle CHOISSELET and Placide VERNET, worked out a more precise time specification and assumed the date of the book's completion to be between the general chapters of the years 1184 and 1186 (Les *Ecclesiastica Officia* cisterciens du XIIème siècle. Texte latin selon les manuscrits edités de Trente 1711, Ljubljana 31 et Dijon 114, ed. D. CHOISSELET / P. VERNET [La Documentation Cistercien 22], Reiningue 1989, pp. 49f.). The importance of this manuscript is also due to a *Collectaneum* with numerous liturgical formulae, which is preserved in it (edited in: Les *Ecclesiastica Officia* cisterciens du XIIème siècle, ed. D. CHOISSELET / P. VERNET [see above], pp. 351-391). It has to be assumed that the manuscript of the university library Ljubljana 31 (Codex manuscriptus 31 Bibliothecae Universitatis Labacensis, ed. C. NOSCHITZKA, in: Analecta Sacri Ordinis Cisterciensis 6 [1950], pp. 1-124), which was edited by Canisius NOSCHITZKA in 1950, was completed on a much

under the title of *De magistro novitiorum*, the reader finds a quite exhaustive description of the master's tasks and activities:

> He has to teach the novices the way of life in the order, wake them up in church and, whenever they have made a mistake, he has to correct them with a word or a sign if possible. [...] As far as he can, he shall provide for their needs. [...] If they ask him for forgiveness for the outward offences, he imposes a penance on them. He has to note down the day of their entrance into the novitiate and to tell the abbot when the rule has to be read to them. [...] After the completion of the year of probation he leads [the novices – M.B.] to monastic profession. [...] In church, he reads out the profession charter for those novices incapable of reading and keeps the ink ready for the cross. [...] If necessary, he leads [the novice] to the feet of the monks and back, prepares holy water and the *cuculla* and helps the novices undress and dress. Afterwards he carries their water mug to the refectory and shows them the bed allocated to them by the prior.[8]

---

earlier date. Researchers generally agree that this redaction probably occurred in the time from 1147 to 1152. An even earlier date has to be assumed for the redaction of the *Ecclesiastica* of the Codex 1711 of the Bibliotheca Comunale di Trento, which was edited by Bruno GRIESSER in 1956 (B. GRIESSER, Die *Ecclesiastica Officia Cisterciensis Ordinis* des Cod. 1711 von Trient, in: Analecta Sacri Ordinis Cisterciensis 12 [1956], pp. 153-288). GRIESSER dated this redaction to the years from 1120 to 1130 (ibid., p. 161). Yet, even if, as it has recently been suggested, this redaction has to rather be dated to the years from 1130 to 1135 (*Ecclesiastica officia*, ed. HERZOG / MÜLLER [see above], p. 7) or also from 1136 to 1140 (Twelfth Century Statutes from the Cistercian General Chapter, ed. CHR. WADDELL [Cîteaux. Studia et Documenta 12], Brecht 2002, p. 510), it would still give an insight in the time under abbot Stephan Harding, as it is a copy of an older original. Further manuscripts such as the Codex Guelferbytanus 1068 of the Herzog-August-Bibliothek Wolfenbüttel or the MS lat. 4346 of the Bibliothèque Nationale de Paris provide complementations of the Trent redaction, although the mentioned manuscripts themselves were written in as late as the middle of the 12th (Paris) or the 13th century (Wolfenbüttel). With regard to this, cf. Les 'Ecclesiastica Officia' cisterciens du XIIème siècle, ed. CHOISSELET / VERNET (see above) pp. 19f. as well as 'Ecclesiastica officia', ed. HERZOG / MÜLLER (see above), pp. 7f.

7 Corresponds to chapter 135 of MS 1711 from Trent; Die Ecclesiastica Officia Cisterciensis ordinis des Cod. 1711 von Trient, ed. GRIESSER (note 6 above), here pp. 272f.

8 *Magister novitiorum debet novicios ordinem suum docere, in ecclesia excitare et ubicunque se negligenter habuerint, verbo vel signo quantum potuerit emendare.* [...] *Necessaria eis quantum potuerit debet procurare.* [...] *De apertis negligentiis cum ante eum veniam petierint, penitentiam*

Several privileges are granted to the master in order to enable him to carry out the tasks assigned to him. Thus, he is not obliged to attend the evening lecture from the *collationes*[9] and may leave the *claustrum* after the bloodletting.[10] However, the novice master, too, has to be present during the assignment of daily tasks after the chapter.[11] He is explicitly mentioned here, as well as *infirmarius*, cantor, sacristan or the brother responsible for taking care of the guests.

After this short overview of the regulations of the *Ecclesiastica Officia*, the next part of this essay looks at implicit information. Explicit descriptions of the master's properties as well as a naming of specific qualifications and terms of suitability recommending him for precisely this office are missing in this book of customs. Similar results are at hand when examining the statutes and other determinations from the Cistercian General Chapter or the later *Libelli definitionum*. These texts characterise the master of lay brothers as a suitable priest-monk accomplished in manners and setting an example to the lays through his way of life and his attire[12], yet not a word is said about the novice master. Neither does the *Carta caritatis* contain information on this matter in any of its redaction versions. Which implicit indications can be taken from what has been said hitherto and be used as clues to the demands on the

---

dare. Diem primum ingressionis in cellulam scriptum habere, et quando eis legenda sit regula abbati prenuntiare [...] *Et anno evoluto ad benedictionem adducere* [...] *Pro ipsis noviciis qui legere nesciunt, professiones in ecclesia legere, et ad crucem apponendam incaustum preparatum habere* [...] *et ad pedes monachorum si necesse fuerit eum ducere et reducere, aquam benedictam et cucullam preparare, et ad eum ibi exuendum et induendum adiuvare. Post hec scyphum eius et iusticiam in refectorium deferre, et lectum ei quem prior iusserit ostendere* [...]. (Ecclesiastica officia, ed. HERZOG / MÜLLER, [note 6 above], cap. 113 [p. 438]).

9 Ibid., cap. 81.8 (p. 310).

10 Ibid., cap. 90.24 (p. 344).

11 Ibid., cap. 75.3 (p. 286).

12 *Provideat abbas, ubi multitudo conversorum exigere videtur, monachum sacerdotem idoneum et discretum, maturis moribus preditum, et qui presertim in victu et vestitu laicos fratres edificet suo exemplo, et eis magistrum constituat et confessorem.* (Libellus definitionum, 1257, dist. 8.7, in: Les codifications cisterciennes de 1237 et de 1257, ed. B. LUCET, Paris 1977, pp. 203-357, here p. 300). An almost identical definition was included in the *Libellus definitionum* of the year 1289 (Libellus antiquarum definitionum ordinis Cisterciensis, dist. 14.1, in: Nomasticon Cisterciense seu antiquiores ordinis Cisterciensis constitutiones. Editio nova, ed. H. SÉJALON, 2 vols., Solesmes 1892, pp. 367-470, here vol. 2, p. 458).

Magister novitiorum? He is, of course, "an experienced senior who is suited for winning souls and watches over them with the utmost care", as was stated in the above mentioned determination from the rule of Benedict. The matter of 'experience' will be discussed further in a later part of this essay.

First, it is indispensable that he be able to write and to read, as he has to note down the day of the novices' entrance into the noviciate and read the profession charter to them should the occasion arise. (At the same time, this may be interpreted as a clue to the sole purpose of the novitiate being the adoption of a new way of life rather than the acquisition of intellectual qualifications such as reading and writing skills.) However, the mere ability to read and write is by far not sufficient, because the *magister* has to record every novice's day of entrance into the noviciate in order to accordingly inform the abbot when the rule has to be read to the novices as well as when the year of probation has ended and the novices can receive their profession. A multitude of novices very much differing in their level of progress without question requires a competence in calendar management, too.

It is not explicitly emphasised in any of the sources that the master has to be a priest: With certainty, the formula *aquam benedictam preparare* contained in the description of the master's tasks can be interpreted as the act of simply providing the holy water but not of the consecration itself, as *preparare* also refers to *cucullam*.[13] In analogous conclusion with regard to the above mentioned *magister conversorum* – who has to be a priest – it nevertheless is safe to assume that the *magister novitiorum* is a hieromonk, too. Additional information on the master's qualifications is obviously not to be found in the Cistercians' normative texts. At this stage, however, narrative sources can provide further help.

The description of the monk and later *magister novitiorum* Achard of Clairvaux († after 1170) in the *Exordium Magnum Cisterciense* by Konrad of Eberbach († 1221) proves insightful: Achard, who above all had gained a reputation as architect of the Himmerod abbey, was "a man, powerful in his words of edification and comfort."[14] According to Konrad, he

---

13 Cf. note 8 above.

14 *Senex quidam Acardus nomine, nobilis genere, sed conversationis dignitate nobilior, novitiorum curam in Clarevalle gerebat, vir potens in verbo aedificationis et consolationis qui etiam in iuventutis suae robore iubente simul et mittente beato Bernardo abbate suo plurimorum*

became a novice master "as a veteran" who had "already been released from active soldier's duty", after he had retired as it were. Achard – "this old one" as he is called here – eagerly fulfilled the task now assigned to him, and "with the help of what he had learnt in a long time of practise, he shaped the still inexperienced senses by daily admonitions". Here, his qualification undoubtedly is his age and the experience resulting from it: The subsequently related three examples by which Achard induced his novices to be "watchful against errors" are those he either had experienced himself or heard about from a competent authority.[15] Their content blends in with quite a number of similar reports of miracles, the centre of which are either unworthy novices or such of exceptional holiness. In this case, Achard's age acts as a guarantee for the credibility of his reports.

In comparison to this, the English Cistercian abbot and theologian Aelred of Rievaulx († 1166) was rather young of age. Aelred, who had served at the court of King David of Scotland, was impressed by the monks' way of life, and in his mid-thirties he entered the Cistercian abbey of Rievaulx, which had been founded as an affiliate of Clairvaux a few years before.[16] At an age of approximately 40 years, the office of the novice master at Rievaulx was assigned to him for one year. His famous

---

coenobiorum initiator et exstructor devotus exstiterat. (Exordium magnum Cisterciense sive narratio de initio Cisterciensis ordinis auctore Conrado monacho Clarevallensi postea Eberbacensi ibidemque abbate, ed. B. GRIESSER [Series scriptorum s. ordinis Cisterciensis 2], Rom 1961, dist. 3, cap. 22 [p. 210]).

15 *Hic iam veteranus et emeritae militiae senex instituendis tironibus deputatus officium suum strenue adimplebat et ex iis, quae longo usu didicerat, rudes adhuc mentes contra triplicem funiculum carnis, mundi et diaboli, qui difficile rumpitur, cottidianis exhortationibus informabat, exemplis etiam tam veteribus quam recentioribus adversus vitia cautiores reddebat, unde et nos aliqua, sicut ex ipsius ore audivimus, perstringemus.* (Exordium magnum Cisterciense, ed. GRIESSER [note 14 above], dist. 3, cap. 22 [p. 210]).

16 The research on the life and work of Aelred of Rievaulx have been made well accessible by means of two exhaustive bibliographies up to the year of 1996: A. HOSTE, Bibliotheca Aelrediana. A Survey of the Manuscripts, Old Catalogues, Editions and Studies Concerning St. Aelred of Rievaulx (Instrumenta Patristica 2), Steenbrugg 1962; P.-A. BURTON, Bibliotheca Aelrediana Secunda. Une bibliographie cumulative (1962-1996) (Textes et Études du Moyen Âge 7), Löwen 1997. According to these, W. G. BUCHMÜLLER, Die Askese der Liebe. Aelred von Rievaulx und die Grundlinien seiner Spiritualität, Langwaden 2001, and D. BOQUET, L'ordre de l'affect au Moyen Age: autour de l'anthropologie affective d'Aelred de Rievaulx, Paris 2005, were published.

Speculum Caritatis[17], which had been commissioned by Bernhard of Clairvaux, was probably written during this time. This work has to be classed with the genre of 'treatises of practical spiritual advice', as named by Caroline BYNUM.[18] One of the peculiarities of the text is a conversation held by the author of the *Speculum* with one of the novices entrusted to him. The starting point of this dialogue, whose degree of fictionality shall not be subject of this essay, is the novice's remark that he had enjoyed the sweetness of God's love in the worldly life more than in the much more pious way of life he was pursuing now, and the question resulting from this observation as to what the reason for this would be.[19] For this study, the form and process of the conversation are more interesting than the content in this context. Aelred does not in the least present the novice with the answer to the problem in form of a clear reply; in classical style and in the Socratic tradition of interlocutory form he guides his counterpart on the way leading to the solution of the paradox, and thus lets the novice find the answer for himself. The essence of this maieutic lies in the reference to experience as well as in the exact and consensual definition of terms. Probably more by instinct than consciously, both are taken into consideration by Aelred. His

---

17 Aelred wrote the final draft of the *Speculum caritatis* within one year; the same year the office of the novice master was assigned to him after his return to Rievaulx (BUCHMÜLLER, Die Askese der Liebe [note 16 above], p. 90).

18 "Works of practical spiritual advice – that is, works about the soul's spiritual and moral progress within the cloistered life. Such works include treatises on the formation of novices, commentaries on the Benedictine and Augustinian Rules, and certain other works that are clearly parallel to these two genre in form and intention." (C. W. BYNUM, Jesus as mother. Studies in the spirituality of the High Middle Ages [Publications of the UCLA Center for Medieval and Renaissance Studies 16], Berkeley, Calif. 1982, p. 35; cf. also ibid. pp. 267-269 [Appendix: Monastic and Canonical Treatises of Practical Spiritual Advice]) According to Caroline BYNUM, all these texts obviously have the same intention, which is: "to explain the cloistered life to those engaged in its practice" (ibid., p. 36).

19 *Cum ante non multum tempus frater quidam abrenuntians mundo, nostro se monasterio contulisset, traditus a reverendissimo abbate nostro meae parvitati disciplinis regularibus instituendus, coepit aliquando admirans quaerere quaenam mihi causa videretur, quod in saeculari adhuc habitu ac conversatione positus ita saepius compungébatur, ac in quemdam divini amoris resoluebatur affectum tantaque spiritus suavitate frueretur, quantum, inquit, modo non dicam diutius retinere, sed ne raro quidem degustare sufficiam.* (Aelred of Rievaulx, Speculum caritatis, ed. CH. H. TALBOT, in: Id., Opera ascetica, ed. A. HOSTE / CH. H. TALBOT (= Aelredi Rievallensis opera omnia 1) (Corpus Christianorum. Continuatio Mediaevalis 1), Turnhout 1971, pp. 1-161, lib. 1, cap. 27 [p. 86]).

didactic abilities cannot have been the least decisive factor leading to him being entrusted with the office of the *magister novitiorum* and to Bernhard of Clairvaux asking him to write the 'Mirror of Love'.

The *vita* by Walter Daniel († ca. 1170) reveals another of Aelred's virtues: his capacity of *discretio*. As novice master, Aelred of Rievaulx even showed this gift of discretion with regard to the instructions of the rule, when he didn't reveal to the abbot that a novice had fled and returned.[20] The granting of rewards was important, too, when signs of weariness appeared.[21]

Adam, the later abbot of the Cistercian abbey of Perseigne († ca. 1221), shall serve as the last example. Adam, who had originally been a regular canon and a Benedictine monk later on, became the novice master in Pontigny after he had joined the Cistercians once more. It is of interest for our question regarding qualifications and capabilities that Adam was given this office, although in a letter to a certain Osmund, a monk and probably likewise the novice master in the Norman Cistercian abbey of Mortemer, he pointed out that he had never been a novice of the Cistercians himself. Unfortunately, we do not know the letter which Osmund had sent and which induced Adam to write the answer handed down to us; yet also in itself this *rescriptum* is an interesting testimony of

---

20 *Venit aliquis illi tempore secularis clericus ad Rievallem monachi nomen et officium desiderans adipisci. Recipitur primo in hospicio, paulo post in cella noviciorum ubi Alredus precibiebat ut magister. Qui clericus valde instabilis animo persepe ad diversa titubabat, et nunc huc nunc illuc, ut arundo, pro aura mutabilis voluntatis ferebatur.* […] *Non multo post frater ille in probatorio improbus factus et in sensum reprobum traditus descendere in Egiptum concupivit et ceptum boni operis deserere propositum. Venit itaque et magistro suo rem illicitam indicat, ex ponit estum animi, desiderium prave mentis revoluit. Cui Alredus "Noli, frater, perire. Nam non poteris quamquam et velis, et stultissimum est hoc ipsum velle cuius contrarium cupiunt omnes sancti. Omnes enim salvari desiderant." Set ille non audiens monita salutis recessit a monasterio inscienter nescius et insipienter indoctus. Ut autem exteriora monasterii claustra pertransiit per devia saltus tota die vacabundus oberrat et parum ante solis occasum ad viam veniens per quam exitum fecit subito infra muralem monasterii ambitum se sensit transpositum. Quem propheta suus* [*sc.* Aelred – M.B.] *clamat et dicit: "Fili, quid fecisti michi sic* […]. *Nam ne abbati quidem hunc fratris excessum per totam diem revelavit, timens patris sanctissimi severitatem revertenti novicio nocituram et sperans illius reversionem mente prophetali profuturam sibi. Quod et factum est.* (Walter Daniel, Vita Ailredi, ed. M. POWICKE, Oxford 1978, cap. 15 [pp. 24f.]). Cf. B. P. MCGUIRE, Brother and Lover. Aelred of Rievaulx, New York 1994, pp. 86f.

21 Aelred of Rievaulx, Speculum caritatis, ed. TALBOT (wie Anm. 19), lib. 2, cap. 19 (p. 93).

the contents of the Cistercian noviciate and above all of the master's tasks.

It is six things that Adam declares to be of essence for the successful instruction of the monastic recruits: Besides the intensity of belief, the fear of God and the love of wisdom – in a manner of speaking, this is what the novices are accountable for – Adam also states three points in which the novice master's responsibility shows itself in an extraordinary clarity: These are the religious behaviour of the master, his eager concern about the novice and, finally, the master's friendly and frequent conversations with the pupils about spiritual matters and the observation of the rule.[22] At this point, Adam's extensive statements on the three mentioned points can be dealt with only briefly: The novice master's conduct ought to be – thus his words – like a mirror for his subordinates; these are to be formed according to his example. The master has to eagerly heed whether the novice is truly sincere or only seems to honestly fulfil his daily religious tasks, as it is the master who bears the responsibility for his pupils' salvation. The frequent conversations he is to hold with the novices serve this purpose, too: They are to be a means of avoiding the danger of the novices lapsing into melancholy. This despondency can often be observed with novices, and it is imperative to prevent this by friendly conversation.

Here, one should probably imagine interlocutory situations like that of Aelred of Rievaulx mentioned shortly before. Therefore, the conversations do not only serve the purpose of instruction, but – as Adam explicitly points out – also that of building a confidential relationship between novice and master, which then again becomes a prerequisite for imparting relevant knowledge effectively.[23]

---

22 *Verumtamen ad hoc opus* [*sc.* successful *conversio* – M.B.] *sex necesaria esse puto, quibus habitis et observatis mutare potest Aethiops pellem suam et in beatam albescere novitatem. Primum, est fidei fervor; secundum, Dei timor; tertium, sapientiae amor; quartum, religiosa magistri conversatio; quintum, pia eiusdem circa novitium sollicitudo; sextum, amica et frequens de spiritualibus aut de observantiis regularibus collocutio.* (Adam de Perseigne, ep. 5.47, in: Id., Lettres I, ed. J. BOUVET [Sources Chrétiennes 66], Paris 1960, p. 112).

23 *Nascitur etiam ex amica frequenti et honesta collocutione commendabilis quaedam familiaritas, per quam magister efficitur ad correppiendum audacior, correptus ad disciplinam patientior, uterque ad intelligentiam Scripturarum eruditu, novitius exercitatior in observantia regulari.* (Adam de Perseigne, ep. 5.57, ed. BOUVET [note 22 above], p. 118).

*

The material discussed above can be summarised as follows: The normative texts used here, such as rules, customs and statutes of the Cistercians, contain numerous statements about the novice master's activities and range of tasks. However, explicit information about certain qualifications and conditions of aptitude is missing. These can be deduced implicitly, but they are not specifically discussed. Yet when examining narrative literature, we encounter multiple descriptions of qualities of the *magister novitiorum* like age – here equivalent to experience – *discretio* or interlocutory capacities. The successful completion of a noviciate in the respective community does not, however, seem to have been a necessary precondition for assuming the post of a master. The sole characteristic that can be recorded as being essential and indispensable probably is the novice master's 'aptitude' for his office, his *virtus* meaning a competence for the successful instruction of the monastic recruits.

Franciscans, Children and the Cloister

Michael Robson

While the ministry of the Franciscan order was directed towards the evangelisation of medieval society through word and deed, its pastoral strategy towards children has attracted relatively little scholarly attention. Children, too, stood in need of religious formation and instruction. The friars' dealings with the younger members of the Church were informed by Jesus's teaching about the innocence of children and the value of child-like trust, which was to be safeguarded from scandal. Children feature in accounts of the friars' pastoral ministry, the order's wider influence in the Church and the locality, the life of the mendicant churches, vocations to the order, which in turn gave birth to the polemical exchanges. Each of these areas is explored in this contribution.

Friars' pastoral ministry

The followers of St Francis of Assisi were penitents who based their lives on the teaching and example of Jesus Christ and the apostles. The monastic orders, whose focus was the cultivation of spiritual values within the cloister, had comparatively few contacts with children, except the oblates who joined their communities or attended their schools. In contrast, the friars' vocation took them to the heart of society and entailed dealings with both boys and girls. Friars carried the Gospel throughout the western Church, preaching to people of all ages and social categories; relatively few sectors of medieval society were closed to the friars. Renowned for their sermons in the cities and the countryside, the friars quickly built up a reputation as attractive and highly gifted preachers. Their colourful and imaginative sermons attracted sizeable crowds to churches or other places where they preached and applied the Scriptures to the circumstances of daily life with a new clarity and vigour. The breadth of St Francis's appeal is emphasised by his first biographer, Thomas of Celano, who attests to the fact that people of every age (*omnis aetas*) hastened to hear his sermons.[1] His disciples followed this example in their ministry of preaching, refreshing each level of the medieval Church. While the vast majority of those who heard the friars' sermons were undoubtedly adults, the mendicant message was presented in a form that was accessible to the younger members present.

The order's chroniclers concentrate largely on the friars' relations with adults for whom they wrote. Children are sometimes mentioned because a thorough programme of evangelisation included them as well. They accompanied their parents to the parish churches, *piazze* or the town squares and the fields, where the friars preached; it is probable the certain friars were deemed to be particularly talented in making the teaching of the Gospel more accessible to the young. There was something of an exotic quality about the friar, a member of a cosmopolitan fraternity whose members travelled not only from one village, town or city to another, but also crossed the seas as missionaries and ecclesiastical envoys. Even the friars, whose lives were strictly circumscribed by their own custodies, were distinguished by their thorough education in the arts and theology, a factor which separated them from the ranks of the secular clergy. Their membership of a vast international order gave them knowledge of events which occurred in foreign lands, such as the Holy Land, China and India, which were described by the memoirs of their confrères.

The friars' sermons had a theatrical quality which may have had a special appeal to the young. A witness to the effective preaching of the first generation of friars in Tuscany is Mansuetus de Castiglione Fiorentino, who grew up to become a friar and a papal penitentiary in the middle of the thirteenth century, serving Innocent IV. Expatiating upon the friars' zeal and reforming energy, he testified that, when he was a boy of about 10 years (*puerulus*), the friars instilled in him an especial reverence for the Body of Christ. As a boy he was accustomed to fasting

---

Dr Alison Binns kindly read the last draft of this paper and made some helpful suggestions. Abbreviations: AFH = Archivum Franciscanum Historicum; BL = The British Library, London; BSFS = British Society of Franciscan Studies; FF = Fontes Francescani, ed. E. MENESTÒ, S. BRUFANI et al. (Medioevo Francescano, Collana diretta da Enrico Menestò, Testi II) Assisi 1995; RS = Rolls Series; TNA: PRO = The National Archives, London, formerly known as the Public Record Office.

1 Thomas of Celano, Vita prima S. Francisci, no. 36, in: FF, pp. 310f.

almost throughout Lent in order to prepare for a good communion on Easter Sunday.[2]

Although the friars were drawn to the urban centres, they were active as preachers and confessors in towns, villages and hamlets, where they met and instructed children. The friars' itinerant ministry is reflected in the policies of Robert Grosseteste, bishop of Lincoln (1235-53), the patron and friend of the order. The bishop explains that, from his consecration, he was accustomed to making a systematic visitation of the archdeaconries and rural deaneries of his far-flung diocese. Clergy and people were summoned to meet him to hear a sermon and to confess their sins. While Grosseteste preached to the clergy, a friar, Franciscan or Dominican, preached to the laity. The friar would be assisted by four others who heard confessions and assigned penances. Children for confirmation were also to be present and it is probable that friars played some part in the final preparation of the candidates for this sacrament.[3] This reference lifts the veil on the instruction imparted to the young by friars not only in their own churches, but also in parish churches, where they assisted the parochial clergy in the ministry of teaching.[4]

The friars' dealings with the younger members of the Church were informed by the mystery of the Nativity, whereby the Son of God entered the world as a child. The fruits of meditation on the circumstances of the birth of Jesus were applied to the young. While the apostles tried to turn away children, Jesus called them to Himself and blessed them, declaring that the kingdom of God belonged to them (Luke 18.15-17). The kingdom of heaven was revealed to children rather than the learned and the clever (Matthew 11.25-26). Those intent on

---

2 Fratris Thomae vulgo dicti de Eccleston Tractatus de Adventu Fratrum Minorum in Angliam, ed. A. G. LITTLE, Manchester 1951, p. 96.

3 S. GIEBEN, Robert Grosseteste at the Papal Curia, Lyons 1250. Edition of the Documents, in: Collectanea Franciscana 41 (1971), IV, no. 3, pp. 340-393, here p. 376.

4 Cf. The Register of Walter de Stapeldon, bishop of Exeter (A.D. 1307-1326), ed. F. C. HINGESTON-RANDOLPH, London 1892, p. 111. On 10 July 1301 the parishioners of Colyton, Devon, informed the diocesan visitators that Robert Blond, their vicar, preached to them as well as he knew, but not sufficiently. Blond's predecessors were accustomed to call in the friars to instruct them for the salvation of their souls. But Blond did not care for the friars, and, if they happened to come, he would not receive them or show them hospitality.

entering the kingdom of God were advised to approach it as little children (Mark 9.35-37). A special rebuke was reserved for those who caused scandals and obstacles for the younger members of the Church (Mark 9.42-43). Children were to be instructed in respect for their parents and schooled in the norms of the Gospel.

Prolonged reflection on the Gospel's application to the young is reflected in the preparation of homilies for them. These are contained in the *ad status* sermons produced by Guibert of Tournai, a Parisian master and an avid collector of materials for *model* sermons in the middle of the thirteenth century.[5] One section of Padua, Biblioteca Antoniana, MS 469, focuses on the needs of the junior members of the Church. Three sermons were addressed *ad virgines et puellas* (ff. 123v-27r), one *ad adolescentes et pueros* (ff. 148v-50r), one *ad adolescentes* (ff. 150r-52v) and another *ad eos qui addiscunt in scholis parvulos* (ff. 152v-54v). The fact that this popular collection of sermons paid particular attention to the place and role of children reflects a significant feature of the friars' preaching.[6] The formation of the young is also reflected in the Tabula of scriptural and patristic materials assembled by Robert Grosseteste, the first lector of the friars' school in Oxford, and Adam Marsh, his friend and collaborator. The heading of *De bene informando pueros* appears in the third distinction and cites corroborative texts from Deuteronomy, Ephesians, Hebrews, Augustine's Confessions and Commentary of the Psalms, St Jerome's letters and biblical commentaries and the Dialogues of Gregory the Great.[7]

Bernardine of Siena, one of the greatest preachers of the fifteenth century and a lynchpin of the Observant reform first in Tuscany and then throughout Italy, cast himself in the role of spiritual father to his children, the people of God, in search of repentance. While parents had a generative role in the formation of the character of their sons and daughters, Bernardine believed that the preacher had a similar

---

5 D. L. D'AVRAY, Sermons to the upper bourgeoise by a thirteenth century Franciscan, in: D. BAKER (ed.), The Church in Town and Countryside, (Studies in Church History 16), Oxford 1979, pp. 187-199, here p. 188.

6 Cf. A. G. LITTLE, A Guide to Franciscan Studies (Helps for Students of History 23), London 1920, p. 46.

7 P. ROSEMANN, "Tabula", in: Opera Roberti Grosseteste Lincolniensis 1, ed. J. MCEVOY (Corpus Christianorum. Continuatio Mediaevalis 130), Turnhout 1995, pp. 250, 295.

responsibility to prepare the field for the implantation of the good seed of the Word of God; he regarded himself as playing an important role in the formation of the young.[8] The Word of God should penetrate the minds of the young. On the first Sunday of his Lenten sermons at Florence in 1424 Bernardine urged parents to bring boys and girls from the age of five to the sermon in the following week. Sermons on the value of study or on the Virgin Mary as a cultural ideal for girls were tailored to the needs of children and youths. The virtues of parental respect and filial obedience were to be fostered among the young. The bonfire of vanities, the culmination of so many of Bernardine's cycle of sermons, was attended by children. Bernardine believed that a child's presence at such a spectacle would remain in his or her memory for the next half a century, long after the content of the sermon had been forgotten.[9]

The heir to the patristic theology of history, Bonaventure of Bagnoregio, the fifth master of the school of the Cordeliers in Paris, articulated his own scheme of seven ages of the history of the cosmos, from childhood to old age.[10] St Francis's sanctity and his rapport with the animal world are perceived as a manifestation of his recovery of a state of original innocence.[11] The young, despite the impact of original sin, are often associated with the miraculous in Franciscan literature. The *puerulus* Mansuetus is a witness of the miraculous. Having explained his own eucharistic piety, he recounted that one Easter Sunday, when all the people had made their Communion, an evil and notorious man named Execius went with them and, having received the Body of Christ irreverently, immediately went off and sat on a bench. Indifferent to the

---

8 C. L. POLECRITTI, Preaching Peace in Renaissance Italy: Bernardino of Siena and His Audience, Washington 2000, p. 26; Le prediche volgari (Florence 1424), ed. C. CANNAROZZI, 2 vols., Pistoia 1934, vol. 1, p. 200; Le prediche volgari (Florence 1425), ed. C. CANNAROZZI, 3 vols., Florence 1940, vol. 2, p. 325.

9 POLECRITTI, Preaching Peace (note 8 above), pp. 53f., 79; Le prediche volgari (Florence 1424), ed. CANNAROZZI (note 8 above), vol. 1, pp. 66, 202, 194f.; Le prediche volgari (Siena 1425), ed. C. CANNAROZZI, 2 vols., Florence 1958, vol. 1, pp. 192, 291.

10 Bonaventura, "Breviloquium", prol. II, no. 3, in: Doctoris Seraphici S. Bonaventurae S.R.E. episcopi cardinalis Opera Omnia edita studio et cura P. P. Collegii a S. Bonaventura, 10 vols., Florence 1892-1902, vol. 5, p. 204.

11 ID., "III Sententiarum", d. 28, a. 1, q. 1, conc., in: Doctoris Seraphici S. Bonaventurae (note 10 above), vol. 3, p. 622b.

fact that the consecrated host was still in his mouth, he began to gossip with bystanders. Mansuetus saw the Body of Christ leave his mouth and fall to the ground some distance away. He immediately notified a well respected priest, who sent him to the place where this occurred. He received the Body of Christ reverently as well as the hosts which remained on the altar and his faith was greatly strengthened.[12] On occasion children witnessed eucharistic miracles. Peter of Tewkesbury, minister provincial of England, was on good terms with Lord Galfrid le Despenser and his family. When he celebrated Mass in the domestic chapel, John, the lord's son, witnessed a miracle in the form of the friar consuming a child at the altar. The boy avoided Peter's company, lest he too, be eaten by the friar.[13]

The devotees of the St Francis of Assisi included children who make numerous appearances in the list of miracles appended to the life of the *poverello*, who also drew St Clare into the ministry of healing.[14] A child who fell into an old well at Celano in the region of Capitanata invoked Francis's name. When his friends obtained help from the neighbouring village, the boy was rescued and he explained that his safety was due to the intercession of the saint.[15] Friars encountered children in the course of their daily activities. The unnamed seven year old son of a notary in Rome wanted to follow his mother to the church of San Marco, but was obliged to remain at home. He jumped out of a window in the palace, suffered multiple injuries and died. His mother had not gone very far, when she heard the commotion and hurried back to her home. Learning of the tragic events, she was overcome with grief, filling the

---

12 Cf. Eccleston, ed. LITTLE (note 2 above), pp. 96f.

13 Ibid., p. 97.

14 St Francis was accustomed to sending people to St Clare for healing, including Stephen, a friar whose sanity had been impaired. Children, too, were taken to San Damiano by their distressed parents. Cf. Legenda Sanctae Clarae Assisiensis, no. 32-33, in: FF, pp. 2434f. Cf. Legenda Latina Sanctae Clarae virginis Assisiensis, ed. G. BOCCALI (Pubblicazioni della Biblioteca Francescana Chiesa Nuova 11), Assisi 2001, c. 22, nn. 4, 8-15, pp. 166-171, recounts how Clare healed Mattiolo, a three-year old boy from Spoleto, who had a pebble stuck in his throat, and a boy from Perugia, whose eyes were covered. In each case Clare blessed the children who were healed. Ortolana, Clare's mother, was also involved in the healing of the second child.

15 Fr Thomae de Celano Tractatus de miraculis Beati Francisci, VIII, no. 51, in: FF, p. 685.

neighbourhood with her shrieks. A friar named Roho was on his way to preach at the church. Hearing the commotion, he went to the scene of the tragedy and asked the child's father whether he had confidence in St Francis's intercession and his powers to raise the child. Receiving an affirmative reply, the friar devoted himself to prayer and the boy gave signs of life. The child was restored to health through the saint's intercession.[16]

Friars and their influence

Children have featured in various missionary strategies in the history of the western Church, from Gregory the Great, especially in his plans to evangelise the Anglo-Saxons at the end of the sixth century.[17] Perhaps aware of this historical precedent, John of Montecorvino, the apostle sent a letter to his confrères in western Europe on 8 January 1305, informing them that he had successively purchased 40 boys (*pueri*) of pagan families; the boys were aged between seven and eleven and had had no religious instruction. He baptised them and instructed them in Latin and the Roman liturgical rite. He transcribed 30 psalters with hymnaries as well as two breviaries for the boys. He trained the boys in the same skills and several of them copied psalters and other suitable things. The boys knew the Divine Office and they kept choir and prayed the offices, as it is celebrated in friaries, regardless of his own presence or absence. John was accustomed to celebrating the Divine Office with a convent of sucklings and infants (Psalm 8.3, *infantium et lactentium*). They sang by rote because they had no books with notes. The Great Khan took delight in the boys' singing. Explaining that he had nothing besides a small breviary with shortened lessons and a little missal, John asked the minister general to send him an antiphonary, the legends of the saints, a

16 Bonaventure, Legenda maior S. Francisci, miracula, II, no. 4, in: FF, p. 921.

17 S. Gregorii Magni Registrum Epistularum, ed. D. NORBERG, (Corpus Christianorum Series Latina, CXL), vol. VI. 10, pp. 378f. In September 595 Gregory had ordered his administrator in Gaul to purchase English boys aged 17 or 18 in the slave markets so that they could be brought to Rome and taught in the city's monasteries. Cf. The Earliest Life of Gregory the Great by an Anonymous Monk of Whitby, ed. B. COLGRAVE, Lawrence/Kansas 1968, cap. 9, pp. 90f.

gradual and a psalter. A single copy would serve as an exemplar to be written by the boys.[18]

The letter of 13 February 1306, addressed to the vicars general of the Dominicans and Franciscans and the friars of both orders in the province of Persia, announces that some of the boys whom he had purchased and baptised had died. The proximity of the friars' church to the imperial court is reflected in the fact that the emperor could hear the boys' singing. The boys were divided between the two churches in the capital city, which was some two and a half miles away. They sang the Divine Office by themselves. John's practice was to celebrate Mass in the two churches on alternate weeks, because none of the boys was ordained.[19] The friars in China informed the papal curia and the general chapter in a letter of 15 May 1323 on the progress of the mission and their pastoral programme. They continued John's practice of purchasing boys as slaves. In addition, they also bought girls (*pueros emimus venales sexus utriusque*). Some of the boys were trained as clerics and others made fine friars (*quorum aliqui sunt modo et fratres optimi conversores*). The letter contrasts the linguistic skills of these boys with those of the friars who were required to master the foreign tongue.[20]

Despite their profession of evangelical poverty, the friars were sensitive to the plight of the needy to whom they ministered in word and deed, dispensing alms at the friaries. Children were among those who received alms from the friars. A layman called John entered the order and served as a porter for many years until he was overtaken by physical infirmity. Reflecting the behaviour of the early friars collecting alms sufficient for the day, he alluded to his practice of distributing surplus alms to children and paupers at the door of the friary.[21] The friars' charitable work, which complemented their programme of preaching, was frequently focused on the care of the young and examples from the foundation of the order to the present abound. One forum for this

---

18 Epistolae Fr. Iohannes de Monte Corvino, ed. A. VAN DEN WYNGAERT, in: Sinica Franciscana 1 (Quaracchi/Florence 1929), Epistola 2, no. 3, 8, pp. 333-355, here pp. 347, 350.

19 Ibid., Epistola 3, no. 1, 3-4, pp. 352f.

20 Textus duarum epistolarum Fr. Minorum Tartariae Aquilonaris an. 1323, ed. A. C. MOULE, in: AFH 16 (1923) pp. 104-12, here p. 109.

21 Fratris Thomae vulgo dicti, ed. LITTLE, (note 2 above), p. 104, *credo… quod parvuli et pauperes quos in ianua refeceram de fratrum relinquiis cito me iuvabunt ad coelum pervenire.*

ministry was the hospital. Peter d'Assisi, an Umbrian friar, preached in the Veneto about 1335. There he began a project to relieve the sufferings of abandoned children, whom he collected near the church of San Francesco de Vinea until such times as a hospice might be constructed. He was an influential figure in the establishment of the Ospedale della Pietà in Venice.[22]

Respect for the friars passed from one generation of a family to the next. It is, however, easier to trace the communication of this attitude towards the friars in the members of the nobility and royalty. For example, Raymond Berengarii IV, count of Provence, was a special benefactor of the order and was described as *pulcher homo et amicus fratrum Minorum*. The count's four daughters, Margaret, Eleanor, Sanchia and Beatrice, married Louis IX of France, Henry III of England, Richard, Earl of Cornwall, and Charles, the Count of Anjou and Provence. Richard subsequently became King of Germany and Charles was later invested with the crown of Sicily and Naples.[23] Queen Margaret had a friar as her confessor, William of St Pathus, who wrote a biography of Louis IX about 1303.[24] Queen Eleanor communicated her respect for the order to her daughters, Margaret, Queen of Scotland, and Beatrice, Duchess of Brittany, both of whom died in childbirth on 26 February and 24 March 1275 respectively.[25] The former's last confession was heard by an unnamed friar[26] and the latter was buried in the London Greyfriars to the left in a northern arch, close to the place in which her mother's heart would be placed in the wall.[27] The kings and queens of

22 Cenni e Documenti su Fr. Pietro d'Assisi, O.F.M. (Fr. Pietruzzo della Pietà) 1300-1349, ed. L. RANZATO DI CHIOGGIA, in: AFH 8 (1915), pp. 3-11. Cf. Documenti riguardanti Fr. Pietruccio d'Assisi e l'Ospedale della Pietà, ed. CECCHETTI, in: Archivo Veneto 30 (1885), pp. 141-147.

23 Salimbene de Adam, Cronica, ed. G. SCALIA (Scrittori d'Italia 232-33), Bari 1966, vol. 1, p. 338.

24 Vie de Saint Louis par Guillaume de Saint-Pathus confesseur de la Reine Marguerite, ed. H. F. DELABORDE, Paris 1899.

25 M. HOWELL, Eleanor of Provence: Queenship in Thirteenth-Century England, London 1998, p. 291; The Chronicle of Bury St Edmunds 1212-1301, ed. A. GRANSDEN (Nelson Medieval Texts), London 1964, p. 57.

26 Chronicon de Lanercost M.CC.I.-M.CCC.XLVI, ed. J. STEVENSON, Edinburgh 1839, p. 97.

27 C. L. KINGSFORD, The Grey Friars of London: Their History with the Register of their Convent and an appendix of Documents (BSFS 6), Aberdeen 1915, p. 71.

western Europe showed a predilection for the friars and recruited them as confessors who resided in the royal households.

Friars in the English province were drawn into royal households as chaplains and confessors. The friars who celebrated Mass for the spiritual welfare of Princes Thomas de Brotherton and Edmund de Woodstock, the sons of Edward I and his second wife, Margaret of France, received 23s.4d. at Clarendon on 26 June 1305.[28] Robert de Moggeston and John de Dunstaple, probably friars of Winchester, received alms and an allowance for new habits in recompense for their work as chaplains in the Winchester household of the same princes. These friars received the royal alms on 10 February and 26 October 1312.[29] Friars served as tutors, chaplains and confessors to Louis, Robert and Raymond Berengar, sons of Charles II, king of Sicily, who were held as hostages first in Provence and then in Aragon between 1286 and 1295. Francis le Brun of Apt in Provence was engaged in 1286 and became the confessor of Louis, who was then aged 12.[30] Two years later he was joined by a second friar, Peter Scarrerii, who taught the princes. Peter Scarrerii was styled as Francis's *socius.*[31] Under the care of these Franciscan instructors the princes passed through the usual course of study prescribed for medieval youth, grammar and logic, to which were added theology, natural science and metaphysics (*logicalia, naturalia, moralia, et theologica*).[32] Classes began after Mass and continued until lunch time.[33] Francis le Brun advised the 14 year old Louis on the composition of a rule of life for himself. Louis fasted on bread and water.[34]

Friars participated in the exequies of some of the younger members of the royal family. Adam, an illegitimate son of Edward II died before 30 September 1322, when the crown gave a piece of cloth of gold to be placed upon his body in the conventual church of the Benedictines at

---

28 BL, MS Add. 37656, f. 1r. The Dominicans received 25s.4d.

29 TNA: PRO, E 101/374/19, f. 3rv.

30 Processus Canonizationis et Legendae variae Sancti Ludovici O.F.M. Episcopi Tolosani (Analecta Franciscana 7), Quaracchi/Florence 1951, p. 106.

31 Ibid., pp. 98, 107, 110.

32 Ibid., p. 98.

33 Ibid., pp. 33, 72.

34 Ibid., pp. 107f.

Tynemouth.[35] Members of the four main mendicant orders attended the funeral on 4 October, each of them receiving five shillings.[36] William de Hatfield, the fourth child and the second son of Edward III and Philippa of Hainault, was born in 1336 and died early the following year. An offering of forty shillings was made to the high altar of the Cluniac monastery of Pontefract on 11 February 1337. The prince's body lay there overnight *en route* for burial in York Minster.[37] Moreover, the friars were engaged to celebrate Masses for the deceased prince at York, probably in their friary. Friars attended the funeral in York Minster and they were listed among the recipients of alms between Hatfield in Yorkshire, Pontefract and York. Payment was made to the mendicants and others on 3 March 1337.[38]

The friars' churches

The friars' churches were popular venues for sermons, the celebration of Mass, the hearing of confessions and other acts of personal or public piety. The grand mendicant churches came to be seen as public places, accessible to the local city or borough authorities, in whom ownership of the land and buildings was frequently vested. The friars were closely intertwined in the events of the local community, whose fortunes they frequently shared and chronicled, especially in times of warfare or pestilence. In some instances the friars supplied water to the town. Apart from the works of art which decorated the walls of the mendicant churches and instructed the young on the principal moments in the drama of salvation, these churches met other needs.

35 BL, MS Stowe 553, f. 113r: *ultimo die Septembr' ponebantur ut supra super corpus Ade dicti filii regis bastardi defuncti die sepulture eiusdem in ecclesia conventuali de Tynemuth – due pani ad aurum ….*

36 Ibid., f. 21v: *fratribus ordinum Predicatorum, Minorum, Sancti Augustini et Mont' Carmeli ville Novi Castri super Tynam exist' apud Tynemouth die sepulture Ade filii Regis defuncti et ibidem sepulti, de elemosina domini Regis cuilibet ordini 5s. per manus fratris Iohannis de Leek de ordine predicatorum ibidem eodem die.*

37 BL, MS Cotton Nero, C.VIII, f. 207r.

38 Ibid., f. 206v.

First, the friars' churches offered a pageant of local history. They were so often the centre of memorable episodes in the life of the city or borough. A visitor to the friars' church at San Lorenzo Maggiore in Naples could familiarise himself with the history of the city and the kingdom of Naples. This sixth century church, which passed to the friars in 1234, housed numerous monuments to the life of the crown and the city. Charles II, king of Sicily, gave the friars grants for the completion of their building in 1284, 1299, 1300 and 1301. His son Raymond Berengar, who had died on 22 December 1305, was buried in San Lorenzo in a chapel constructed by the king. When Robert acceded to the throne, he continued to show his respect for the friars, who had educated and guided him in his exile. Simone Martini's painting of St Louis of Toulouse's renunciation of his right to the crown of Naples in favour of his brother, Robert, was displayed in the church, where the saint had been ordained to the diaconate there by Ralph II of Granville, the Dominican patriarch of Jerusalem.[39] Louis subsequently celebrated his first Mass publicly in 1296.[40] In addition to San Lorenzo's links with the crown, the church and its side chapels provided a burial place for paupers and important citizens of Naples.

Secondly, the mendicant churches offered the younger members of the community a visible guide to the history of the family. The friary provided a place of burial for all sectors of medieval society. Graves were numerous in the church, the cloisters, cemeteries and the chapter houses. They were visited regularly by members of the family, especially on anniversaries. There a young person would be taken to pray at the graves of grandparents, aunts and uncles and the other relations, who chose to be buried close to each other and frequently in the same chapel. The wealthier families enjoyed access to the numerous side-chapels or altars where their relations had been laid to rest. Some wealthy families were responsible for the construction, decoration and maintenance of these chapels, where Mass was celebrated daily for donors.[41] The links between

---

39 Processus Canonizationis (note 30 above), pp. 102, 111, 360.

40 Ibid., p. 38.

41 D. NORMAN, Those who pay, those who pray and those who paint: two funerary chapels, in: ID. (ed.), Siena, Florence and Padua: Art, Society and Religion 1280-1400, vol. 2. Case Studies, New Haven/London 1995, pp. 169-193, here pp. 169-174; J. C. LONG, The Program of Giotto's Saint Francis Cycle at Santa Croce in Florence, in: Franciscan Studies 52 (1992), pp. 85-133.

the chapel and the family were made visible in the shields or coats of arms on display there. The chapels flanking the high altar of Santa Croce in Florence were known by the names of the families buried there rather than the saints in whose honour they had been constructed.[42]

On occasion, the friars' churches were the venue for the sacrament of Confirmation. The friars of Worcester took part in the official welcome and enthronement of William Gainsborough, their confrère and former minister provincial in England, when he entered his cathedral city. Gainsborough confirmed boys in the Worcester Greyfriars on 10 June 1303, two days after his installation as bishop of that city.[43] The friars' churches were not merely the venue for spiritual activities. This practice was exemplified when Francesco di Marco Datini, the celebrated merchant of Prato, solemnly promised Lionardo his daughter's hand in the church of San Francesco at Prato in the presence of many witnesses on 24 April 1399.[44]

Excavations of the friaries in England and Wales reveal the presence of children's graves in the churches, cemeteries and chapter houses. The lay cemetery at the Cambridge Greyfriars contained the bodies of women and children.[45] Two of the 24 graves inspected at the Northampton Greyfriars in 1972 were occupied by juveniles; two small children were buried there.[46] There were children's graves in the cloister of the Carmarthen Greyfriars. Five of the nine skeletons excavated east of the cloister alley were aged between 14 and 16 years. The predominance of juveniles in this part of the friary complex reflects patterns in other friaries; one hypothesis is that they were novices. Two

42 Giorgio Vasari, Le vite de' più eccellenti pittori scultori e architettori nelle redazioni del 1550 e 1568, ed. R. BETTARINI / P. BAROCCHI, Florence 1966, vol. 2, p. 98.

43 The Register of the Diocese of Worcester during the vacancy of the See, usually called 'Registrum Sede Vacante', 1301-1435, ed. J. W. WILLIS BUND (Worcestershire Historical Society 8), Oxford 1897, p. 54.

44 I. ORIGO, The Merchant of Prato, London 1957, pp. 192f.

45 P. SALWAY, Sidney before College, in: D. BEALES / H. S. NISBET (eds.), Sidney Sussex College Cambridge: Historical Essays in Commemoration of the Quatercentenary, Woodbridge 1996, pp. 3-34, here p. 23.

46 J. H. WILLIAMS, Excavations at the Greyfriars Northampton 1972, in: Northamptonshire Archaeology 13 (1978), pp. 96-160, here pp. 155f.

juveniles were buried in the chapter house.[47] Children, possibly from benefactors' families, were interred at the west end of the chapter house of the Oxford Greyfriars.[48] Recent excavations of the Greyfriars of Norwich have identified an unusually large number of skeletons of the young, some of whom may have been boys preparing to join the community. Fuller information is eagerly awaited and will be made available when the archaeological report is published.[49]

Children feature prominently in the miracles attributed to Franciscan saints. An early miracle of St Francis, read out at his canonisation on 16 July 1228, concerned a girl from Gubbio who was carried to the tomb in San Giorgio, Assisi, by her nurse, bearing a wax image. After spending eight days there, the use of all her limbs was restored. A boy from Montenero lay for several days before the doors of San Giorgio, Assisi, the church in which the saint was buried prior to his translation. One day he entered the church and touched the tomb. He was restored to health.[50] While the tombs of Saints Francis of Assisi and Anthony of Padua drew large numbers of pilgrims, several of the friars' churches contained the bodies of friars and members of the third order associated with miracles. The cult of Odorico da Pordenone († 1331), the friar and missionary who kept an account of his travels in China, flourished in the fourteenth century, when 64 miracles were recorded. Children accounted for 31.3% of these miracles which occurred at his shrine in San Francesco, Udine, in Friuli.[51] For instance, Nicolay de Pirano John, a boy aged 10, was the son of Anthony Vercii de Pirano. Having been taken to the shrine where he passed one night, he regained the use of his limbs.[52] The practice of pilgrims remaining at the shrine around the clock is

---

47 T. JAMES, Excavations at Carmarthen Greyfriars, 1983-1990, in: Medieval Archaeology: Journal of the Society for medieval Archaeology 41 (1997), pp. 100-194, here pp. 137f.

48 L. BUTLER, The Houses of the Mendicant Orders in Britain: Recent Archaeological Work, in: P. V. ADDYMAN / V. E. BLACK (eds.), Archaeological Papers from York presented to M.W. BARLEY, no. 52, York 1984, pp. 123-136, here p. 131, n. 52.

49 Andy HUTCHESON, Head of Archaeological Planning, Norfolk Museums and Archaeology Service kindly furnished this information by e-mail and telephone.

50 Celano (note 1 above), nn. 132, 133, pp. 409f.

51 A. TILATTI, Odorico da Pordenone, Vita e Miracula (Centro Studi Antoniani 41), Padua 2004, pp. 65-68.

52 Ibid., cap. 5, pp. 117- 121.

exemplified by John, son of Anthony Vercii of Pirano who remained *iuxta sepulcrum* for seven days and nights.[53] Altigarde of Pironio was aged five when she was brought to the tomb of Odorico.[54] The cult of Gerard Cagnoli († 1342), a Sicilian friar interred at San Francesco, Palermo, flourished towards the middle of the fourteenth century. Gerard's arm was venerated in the sacristy of San Francesco, Pisa. Towards the end of June 1348 Lapus Pucii of Vico Pisano promised to name his new born son after the saint in the waters of Baptism. The boy duly recovered from his life-threatening ailment.[55]

Boys were engaged to do routine tasks at friaries before the end of the thirteenth century. For example, Maurice de Lond' was the *garcio* of the London Greyfriars who carried apples and pears from the friary to Queen Margaret, the second wife of Edward I. The king gave him six shillings and eight pennies on 29 December 1300.[56] There is fuller documentation regarding the employment of boys engaged to assist friars outside their friaries. Three friars served as lectors to Christ Church cathedral priory in Canterbury between 1275 and 1314. The priory's accounts record payments to the boys who helped the friars. A boy, described as the *puer fratrum minorum*, received a payment of 6 pennies for the financial year of 1275/76, which ran from Michaelmas to Michaelmas.[57] Annual payments for the clothing of the lector and his *socius* included the boy. For example, the cost of clothing for the two friars in 1277/78 amounted to 32 shillings, with a further three shillings for the master's tunic. Six shillings and six pennies were paid for the boy's clothes. In 1287/88 the cost of the boy's clothing exceeded that of the lector and *socius*. Expenses were also incurred *ad opus pueri lectoris*. The following year the cost of the boy's clothing was 12 shillings.[58] In 1280/81 there was a payment of six shillings and two pennies *pro calciamentis et aliis minutis pueri lectoris nostri*. The accounts for the year

---

53 Ibid., cap. 4, pp. 113- 116.

54 Ibid., cap. 6, pp. 121f.

55 F. ROTOLO, Il trattato dei miracoli del B. Gerardo Cagnoli, O. Min. (1267-1342) di Fra Bartolomeo Albizi († 1351), in: Miscellanea Francescana 66 (1966), pp. 128-192, here p. 141.

56 BL, MS Add. 7966A, f. 66v.

57 W. A. PANTIN, Canterbury College Oxford, (Oxford Historical Society, new series, 30), Oxford 1985, p. 167.

58 Ibid., p. 168, 170.

1281/82 supply the name of the lector's boy, Thomas de Toting (?).[59] In 1284/85 the *puer* received two shillings for carrying letters of the friars' provincial chapter.[60] The confessor and the *socius* of Queen Isabella, wife of Edward II, were assisted by at least four named boys (*garciones confessoris*) who performed menial tasks and took messages in 1311/12.[61] Thomas de Normand' was described as the friars' *garcio*.[62] Thomas Motte, John Bere, John de Coderstok and John de Aumbely were granted robes by the queen for their services. John de Puseaux, the royal confessor, received 40 shillings for them on 5 August 1314.[63]

Mendicant images of childhood

A mendicant view on the formation of young minds was articulated by Thomas of Celano. The *vita prima*, composed to celebrate the canonisation of *il poverello*, wastes no time in declaring the customary friction between *mundus* and *religio*. Echoing the opening words of the fourth Gospel, the biographer announces that Francis, from his earliest years, was brought him up to be proud of spirit, in accordance with the vanity of the world. Imitating his parents' life and habits for a long time, he became even more vain and proud. The friar's disapproval of parental failings leads him to denounce the practice whereby nominal Christian parents educate their children from the cradle in a negligent and dissolute manner. Some parental aspirations were deemed injurious to their children and thus, from an early age, children sank into worse deeds

---

59 Ibid., p. 169.

60 Ibid., p. 170.

61 The Household Book of Queen Isabella of England for the fifth regnal year of Edward II, 8th July 1311 to 7th July 1312, ed. F. D. BLACKLEY / G. HERMANSEN (The University of Alberta Classical and Historical Studies 1), Alberta 1971, pp. 172f., 192f.

62 TNA: PRO, E 101/375/9, f. 3r: *eidem clerico in participacionem unius ville sigillo suo signate de liberacionibus confessoris regine et socii sui fratrum minorum panetr' et lit' deficient anno vi usque xv diem Novembr anno vii per manus Willelmi de Normand' garcionis eorum fratrum' recipient' apud Eltham 7 January 11s.10d.*

63 Ibid., f. 29v; cf. ibid. ff. 31r, 32v; cf. The Household Book of Queen Isabella, ed. BLACKLEY / HERMANSEN (note 61 above), pp. 192f. The same boys had been in the queen's service in 1311/12.

than those of their parents; these children followed their own impulses. Neither support nor guidance was given to the young on entering adolescence and this resulted in a disordered life and an enslavement to sin. Francis was brought up in such wretched circumstances (*misera rudimenta*). Pietro and Pica Bernardone make a relatively late entrance in the *Vita prima* in the context of the dispute following Francis's illicit sale of cloth at the fair in Foligno and they disappear for good in the aftermath of the scene enacted before Bishop Guido in the vescovado.[64] The *Vita secunda* or *Remembrance* offers a more conciliatory account of Francis's parents.[65] The *Legenda Latina*, which is also linked with Thomas of Celano, attributes a strong piety to Ortolana, the mother of Sts Clare and Agnes, whom she subsequently followed to San Damiano, where she took the veil. She had been on pilgrimage to the Holy Land, Rome and the shrine of St Michael the archangel in Apulia and communicated to her children a strong conventional piety, which contained the seeds which germinated under the guidance of St Francis.[66]

A different model of Christian childhood is projected by John of Orta, a friar, in his biography of St Louis of Anjou, the son of Charles II, king of Sicily. Discarding the ways of children, Louis displayed a maturity beyond his years. From his first years he aspired to the divine service and avoided the games in which his two brothers indulged. Acts of penitence and asceticism replaced the more usual pastimes of the young. Louis seemed like another St John the Baptist. His mind was intent on visits to monasteries and churches. He was given to meditation and attended the celebration of the Divine Office. In addition, he also prayed the penitential psalms with their litanies, weeping warm tears of devotion. At the conclusion of the Office of Compline he sang the *Salve Regina*. He was accustomed to joining the friars in their Offices and received the Body of Christ frequently and with remarkable devotion. His preparation for Mass included a daily confession of his sins. His devotion moved others to fervour. He was tested with temptation, particularly during his

---

64 Celano, Vita prima, nn. 1-2 (note 1 above), pp. 277ff.

65 Celano, Vita secunda Sancti Francisci, no. 3, in: FF, pp. 445f. The text, composed about 1247/48, incorporates a more conciliatory view of Peter and Pica Bernardone. There is a gentler start which focuses on the virtues of Francis's mother, Pica, who was depicted as a second Elizabeth.

66 Legenda Sanctae Clarae Assisiensis, cap. 1-2, in: FF, pp. 2416f.; cf. Legenda Latina Sanctae Clarae, ed. BOCCALI (note 14 above), cap. 1, pp. 92-95.

period as a captive in Aragon. The Scriptures were read during meals. During a bout of sickness he promised the mother of God and St Francis that he would take the Franciscan habit if he recovered.[67]

The vices and virtues of children appear in the *exempla* collections of the Middle Ages.[68] Children featured in the friars' *exempla* or sermon materials recounted by Adam Marsh and Albert of Pisa. Adam narrated the story of a boy, who had been brought up in comfort. When he fell ill, his parents tried to persuade him to eat. The boy became so disturbed that he declared that he was not his parents' son, however much they regarded him as their favourite. When questioned further by his parents about whose son he was, he replied that he was his own son. Those guided solely by their own inclinations resembled the stupid boy. The conceit of the young featured in an anecdote rehearsed by Albert at the friars' *collatio*. A young bull enjoyed the freedom to wander from meadow to meadow each day. One day he entered a ploughed field and observed some oxen at work; the oxen, advanced in years, were making slow progress. The bull belittled the oxen and boasted that he would accomplish much more. When he assumed the yoke, the bull quickly grew weary and was reproached and mocked by the oxen.[69]

Vocations

The biographers of St Francis describe the range and the number of the men who responded to his challenging vocation. The young were also drawn by his ideals and took their place in the queue to be clothed in the friar's habit. An unnamed *tenerrimus puer* was admitted to the order. The mother of God appeared to him and indicated that he would become a distinguished preacher and lector.[70] Stephen, an English friar who filled the office of lector in Genoa and Rome as well as the papal court in the middle of the thirteenth century, entered the order at a relatively young age as a *puerulus*.[71] Peter Olivi was another early recruit to the order,

---

67 Processus Canonizationis (note 30 above), cap. 1-2, nn. 2-13, pp. 336-343.

68 Cf. BL, MS 27336, f. 3r.

69 Eccleston, ed. LITTLE (note 2 above), p. 84.

70 Ibid., p. 88.

71 Salimbene de Adam, Cronica, ed. SCALIA (note 23 above), vol. 1, p. 430.

which he joined at the age of 12. While the general chapter of 1260 in Narbonne promulgated its constitutions and ordained that no one should be admitted to the order below the age of 18, youths of 15 might be clothed in certain circumstances.[72] There were exceptions. Garin of Orwell entered the order in his youth (*iuvenis satis*).[73] Friar Fortis, a friar interviewed in the cause of canonisation of St Louis of Anjou, entered the order at the age of approximately 13 or earlier.[74] The son of the Pisan noble, Guido Zacci, protested that his son, Vanni or Giovanni, had been admitted to the order before his fourteenth birthday. On 13 January 1279 his vow of profession was abrogated by the custos of Florence.[75] The monastic practice of oblates quickly entered the Franciscan cosmos.[76] The reception of a boy of eleven and his clothing in the friar's habit caused outrage at Sienna, prompting twelve defenders of the people to protest to the minister provincial of Tuscany, Gabriel de Volterra, on 11 April 1372. Four days later Gabriel replied that he would review the case.[77]

The constitutions of the general chapter of Assisi in 1354 ordained that candidates should be at least 14 years of age.[78] From the middle of the thirteenth century to the end of the fourteenth the friars' policy on admissions, particularly the young, was hotly debated in circles from the parish to the new universities; it even reached the forum of national government. Such young vocations soon featured in the polemical exchanges, which proliferated from the 1250s and remained vigorous for

---

72 Statuta generalia Ordinis edita in Capitulis generalibus celebratis Narbonae an. 1260, Assisii an. 1279 atque Parisiis an. 1292, ed. M. BIHL, in: AFH 34 (1941), pp. 13-94, 284-358, here p. 39.

73 Eccleston, ed. LITTLE (note 2 above), pp. 97f.

74 Processus Canonizationis (note 30 above), p. 59.

75 G. TREGLIA, I documenti del convento di San Francesco di Pisa dalla fondazione al 1350 circa (Tesi di laurea in istituzioni medioevali, Università di Pisa) 1994/95, pp. 140f.

76 L. OLIGER, De pueris oblatis in ordine Minorum Additamentum, in: AFH 10 (1917), pp. 271-288.

77 G. MOLLAT, Reception d'un oblat au couvent de Sienne (1372), in: AFH 48 (1955), pp. 195f.

78 Statuta generalia Ordinis edita in Capitulo generali an. 1354 Assisii celebrato, communiter Farineriana appellata, ed. M. BIHL (Editio critica et analytica), in: AFH 35 (1942), pp. 35-112, 177-253, here p. 83.

much of the fourteenth century. Some of the friars were disposed to interpret the number of younger vocations in apocalyptic terms. Joachim of Fiore's prophecy that children would be appointed to preach the Gospel in the third age is quoted by Salimbene. Referring also to the feast of the innocents, 6 December, when a boy was enthroned as a bishop, the chronicler adds that learned, honourable and noble children entered the Dominicans and Franciscans [*pueri litterati, nobiles moribus et honesti*]. These children fulfilled the prophecy of Isaiah 8.18.[79]

Dreams concerning boys were sometimes instrumental in accounts concerning vocations to the order. Ralph of Maidstone, archdeacon of Chester and future bishop of Hereford (1234-39), dreamed of sitting in a synod and appointing the clergy, when he was checked by a boy (*quidam puer*), who hurled water into his face. He found himself changed into a ragged little boy who asked permission to share a pallet with Haymo of Faversham.[80] Maurice of Dereham, a confessor, found a boy who for a long time had been wasting away with an incurable disease. When the friar heard the boy's confession, he instructed him to recite the *Ave Maria* thrice daily and to seek the restoration of his health through the intercession of the mother of God so that he might be clothed as a friar. The boy did as he was instructed. About the age of 15 he pledged to embrace the mendicant discipline until he had attained the age of 18, when he might be admitted. The boy duly received the habit from Agnellus of Pisa.[81] A young man (*iuvenis*) called Ubertino from Rivarolo Canavese, near Susa, joined the order and was miraculously healed of madness during his novitiate.[82]

Some boys or adolescents were not only healed by the saint's intercession, but also joined the order at a later stage. Bartholomew, an eight year old boy, brought food to the men who were casting a bell at Tarquinia. A powerful gust of wind struck the house and knocked down a heavy door, which fell on top of the boy. People hurried to the place and invoked the intercession of St Francis for the welfare of the boy, who could not be seen beneath the door. Bartholomew's father commended him to the saint's intercession. When the heavy door was

---

79 Salimbene de Adam, Cronica, ed. SCALIA, (note 23 above), vol. 1, p. 387.

80 Eccleston, ed. LITTLE (note 2 above), p. 85.

81 Ibid., p. 62.

82 Bonaventure, Legenda maior S. Francisci, miracula, X, no. 5a, in: FF, p. 959.

lifted, the boy emerged unscathed and at the age of 14 he entered the order. In later years he became a learned man (*litteratus*) and a distinguished preacher (*famosus praedicator*).[83] Some of the most distinguished friars of the thirteenth century entered the fraternity in their youth. James de Iseo was inspired to join the order at a tender age (*puer* and *iuvenis*), despite his physical infirmity from which he was healed during the translation of the founder on 25 May 1230.[84] Iluminato, the son of a nobleman, obtained sight through the intercession of the saint. When he was old enough, he, too, joined the order.[85] In two places Bonaventure of Bagnoregio describes his own miraculous healing through the intercession of St Francis. As a child (*puerulus*) he fell seriously ill. His mother made a vow to the newly canonised St Francis. Bonaventure believes that he was snatched from jaws of death and restored to perfect health and strength through the intercession of the saint. He was old enough to remember the event and place it on record. The recollection of his debt to the saint helped him to overcome his diffidence in compiling the *Legenda maior*, in conformity with the wishes of the general chapter of Narbonne in 1260.[86]

The diary of Francesco da Lendinara offers illustrations of the practice of children and adolescents being admitted to the order, demonstrating the attractiveness of the order to the young. Francesco, then guardian of Lendinara, received the 12 year old Louis de Castelis, into the order in 1402. He was the visitator of the custody of Padua, when he received Laurence da Lendinara, a nine year old orphan into the order in 1406. As a definitor of his province and custos of Padua in 1422, he admitted several *pueros*, including the ten year old Anthony de

83 Fr Thomae de Celano Tractatus de miraculis Beati Francisci, VIII, no. 54; Bonaventure, Legenda maior S. Francisci, miracula, III, no. 5, in: FF, pp. 686f., 927f.

84 Fr Thomae de Celano Tractatus de miraculis Beati Francisci, XIII, no. 109; Bonaventure, Legenda maior S. Francisci, miracula, VIII, no. 2, in: FF, pp. 714f., 947f.

85 Fr Thomae de Celano Tractatus de miraculis Beati Francisci, XIV, no. 123, in: FF, p. 722.

86 Bonaventure, Legenda maior S. Francisci, miracula, prol., no. 3; Legenda Minor, c. 7, no. 8, in: FF, pp. 779, 1011f.

Luxia at Lendinara.[87] The order was required to make provision for the welfare of these boys and adolescents, whose number is difficult to estimate, until they were old enough to be admitted to the novitiate. The provincial and custodial chapters assigned teachers and tutors to attend to the intellectual formation of these young men. The education of the younger members of the community is reflected in the appointments made by the provincial chapter of Tuscany held at Figline in 1394. The major friaries in the province had a range of academic appointments, some of them focusing on the younger members of the community. The Florentine friary of Santa Croce had a *lector biblie*, a *magister studii*, a *magister novitiorum* and *a magister iuvenum*; the smaller friaries in that custody lacked most of these offices. The positions of master of novices and the young were combined at San Francesco, Pisa, and Montepulciano.[88]

The friars' schools may have offered some instruction to the young men of the neighbourhood. Scholars have interpreted the young Dante Alighieri's observation that he had attended the schools of the religious and had participated in their philosophical disputations[89] as evidence that he was associated with the mendicant schools of Santa Croce and Santa Maria Novella in Florence.[90] Such contacts with the young became a polemical matter at an early stage. Elizabeth, aged six, was educated among the Poor Clares at Bruisyard. Her grandmother, the dowager countess of Suffolk, paid 6s.8d *uni fratri ibidem vocato le President* on 10 May 1417.[91]

---

87 Fra Francesco da Lendinara e la storia della Provincia di S. Antonio tra la fine del s. XIV e l'inizio del s. XV, ed. C. CENCI, in: AFH 55 (1962), no. 28, 32, 48, pp. 103-192, here pp. 123f., 127, 134.

88 B. BUGHETTI, Tabulae Capitulares Prov. Tusciae O.M. (saec. XIV-XVIII), in: AFH 10 (1917), pp. 413-497, here pp. 416, 418, 420.

89 Dante Alighieri, Opere Minori, I, ii, (La Letteratura Italiana Storia e Testi, 5, iii) Convivio, II, XII, 7, ed. C. VASOLI / D. DE ROBERTIS, Milan 1988, pp. 205-210: *cioè ne le scuole de li religiosi e a le disputazioni de li filosofanti.*

90 C. T. DAVIS, Education in Dante's Florence, in: Speculum 40 (1965), pp. 415-435. The article was revised in: ID., Dante's Italy and other Essays, Philadelphia 1984, pp. 137-165, here pp. 146-154.

91 K. B. MCFARLANE, The Nobility of Later Medieval England, Oxford 1973, p. 245. BL, Egerton Roll 8776.

Family opposition to a religious vocation is a *topos* of hagiographical literature and it informed the friars' chronicles and *exempla*. One of the best documented cases involved Guido de Adam, a crusader in the time of Baldwin, Count of Flanders. His son, Salimbene de Adam was admitted at the age of 15 on 4 February 1238 and was clothed by Elias, minister general at Parma. This was to the dismay of his inconsolable father, Guido, who continually lamented the loss of his son and heir. Guido complained to the emperor who was then visiting Parma, protesting that the friars had stolen his son. Frederick II wrote to Elias, asking for Salimbene to be restored to his father. Guido went to Assisi to hand a copy of the emperor's letter to Elias. When Guido was passing through Fano *en route* for Assisi, the friars hid Salimbene and his brother at the house of Lord Martin, a master of law. After reading the letter, Elias wrote to the friars of Fano to state that, if Salimbene wished to leave the order, he was free to do so at once. Conversely, if he wished to stay, he was to be allowed to do so. Accompanied by a large group of knights, Guido then proceeded to Fano to speak with his son in the presence of a crowd of friars and others in the chapter house. He produced Elias's letter in the presence of the custos and urged his son to go home with him. When Salimbene declared that his vocation was a matter of his salvation, his father accused the friars of brainwashing his son. A private meeting achieved nothing and eventually Guido prostrated himself on the ground and cursed his son. The convent of Fano was outside the city walls and close to the sea. It was vulnerable to manoeuvres by Guido, who had arranged for pirates from Ancona to kidnap his son if he ever took a walk along the beach. Moreover, Guido had offered a reward for his son's capture. For this reason Salimbene left Fano and went to the friary at Iesi, where he spent the whole of Lent. Even after Salimbene's move to Pisa, his father continued to lay traps to detach him from the order and was never reconciled with him.[92] Guido spent the rest of his life in trying to remove his son and sought the intervention of Innocent IV.[93]

---

92 Salimbene de Adam, Cronica, ed. SCALIA (note 23 above), pp. 52-58, 136. Salimbene's eldest brother, Guido de Adam, was a judge who had married Adelasia, the daughter of Lord Gerard de Baratti; they had an only daughter, Agnes. He became a friar while his wife and daughter of Guido junior became Poor Clares at Parma; he was subsequently ordained and then appointed to the office of preaching.

93 Ibid., p. 85f.

Polemics

Professor Donald LOGAN explains that the age for entering the novitiate of a religious order was the same as the discernment required for marriage; this was not to be confused with the age of profession.[94] The admissions policy of the Franciscan order, particularly in relation to youths, was a part of the controversy between the secular masters and the mendicants in the University of Paris from the middle of the thirteenth century. William of St-Amour and Nicholas, treasurer of Lisieux explained the complaints of the secular master. The order's policy was defended by John Pecham, formerly regent-master at Oxford and then Paris.[95] Debate smouldered for some time before being re-ignited in the second quarter of the fourteenth century. Richard de Bury, bishop of Durham, had reason to be well disposed towards the friars because the Cordeliers of Paris had sheltered him in their campanile for a week, when Edward II's lieutenant in Gascony was pursuing him in 1325. Nonetheless, he reproved the friars' practice of attracting boys to their order and failing to impose on them an academic discipline appropriate for their age. Instead of educating such recruits, the friars were accustomed to send them on begging expeditions and seeking the favour of friends. These bad habits provided no foundation for the ministries of preaching and hearing confessions.[96]

This theme was taken up by one of the friars' most vigorous and eloquent critics, Richard FitzRalph, Dean of Lichfield and then Archbishop of Armagh (1346-60). FitzRalph was an Oxford master and expressed the criticisms of both the secular clergy and the universities about the mode of the order's admission of the young. Dr Kathleen WALSH believes that the archbishop was intending to add this to his list of complaints against the mendicants. FitzRalph painted an evocative picture for the pope and cardinals in his sermon delivered at Avignon on 8 November 1357. On that very day he had been accosted by an Englishman whose 12 year old son had been drawn to the friars during

---

94 D. LOGAN, Runaway religious in Medieval England, c. 1240-1540 (Cambridge Studies in Medieval Life and Thought), Cambridge 1996, p. 12.

95 De pueris oblatis in Ordine Minorum (cum rextu hucusque inedito Fr. Iohannis Pecham), ed. L. OLIGER, in: AFH 8 (1915), pp. 389-447; De pueris oblatis in Ordine Minorum. Additamentum, ed. ID., in: AFH 10 (1917), pp. 271-288.

96 E. C. THOMAS, Philobiblon Richard de Bury, Oxford 1960, VI, p. xiii, pp. 64f.

his studies at Oxford. The anguished parent set out for the papal court and claimed that he and his wife were not permitted to talk to their son alone; everything was conducted under the surveillance of a friar. Although the parents believed that the boy was being kept against his will, they were powerless to act. The prelate argued that such cases were common in England and were a contributory factor in the decline of young men attending the University of Oxford.[97]

Faced with dwindling numbers of students, the University of Oxford took strong action in 1358, passing a series of statutes preventing the friars from admitting undergraduates below the age of 18; similarly, the mendicants were not permitted to circumvent the ruling by sending such students to be admitted in convents away from Oxford. Failure to conform would result in their banishment from the university.[98] Richard FitzRalph argued for the revocation of the friars' privileges and for the case to be delegated to a commission of cardinals rather than the curial court.[99] The friars' policies towards the recruitment of the young provided Wyclif's followers with ample ammunition.[100] In 1401 parliament addressed the issue, but the new statute did not forbid the friars from accepting under-age boys. It forbade such boys being taken without the consent of parents or guardians. In 1402 John de la Zouche, minister provincial and the provincials of the other three mendicant orders, swore to observe the statues against boys under the age of

97 R. FitzRalph, Defensorium Curatorum contra eos qui privilegiatos se dicunt, in: E. BROWN (ed.), Appendix ad Fasciculum Rerum Expetendarum et Fugiendarum, II, London 1690, p. 1397; K. WALSH, A Fourteenth Century Scholar and Primate: Richard FitzRalph in Oxford, Avignon and Armagh, Oxford 1981, pp. 424f.

98 Ibid., pp. 424f.; J. COLEMAN, FitzRalph's Antimendicant *proposicio*, in: Journal of Ecclesiastical History 35 (1984), pp. 376-390.

99 R. FitzRalph, Defensorium Curatorum, ed. BROWN (note 97 above), pp. 466-486, here pp. 468, 472-476.

100 Cf. John Wiclif's Polemical Works in Latin for the first time edited from the Manuscripts with Critical and Historical Notes, ed. R. BUDDENSIEG, London 1883, vol. 1, p. 55.

fourteen being admitted.[101] Nonetheless, two years later Jack Upland asked why the friars stole children, contrary to the divine laws.[102]

The custom of clothing boys in the habit was too well entrenched for the liking of some reformers. Its durability is reflected in two examples drawn from the last generation of the friars in England. The pope intervened in the case of John Sillow, who at the age of about seven and under the care of his stepmother, was induced to become a Franciscan with childish levity. Aged 14, he made several attempts to leave the order, but he was not allowed to do so and he was compelled to make profession. About 1476 he fled and the friars judged him to be an apostate. Sillow was a scholar in the diocese of York on 29 May 1490 when Innocent VIII cleared him of any taint of apostasy on the grounds that his profession had been invalidated by force and fear.[103] Henry Hill entered the order as a boy (*impubes*) at the friary of St Francis in Hereford. Aged 15 he protested that he was not permitted to leave. In due course he was ordained to the priesthood and was working in the diocese of Worcester. Because he had been constrained to remain in the friary the pope dispensed him to live as a secular priest. Leo X wrote to Charles Bothe, bishop of Hereford, on 18 March 1518 and authorised him to release Hill from his vows as a friar in order that he might obtain a benefice.[104]

Throughout the Middle Ages the order continued to attract boys and adolescents, a fact reflected in the polemical exchanges between the friars and the secular clergy. This aspect of the friars' dealings with the young is well rehearsed in the mendicant controversy, although the number of boys below the age for the novitiate can be reckoned only in approximate terms. Evidence of the friars' wider policies for dealing with the young merit closer inspection. Although much of the evidence is

---

101 Rotuli Parliamentorum ut et Petitiones et Placita in Parliamento tempore Ricardi R.II., vol. III, ed. P. MORANT / T. ASTLE / J. TOHAM, London 1783, no. 62, p. 502.

102 T. WRIGHT (ed.), Political Poems and Songs relating to English History composed during the period from the Accession of Edw. III to that of Ric. III, (RS, 14), 2 vols., London 1859-61, vol. 2, pp. 22, 83f.; C. M. ERICKSON, The Fourteenth-Century Franciscans and their Critics, in: Franciscan Studies 35 (1975), pp. 107-135.

103 Bullarium Franciscanum, ns. IVii, no. 1845, ed. C. CENCI, Rome 1990, pp. 690f.

104 Registrum Caroli Bothe, episcopi Herefordensis, A.D. MDXVI-MDXXXV, ed. A. T. BANNISTER (The Canterbury and York Society 28), London 1921, pp. 115f.

fragmentary, the extant sources illuminate spheres of the order's ministry and pastoral strategy. The six sections of this paper point to a significant investment of the friars' time and energies, as they sought to shape and inculcate Christian principles in the minds and hearts of the younger members of the people of God.

INDEX

D

E

F

G

K

L

M

N

S

T

U

V

W

Y